THE CZECHOSLOVAK EXPERIMENT

IVAN SVITÁK

The Czechoslovak Experiment

1968-1969

NEW YORK AND LONDON
COLUMBIA UNIVERSITY PRESS
1971

Ivan Sviták was, until the recent Soviet occupation of Czechoslovakia, a Fellow of the Institute of Philosophy of the Czechoslovak Academy of Science and a lecturer in modern philosophy at Charles University, Prague. He has been attacked many times in the Soviet press as a leading dissenter, and the new post-Dubček government has deprived him of his Czechoslovak citizenship.

*Dedicated to the memory
of the living torches of 1969—
to the memory of Jan Palach and Jan Zajíc
who knew that freedom and truth
are higher values
than an individual's life*

Acknowledgments

Work on this book was begun in the Institute of Philosophy of the Czechoslovak Academy of Science in Prague and completed at the Research Institute on Communist Affairs, Columbia University. I owe much to the excellent conditions for research and writing offered by both institutes. The Czech edition of this book, *Hlavou proti zdi* (Heads Against the Wall), was already in the press when the Russian occupation made its publication in Prague impossible. It is a pleasure to record my appreciation for the help I have received from Columbia University, which offered me a senior fellowship from September 1968 to June 1969, so that I might complete the book and prepare the English translation. I wish, also, to thank the translators, Mrs. Eva Vanek, Jarmila Veltruský, Vilém Brzorád, and Jiří Neděla, for their work. I am especially grateful to Mrs. Christine Dodson, Jerry Brin, Sophia Sluzar, Toby Trister, and Myron Gutmann, who helped me prepare the manuscript for publication.

IVAN SVITÁK

Prague—Ljubljana—Vienna—New York
1968—1971

Contents

Illustrations

Cartoons from Literární listy

Jan Palach

Prologue

Seek the truth,
Speak the truth,
Hear the truth,
Protect the truth,
Love the truth,
Learn the truth,
And defend truth unto death.
JAN HUS, 1369–1415

—Keď' nenastanú komplikácie, malo by to byť' v deviatom mesiaci donosené

(Dubček to Czechoslovakia:
  "If there are no complications the child should be born in the ninth month.")

The Strategy of Truth ᖇᖇᖇᖇᖇᖇᖇᖇᖇᖇ

> The philosopher asks, What is truth?
> he does not ask, What is currently ac-
> cepted?; he asks, What is true for every-
> body? not What is true for one man?
> Truth does not know the frontiers of
> political geography.
>
> KARL MARX

Truth in Politics

1. Political theories are a rationalization of social group interests. Hence political theories are only as objective or as biased as are the social groups, parties, classes, strata, nations, blocs, and races whose interests such theories defend or oppose. If there is still talk of "political science" in academic circles, the term is a polite form like that used by diplomats forced to speak of France as a great power.

2. Political theories which purport to express, scientifically and ob-jectively, the plurality of interests, conflicts, and contradictions in present-day social groups, classes, strata, nations, blocs, and races exist only as ideological illusions, provoking the resistance not only of the radical students, but also of common sense. If political theories are an expression of subjective interests, then the theories of those groups that are frankly partial will be nearest to the truth. Such groups will regard as the source of political and power motivations their own, as well as alien interests, and the interests of elites, as well as masses; and their theories will express the interest of the widest possible range of groups in a given country, and on our planet as a whole.

3. In political theory, as contrasted with the unequivocal character of the natural sciences, we face an elementary plurality of possible solutions and *a priori* views, depending on our point of reference in judging basic facts and on the regional viewpoint from which we look at the empirical surface of reality. This sociological determination for every political theory is very apparent in the *a priori* approaches to the

(3)

unique history of the Czechoslovak experiment of 1968. The Czecho-slovak experiment has been interpreted in three different ways.

Western theories interpreted it as a democratic revolution; Soviet propaganda saw it as a counterrevolution; and the Chinese press called it a factional struggle between revisionist power elites, a view which is closest to the truth. All three *a priori* theories are an interpretation of a certain local historical process seen from the viewpoints of differing political power-bloc interests; they are ideological projections of the American, Soviet, and Chinese global political strategies with regard to a small Central European country which in 1968 forced the world to face elementary problems concerning structural changes within indus-trial society.

4. The first key to understanding the Czechoslovak experiment is to realize that in 1968 there were several democratization movements in Czechoslovakia, other than the one that operated under the leadership of the Communist Party; political activities expressed a mosaic of various interests. These interests merged into an illusive unity, thanks to the hollow symbols put forth by the politicians in power, who, at the beginning, aimed at representing the whole nation—a spectrum ranging from Maoists to veterans of the Czechoslovak Legion who had fought the Russians during World War I. The condition set for this undertaking was, of course, that no faction would attempt to influence the real and unsymbolic power relations within the power center—the Politburo of the Czechoslovak Communist Party. Political activities, however, were expressions of three different tendencies with different interests and goals.

The first tendency was represented by the official reform policy set by the power elite of the Party apparatus; the second was represented by the intelligentsia, increasingly expressing the opinion of the nation; and the third tendency was the radically democratic and spontaneously socialistic movement of the youth. The goal of the first tendency was economic reform and change in the political leadership; the second tendency aimed at a socialist democracy; and the third, at integral structural reform.

5. These three tendencies were backed not only by various organiza-tions, but also by different social strata and different interest groups. The democratization movement provided the common cover for vari-

ous contradictory tendencies, frequently hazy, but not antisocialist, anticommunist, or anti-Soviet. Communists were the mainspring of this process, and the toleration of opposing views was rather an expression of their force than of their weakness.

6. The second key to an understanding of the Czechoslovak experiment is a consideration of what the essence of this experiment was. The variety of tendencies was an expression of the different group interests of three main strata of Czechoslovak society: a) The power elite, identified with the Party, state, and military apparatus (that is, the establishment—some 100,000 persons); b) the middle class, the so-called intelligentsia, including technical workers and comprising at least one third of the entire population (with data varying according to the criteria used to determine what is the middle class or the intelligentsia); and c) the working class—i.e., the blue-collar workers in industrial plants, including workers on collective farms. The dialectical interplay of substance and phenomenon, the distinction between an empirical investigation of the political surface and the investigation of deep-rooted social dynamics—these are not merely the metaphysical embellishments of Hegelian jargon. In this situation they are rather the concrete, provable reality of a social movement whose substance—a structural change in the society—is hidden behind various partial interests, goals, and groups.

7. Although all of these components were merged in one dynamic process of social change and produced the crisis of the given society, they aimed at different goals and had different opinions as to how the crisis should be resolved. The power elite represented an interest group —narrow and powerful—which regarded the societal crisis as a crisis of the economic system, and was incapable of overstepping this horizon when not pressed to make concessions. The intelligentsia (the middle class) believed the crisis was far deeper, because the representatives of its reform wing knew that economic reform depended on the political solution of the crisis; they had to go further than the technocrats and concentrate on socialist democracy, i.e., on the transformation of the political system. The modern, democratically and humanistically oriented radicals did not represent partial interests only. Increasingly, they functioned—rightly—as the spokesmen of the nation as a whole, on behalf of national interests and goals.

(5)

8. The third and largest group of the population, the working class, during the peak of the Czechoslovak experiment represented a spontaneous, popular, national, socialistic, and democratic movement with a tremendous political potential. The most radical defenders of its interests, who were at the same time defenders of national and international interests, were the radical students and workers who aspired to a structural change in the society, in alliance with other workers and with the intelligentsia.

9. These three main social forces corresponded to three different political programs which gradually appeared on the Czechoslovak political scene—first, as a program of change in the political leadership; later, as the April program of the struggle for reforming society; and, finally, as the program of a socialist democracy, as expressed in the *Two Thousand Words* manifesto.

10. The last decisive key for understanding the Czechoslovak experiment is comprehending the rapid sequence of the successive phases of democratization. (There were five main phases, reminiscent of the sequence of events in a classical tragedy: Exposition, January 5 to March 21, 1968; Collision, March 22 to June 27, 1968; Crisis, June 28 to August 20, 1968; Peripeteia, August 21 to January 16, 1969; Catastrophe, January 17 to April 17, 1969.) The individual phases had different goals. The contribution of individuals, groups, and organizations was different. Tactics, methods, and programmatic principles changed in individual stages. Radicalization and collaboration, hope and despair, activity and passiveness, violence and nonviolence, resignation and faith, apathy and enthusiasm, love and hate, emotion and reason—all alternated in a kind of pendulum motion during the one-year experiment, with a powerful dynamic of structural change—a dynamic that came to an abrupt stop through the irrational logic of violence.

11. As during the last three decades Czechoslovakia went through fascism, Stalinism, de-Stalinization, and re-Stalinization, so now during the individual phases there was an intertwining of reform, occupation, and resistance—the triad of revolution, invasion, and "counterrevolution"; the bizarre *pas de trois* illustrated the specific nature of a modern revolutionary process in which the humanistic content of socialism must once again unite with democracy if it is not to succumb to a totalitarian degeneration of the Soviet neo-Stalinist type.

12. Will the movement for structural reforms and civil rights over-

come the huge obstacles in its way? Those who have faith in socialism as a revolutionary movement inseparable from democracy and humanism must believe that it will, despite hard facts. Their historical commitment is based on the assumption that the personal dignity of man is not derived from the state, that freedom is a natural right, and that people must therefore resist any totalitarian dictatorship based on a total right to control man. If we are mistaken and the twentieth century is not a time of world structural changes, but, on the contrary, a time for the constitution of new elites, we must resist the triumphant trend of history even more energetically. If we accept the premise that the dignity of free men is at stake, we accept the logical conclusion that to die with these values of freedom is better than to live as members of the elites of tomorrow's totalitarian dictatorships.

Tactics of Truth

To think means to change.
BERTOLT BRECHT

1. After a violent occupation of his country, even an objective scientist cannot stay objective, if he does not want to be a collaborator with the occupant. How is one to unite the requirements for academic reliability and scientific honesty with the reality of violence? "Political objectivity" (if this round square exists) is an unattainable aim for anybody who has lived through the events he is writing about, because the way he experienced these events and was engaged in them cancels any possibility of seeing them from a distance, a necessary prerequisite for objectivity. It is impossible to be angry and at the same time describe one's own anger.

2. If, then, the author is a Marxist philosopher, socialist humanist, and Czechoslovak citizen he cannot pretend to be objective or to be above considering the global strategy and national interests of his own country. He will best serve the Czechoslovak experiment if he presents a mirror in the form of documents. All the documents presented in this volume were written by the same author, for the radically democratic Czech intelligentsia, especially the left democratic students; most of the documents were published in the Czech or foreign press, especially in *Student* and *Literární listy*, during 1968.

3. Documents in this book express only the personal opinion of an

(7)

individual. Their author did not hold any public or other political position during the entire democratization process; he did not accept any position of power and made no attempt to obtain one. He had no direct political connections, and was excluded systematically from academic and political life.

4. The documents were formulated during that dynamic Prague Spring which made the city of Jan Hus the capital of truth and therefore a natural terrain for philosophy. Later, the Soviet tanks turned the same city—the birthplace of Kafka—into a metropolis of the absurd. At the beginning of the democratization process radical viewpoints were regarded as utopian. On the eve of the occupation the radically democratic viewpoints became the decisive political force with a mass base. The more extreme the situation became, under the Soviet pressure, the more the views of the student group became the views of the whole nation expressing the national interest.

5. The radical opposition against the totalitarian dictatorship was the only political platform based on a consistent political concept; it was to grow in importance. The conservative *apparatchiks* in Czechoslovakia and the Soviet Union understood very clearly that the small pressure groups of students and writers could produce a pressure of thought that would drive the democratization process forward—over their heads.

6. Thoughts are an unforgivable and deadly sin of intellectuals in the eyes of any power elite anywhere in the world, because thoughts transcend the manipulative bureaucratic routine. The degree of hatred shown in the Soviet press against Czech intellectuals becomes logical as soon as the reader understands that the documents contained in this volume asked precisely those questions that the reform wing of the power elite would never have posed. These documents were always one step ahead of the power elite in formulating the concept of expanding freedom.

7. When reformers spoke of so-called "deformations in socialist society," we posed the question of the nature of the totalitarian dictatorship; when they rehabilitated murdered Communists, we brought up the question of the murder of Jan Masaryk; when they tolerated freedom of artistic creation in art clubs, we posed the question of the unity of intellectuals and workers. When the Communist Party formu-

(8)

lated its program, those outside the Party formulated their demands, and when the enthusiastic representatives of the reform wing returned from negotiations in Čierná and Bratislava and preached official optimism, we warned openly that the country was threatened by invasion.

8. The duty of a philosopher in a revolutionary process must be the same as his duty everywhere else—to speak the truth. People who trust the socialist program as a program of human freedom for the future, and as a system of public ownership, political democracy, and freedom of information, have no other alternative but to rely on truth as their only tactic—a tactic that requires using our "minds against the wall." There is only one way for us to tear the wall down—that is by using our heads.

9. The leading role of truth is above the leading role of the Party, because truth has always been revolutionary, whereas the Party power elite can be revolutionary only for a limited period of time. The discipline of recognized truth is the hardest of all disciplines and is superimposed on the discipline of a Party member.

10. By its very nature, truth is not tactful and has no tactics. This answers the question, Which is preferable—truth or tactics? Under any circumstances, and no matter how shocking or inconvenient it may be, truth is preferable. In the long run, truth is the best political solution because it forces man to understand his own illusions as self-deception. *Truth is the best of tactics because it excludes tactics.*

First Act: Exposition

PROBLEMS OF INTELLECTUALS

The first condition of philosophy is a
free spirit.

KARL MARX

Contents

Chronology

January 3–5

Czechoslovak Communist Party Central Committee unanimously elected Alexander Dubček as its First Secretary. Novotný remained president of the Republic.

January 29

Dubček left for Moscow.

February 7

Dubček and First Secretary Gomulka of the Polish Communist Party met at Ostrava.

February 14

First public political discussion held in Prague.

February 25

Major-General Jan Šejna escaped from Czechoslovakia.

March 5

First issue of *Literární listy* appeared, containing answers to an inquiry, "Wherefrom, with Whom, and Whither?"

March 10

Students demonstrated at Jan Masaryk's tomb in Lány, with the slogan "Will truth prevail?"

March 13

Parliament asked the president of the Supreme Court to complete the rehabilitation of former political prisoners.

March 14

Deputy Minister of National Defense Col.-General Vladimir Janko shot himself.

March 20

Lecture "Heads Against the Wall" delivered at Charles University, Prague.

March 22

President Novotný resigned.

March 28

Extraordinary Conference of the Union of Film and Television Artists held in Prague.

March 31

Club 231 (or K-231) founded, with membership of former political prisoners.

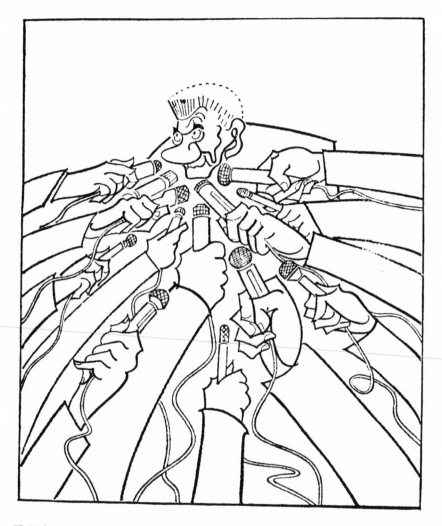

Tak já vám teda něco povím, že jó, ale moc to nikde nikomu nevykládejte . . .

(Smrkovský:
  "Sure I'll tell you something, but keep it quiet . . .")

"Wherefrom, with Whom, and Whither?" * ❧

From totalitarian dictatorship toward an open society, toward the liquidation of the power monopoly and toward the effective control of the power elite by a free press and by public opinion. From the bureaucratic management of society and culture by the "hard-line thugs" (C. Wright Mills) toward the observance of fundamental human and civil rights, at least to the same extent as in the Czechoslovakia of bourgeois democracy. With the labor movement, without its *apparatchiks;* with the middle classes, without their groups of willing collaborators; and with the intelligentsia in the lead. The intellectuals of this country must assert their claim to lead an open socialist society toward democracy and humanism; if not, the reinstatement of the editorial board of this literary magazine will become just another page in an irrational comedy based on the dialectic of arbitrariness and power.

* Published in the new weekly, *Literární listy* [Literary papers], Prague, on March 5, 1968. [Brief replies to the question, "Wherefrom, with Whom, and Whither?" had been requested by the editors of *Literární listy,* and were published in its first issue. The question elicited approximately a hundred replies from leading intellectuals, but this reply, particularly, provoked an immediate negative reaction from various professional Party functionaries (or *apparatchiks*), especially among the technicians of the Doubrava mine in the Ostrava region. A resolution objecting to the point of view presented here was signed by sixty-two technicians of this mine. The author's response to the resolution, "Open Letter to the Workers . . . ," appears in the following section of this volume.—Ed.]

Ten Commandments for a Young Czecho-slovak Intellectual*

> There are no more knaves than before;
> it is only that their field of activity is
> larger. . . . And so all of us are living in
> close collaboration with a few knaves.
> LUDVÍK VACULÍK, *in* Orientation, *1967*

1. Do not collaborate with knaves. If you do, you inevitably become one of them. Engage yourself against the knaves.

2. Do not accept the responsibility forced upon you by the knaves for their own deeds. Do not believe such arguments as "we are all responsible," or the social problems touch "all of us," or "everyone has his share of guilt." Openly and clearly dissociate yourself from the deeds of the knaves and from arguments that you are responsible for them.

3. Do not believe any ideology that consists of systems of slogans and words which only speculate about your feelings. Judge people, political parties, and social systems concretely, according to the measure of freedom they give, and according to how tolerable the living conditions are. Judge them according to results, not words.

4. Do not solve only the narrow generational problems of youth; understand that the decisive problems are common to all human beings. You cannot solve them by postulating the demands of young men, but by vigorously defending the problems of all people. Do not complain about the privileges of one generation, but fight for human rights.

5. Do not consider the given social relations as constant. They are changing in your favor. Look forward. If you do not want to be

---

* Circulated illegally at a literary evening in Prague, April 24, 1967; published in the weekly *Student*, Prague, in March, 1968. [For some of the previously published articles included in this volume exact publication dates were, unfortunately, unavailable. Approximate dates are therefore given here.—Ed.]

wrong today, you must think from the point of view of the year 2000.

6. Do not think only as a Czech or a Slovak, but consider yourself a *European*. The world will sooner adapt to Europe (where Eastern Europe belongs) than to fourteen million Czechs and Slovaks. You live neither in America nor in the Soviet Union; you live in Europe.

7. Do not succumb to utopias or illusions; be dissatisfied and critical. Have the sceptical confidence of a negotiator, but have confidence in the purpose of your negotiations. The activity has its own value.

8. Do not be afraid of your task in history and be courageous in intervening in history. The social changes and transformations of man take place, no doubt, without regard to you, but to understand these changes and to influence them with the limited possibilities of an individual is far better than to accept the fatal inevitability of events.

9. Do not negotiate out of good motives alone; negotiate with sound arguments and with consideration of what you can achieve. A good deed can rise from a bad motive and vice versa. The motives are forgotten, but deeds remain.

10. Do not let yourself be *shot* in the fight between the interests of the power blocs. *Shoot* when in danger. Are you not in danger right now when you collaborate with the few knaves? Are you a knave?

Masaryk's Death * ᔰᔰᔰᔰᔰᔰᔰᔰᔰᔰᔰ

Dear Comrade General Prosecutor:

According to recent appeals published in the newspapers, rehabilitation proceedings will be instituted on behalf of persons unjustly sentenced and victimized during the years of Stalinism. Some of these people are, of course, not alive, and it will be necessary for the State Prosecutor to take up the defense of their interests. This is especially important in those cases where the reconstruction of the true course of events will necessitate action by the authorities against some of the investigatory organs that conducted the prosecution. In the interest of the authority of an independent judiciary and of the new democratization process, I ask you immediately to initiate an investigation into whether or not the Foreign Minister of Gottwald's post-February [1948] government, Jan Masaryk, was assassinated twenty years ago, thus becoming the first victim on our country's road to totalitarian dictatorship. I urge you to publish the court depositions of persons who made sworn statement in European courts, and to initiate further investigations leading to the reconstruction of the events of the critical night of March 9–10, 1948. An imperfect attempt at such a reconstruction was published on April 7, 1965 in the magazine *Spiegel* in an article by Michael Rand, "Fünf Männer kamen nach Mitternacht" (Five Men Came after Midnight), with the unequivocal conclusion that Masaryk was assassinated. To verify these statements, to reject them, or to supplement them, I consider to be the basic question of prestige for further possible rehabilitations, and the first step toward gaining the confidence of thousands of victims that their appeals for rehabilitation will not become further traps leading to further difficulties for them.

To initiate such an investigation is an easy step for an experienced policeman, especially if he uses as a starting point the basic data con-

---

* Appeal to the Office of the General Prosecutor, March 10, 1968; published in *Student*, April 2, 1968.

tained in the article by Rand mentioned above. Permit me to recapitulate these data briefly without in any way evaluating them. To obtain a full picture it will be necessary to study extensively the testimony of witnesses published in this article and other documents of the Ministry of the Interior.

Let us start from the fact that Karel Maxbauer, heating attendant in the Czernin Palace, claimed at the police station of the Ministry of Foreign Affairs that at 5:27 A.M., when he went to raise the flags in the early morning, he found Jan Masaryk lying dead in the courtyard. Six hours later, the official version of Masaryk's "suicide," a suicide allegedly committed as a result of insomnia, illness, and overexcitement over some cables from reactionaries, was already circulating. This version conflicts with a number of testimonies by persons who were in contact with Jan Masaryk in the twenty-four hours preceding his death and with the results of the police investigation itself. From a number of testimonies, I introduce only those relating to crucial events and testified to by direct witnesses who saw Masaryk's body and his bedroom immediately after the investigation had started at seven o'clock in the morning.

1. Dr. František Borkovec, Deputy Chief of State Security in the Ministry of the Interior, who, together with Dr. Jaroslav Teplý, police physician, came as an investigating official to the Czernin Palace and noted, as did all the others, that the bedroom of Jan Masaryk was in unusual disorder, that there was broken glass in the bathroom, that there were no pillows on the bed, and that the window in the bathroom was open. Were there signs of struggle?

2. Dr. Jaromir Teplý, police physician, examined the body and found some physiological symptoms of deadly fear which are never present in suicides.

3. Bohumil Příhoda, personal servant of Jan Masaryk, found the bedroom in extreme disorder, which was very unusual, and he was particularly startled by the open window in the bathroom, which was never opened because it was very high. The pillows were in the bathroom. Why?

4. Vilibald Hoffman, a police physician, measured the distance of the window frame from the floor in both rooms and found that the window in the bedroom was 60 centimeters from the floor and the

window in the bathroom 130 centimeters from the floor. The reason why a man about to commit suicide in his own apartment should use a window which is accessible only with difficulty has never been given. The same Vilibald Hoffman counted fourteen cigarette butts from different brands of cigarettes.

5. Dr. Oskar Klinger, Jan Masaryk's personal physician, was not allowed to see the body. The same physician visited Masaryk on March 8 and noted his good physical condition.

6. The autopsy, signed by Professor Hájek, a pathologist, was a forgery. Professor Hájek was never closer to the body than a distance of three meters. This he admitted in his later testimony.

7. The cables which were supposedly the cause of Masaryk's death were never published.

8. On the day of Masaryk's funeral, an official photograph of Masaryk, distributed earlier to the editorial offices of the news publications, was confiscated by the police; in this picture, taken from the right, Masaryk was wearing a flower near his right ear. There was no apparent reason for this police action.

9. The official communique on Masaryk's death was drafted with no regard to the results of the investigation; it was issued six hours after the discovery of the body without any attempt to evaluate the suspicious factors.

10. The Minister of the Interior, Václav Nosek, forbade further police investigation immediately after the funeral. The examining physician, Dr. Borkovec, continued his investigation despite the interdiction and discovered some signs of a connection between Major Franz Schramm and Václav Sedm, who could have been directly connected with the possible murder.

11. Major Franz Schramm, liaison officer of the State Security Forces and the NKVD, who, according to Rand, organized Masaryk's murder, was assassinated in the summer of 1948 by unknown persons, possibly Western agents.

12. Václav Sedm, member of the guard of the Czernin Palace, died in June in an unexplained car accident; there was no autopsy. Václav Sedm left his post during the night of March 9–10 explaining he was going home because of a toothache. Soon afterward, he became the supervisor of a nationalized jewelry store; when he was to be investi-

gated for blackmarketeering in gold, the investigation was dropped on Major Schramm's request.

13. Police Commissioner Josef Kadlec, on the basis of Borkovec's findings, suggested exhumation and an investigation by experts to determine whether the region behind Masaryk's right ear was damaged by a blow or whether it bore traces of an injection. Commissioner Kadlec died soon after, during a police interrogation.

14. Dr. František Borkovec, toward the end of 1948, was accused of organizing an uprising in Litoměřice and was executed without regular trial on the basis of an alleged confession that he was the leader of the uprising.

Dear Comrade General Prosecutor, you will certainly admit, after reading this simplified listing, that it can be assumed with some justification that Jan Masaryk was murdered. Whether the murderer was an NKVD agent, Major Schramm, and his accomplice was Sedm; whether they themselves, as potential witnesses, became the victims who had to be removed as a preventive measure; whether František Borkovec and Josef Kadlec were also murdered—this is the difficult judiciary-police task that I am requesting you to undertake in the name of truth and justice. You have an excellent opportunity to become a Czechoslovak Garrison,* and your position is much stronger since the archives of the Ministry of the Interior will be at your disposal directly because of our new leadership's interest in removing injustices and errors of the past. I am not certain that you will consider this appeal for investigation adequate, but to a layman's mind it seems that there is enough reason to launch such an investigation: the signs of struggle in the bedroom and bathroom; the physiological symptoms of deadly fear; the bed pillows which were possibly used to silence the victim as he was defending himself; the masking of an abrasion behind the ear; the toothache of the guard exactly around midnight of the critical day and his later connection with the liaison officer of Beria's police; his mysterious death, then the no less mysterious death of Major Schramm, ascribed to Western agents (but not proven); the sudden death of the man who suggested exhumation; the execution of the chief investigator,

* Reference to New Orleans District Attorney James Garrison, and his investigation of President Kennedy's assassination.—Ed.

the falsification of the autopsy report, the Minister of the Interior's interdiction against continuing the investigation, etc. Are these naive arguments or sound reasons for Mr. Bartuška, a professor of law at Charles University, the General Prosecutor of the Czechoslovak Socialist Republic, and the chief guardian of legality, to do that which has long been his duty? This question is being raised on March 10—the anniversary of Masaryk's death—by only a few people; but it is appropriate to put this question to the whole nation, to the students, and to the representatives of the democratization process, the purity of which shall be judged more by action on such cases as Masaryk's than by discourses on democracy; we cannot overlook the diminishing value of such words when overused.

I greet you as my former interrogator with comradely greetings and I assure you of my assistance, if required.

Ivan Sviták

Heads Against the Wall* ❧❧❧❧❧❧❧❧❧

> The friends of Chaos owed most of their success to Chaos; they wanted to repay him in some way. They consulted each other and arrived at an agreement: They found out that Chaos had no sensory organs with which to perceive and define the external world. So, one day they gave him eyes, the next a nose and in a week's time they had completed their task of turning Chaos into a sensitive personality just like themselves. While they were congratulating one another on their success, Chaos died.
>
> CHUANG-TSE (Chinese philosopher, Fourth Century B.C.)

I. Paradoxes of Reality

1. The friends of chaos who give it human form destroy it. It is not the enemies of chaos who cause its death, but its friends, its loyal, devoted friends.

2. This paradoxical peculiarity of the old Chinese riddle is at the same time the harsh truth of the political events in Czechoslovakia in early spring, 1968. Leading the efforts to liquidate chaos in economic and political life stand not its enemies, but its former friends, who destroy it in their desire to repay its many favors to them. The enemies of chaos support them in this, although they realize that the friends of chaos will disavow their own deeds as soon as they realize what they are doing.

3. Reality is paradoxical and "to expose ourselves to paradox means to expose ourselves to truth." Without being conscious of the paradoxical character of the present changes, one is incapable of understanding either the meaning of contemporary events or their inevitable

---

* Lecture at the Faculty of Philosophy, Charles University, Prague, March 20, 1968; published in *Student*, April 10, 1968.

—and unwelcome—further development. The friends of chaos, who today so earnestly present themselves as apostles of democracy compared to whom Masaryk would seem a second-rate bungler, have their limitations; these will begin to reveal themselves when they have to face the basic problems.

4. In the coming year, this paradoxical reality will find the present leaders of the political renewal as ministers, ambassadors and secretaries of the Czechoslovak state, with a direct interest in the preservation of the status quo, just as today they have an interest in going beyond the bounds of the existing totalitarian dictatorship. We support the "young guard" who want to displace the old bureaucrats in the Party; but it must be clearly understood that we support the program of the new team, not their personalities, and that their maximum program is our minimum one.

5. The collaboration between the social critics-intellectuals and the high Party officials of the state bureaucracy is the momentary expression of an identity of interests between these two groups. This identity of interests will vanish at the point where, having consolidated their power, the Party officials will come to consider democratization a closed subject. At that point, democratization will have ended and democracy never begun.

6. Therefore, intellectuals who can see what is happening behind the scenes of the power struggle and who understand the historical processes at work must speak to the nation about something more than democratization. Their political program must run roughly along these lines: *"We want democracy, not democratization. Democratization is our minimum program on the road to democracy."*

7. To the extent that democratization is a true road toward democracy, we support everything that leads toward an extension of civil and human rights. But we do not know enough about what democratization is. In the three months since the stirring events took place, we have still not learned what has actually happened. Is this democratization?

8. On the other hand, we know exactly what democracy is, and two hundred years of experience with this form of government permit us to state with assurance that, except for the temporary lifting of censorship, which could be reimposed at any moment, all the attributes of

democracy are still missing in this country, None of the demands in any programatic proposal has this perspective in view—not even those of our apparently very prudent writers!

9. The slogan of "democratization" is an improvisation born out of abnormal circumstances involving personality conflicts within the Politburo. It is the fruit of empirical politics and at the same time a fortuitous development serving to channel the citizens' dissatisfaction in a desirable direction. Democratization has never been and still is not the political aim of the young guards in their struggle for power; it is at most an accidental by-product which at this particular juncture in the political life of the country could not be avoided. It is consequently tolerated, and used against individuals in leading posts.

10. The bizarre character of this democratization is apparent as soon as we realize that events such as the suicide of Colonel-General Vladimir Janko and the defection of Major General Jan Šejna are attributed to such trivial causes as, for instance, the Major-General's speculations in anemone seeds! Furthermore, no justifiable grounds are given for the resignation of leading officials. Such explanations would enable us to understand why they are criticized and why they resign, since those who criticize them are of the same ilk. In other words, we do not need lessons in democratization to become democrats. The defenders of totalitarian dictatorships, who do need such lessons, are superfluous in a socialist democracy. Any attempt to democratize the cultural terrorists of totalitarian dictatorship would be tantamount to an attempt to square the circle. Round squares do not exist.

II. Totalitarian Dictatorships

1. Dictatorships are as old as mankind. Unchallenged control over the state by one person, clique, or organized power elite is the essence of dictatorship, and it is immaterial whether or not parliaments exist, elections are held, and various forms of state function take place. Modern dictatorships are not merely lineal descendants of the old forms of autocracy, despotism, and tyranny; they also contain new elements. Modern dictatorships—that is, totalitarian dictatorships—consist of a monopoly of a ruling minority over the government; but unlike historical forms of dictatorship, they additionally control mass

movements and have at their disposal a mass ideology; they govern the state from the center and interfere in every aspect, however private, of the citizens' lives. Totalitarian dictatorships and their ideologies do not purport merely to offer the individual a higher standard of living and a better form of government; they also offer a solution for every problem in life. Thus, they are the secular substitute for religion, the messengers of salvation through a new faith in ideology, the party, and the leader.

2. Totalitarian dictatorship is the new form of absolutism, the modern shape of despotism. The essence of a totalitarian dictatorship is the reduction of the human being to a tool of the power apparatus. Thus, every totalitarian dictatorship must destroy personality and individuality—not because the leaders are sadists (they are that, too) but because this trend results from the character of absolute, centralized, and unlimited power. Propaganda and terror, the control of mass information and the secret police are the most important means used for the functionalization of man.

3. Totalitarian dictatorship does not know how to govern indirectly; it rules by terror, fear, and direct interference. Therefore even the common-interest associations, created originally in the interest of their founders, are transformed into bureacratic *apparats*, which serve the purpose of increasing bureaucratic control over all groups of the population—youth, workers, and so forth. Totalitarian power is exercised on the assumption that everything is permitted in the name of race, class, or nation, and that humanitarian considerations or concerns are a mere sign of weakness. The dictatorships of Metternich, Caesar or the tsars were much more humane regimes than the modern ones.

4. Totalitarian dictatorship is an uncontrollable and closed system of power led by the people who believe they know the real interests of race, nation, or class, the meaning of progress for mankind—in fact, what is good for the whole world. In their fanaticism, they think they have the right to impose their program on the masses. Conflicts within the ruling group are resolved by a dialectic of orthodoxy and heresy, by periodical purges, and by tricks, since they cannot be resolved in an un-controlled manner. People, the masses and the classes, do not participate in decision making, but they are encouraged to express their thanks as loudly as they please to the party and the government.

5. Totalitarian dictatorship is based upon terror, and without terror it cannot survive. Terror is not merely a temporary means of arriving at certain ends under abnormal circumstances; it is the specific, the characteristic form rule for the totalitarian dictatorship. The basic meaning of terror is to ensure the functionalization of the citizen and to transform him into a compliant instrument of the power elite. Even when a totalitarian dictatorship is tottering, its secret police—the chief instrument of terror—continues to function efficiently. The result is a complete politicization and militarization of life.

6. Totalitarian dictatorship bases its support on the emotionalism of the masses, on the fragmentation of rational attitudes, and on the disintegration of standards of value. It acts as an imaginary remedy for the symptoms of the crisis. The total effectiveness of totalitarian dictatorship is safeguarded by full control over public opinion and attitudes, by means of propaganda spread through the mass media. Constantly repeated clichés of thought and stereotyped simplifications become generally accepted truths which are exposed neither to verification nor to criticism.

7. Totalitarian dictatorship operates with an *a priori* assumption of unity within the people, nation, party, or bloc; that is, with a postulate of moral-political unity, which in reality does not exist. A difference of opinion is therefore considered heresy and any opponent is considered an enemy and a traitor. Not only are the liberties of the individual and his civil rights discarded, but this very suppression of freedom is extolled as a triumph of progress and the hallmark of a higher social order.

8. The functionalization of man in the totalitarian dictatorship is ensured further by propaganda directed at the citizen through the mass media. Constant allegations concerning fictitious enemies create a psychosis of continual and abnormal threats to all the achievements of the revolution, the race, nation or class, a distant threat which is used to justify a permanent state of martial law over ideas and people. If the citizen is to be permanently disoriented, it is necessary to use the fiction of an enemy (the Jews, the imperialists, foreign nations, the whites, the blacks, the Chinese, the Europeans, and so on) who threatens the citizen and against whom the dictatorship defends him.

9. Totalitarian dictatorships are born out of the internal weak-

nesses of democratic regimes, the fall of which is the precondition for the rise of dictatorships, just as the establishment of democracy is the precondition for the fall of a dictatorship. Totalitarian dictatorships, mass movements and party *apparats* experience basic functional changes after coming into power. In the struggle for power, any such movement transforms itself into a bureaucratic governmental machine, power is institutionalized, and the differentiated apparatus of totalitarian organization arises. The spontaneous movement and its stimulus are replaced by a monopoly system based on party views, surrounded by a system of satellite organizations. The state becomes the instrument of the totalitarian elite, which in turn maintains a decisive influence over its own political institution—the party. This is the origin of the dual power of state and party so characteristic of dictatorships.

10. As soon as the ruling elite has seized power and organized itself, it begins to govern autocratically and to influence public opinion in its own interest, which is, however, presented as the interest of the masses. The tendency to accumulate power necessarily leads to an uncontrollable accumulation of power, which becomes an instrument of oppression, to be turned even against groups that may have helped to create this new elite. The praxis of the totalitarian state is based upon the use of efficient violence against both people and ideas. Totalitarian states have been, are, and will always be the greatest danger that man has ever faced; they constitute a total threat to human values, to European culture, and to the meaning of freedom.

III. The Nature of the Czechoslovak Dictatorship

1. The totalitarian dictatorship in which we have lived for the past twenty years has, by nature, several national peculiarities. The first great advantage of the regime was especially the fact that it was headed by full-blooded Czechs, who combined their Austrian tradition of joviality with the sluttish incompetence of concierges. To define in more specific detail this specific quality of the Czech leaders would require a team of brilliant men developing in depth C. Northcote Parkinson's law of the inevitable growth of inefficiency.

2. The Czechoslovak dictatorship has been totalitarian in the measure of the chaos it created; to attribute to it the term "dictatorship" is a

rather comical paradox. Apart from the several assassinations it did carry out, the government, despite its absolute power, has been as helpless as a baby with a slide rule. The occasional fits of democratization, periodically installed and withdrawn, never brought about any basic changes, and the foundations of this regime were undermined again and again by its aggressive stupidity.

3. The spontaneously spouting geyser of this stupidity, tirelessly gushing forth for twenty years in the official press and the tolerated cultural publications, and in the speeches of politicians and of youth leaders, has not been able, nevertheless, to undermine the foundations of the socialist system. The common sense of good-natured Slovaks, Moravians, and, to an extent, also Czechs has always corrected the worst excesses and reduced them to a tolerable level.

4. Thus our history of the last twenty years may be likened to a phase of marking time; sometimes we would raise our feet as if marching, sometimes as if running—yet we did not move from the spot. Under such circumstances, one might ask one's compatriots what the purposes of the "march" might be. It is like the question that a mischievous girl I know used to ask the soldiers confined in the barracks. When she asked them over the fence whether they liked the service, and they answered "No," she would ask them why did they not leave. To voice this kind of question is now the duty of everyone.

5. The second characteristic peculiarity of this totalitarian dictatorship is that it has in the past twenty years avoided any internal political shock, having succeeded, during the critical years 1956–1957, in reducing the price of salami sausage (*tsabajka*) and in blackening all critics as "intellectuals." It has repeated this method in every crisis that has arisen. Capitalists, kulaks, Jews, and intellectuals became the scapegoats and these scapegoats, together with cut-rate sausage, made up the essence of our statesmen's political philosophy. Hence a politician's inability to cut the price of sausage might have fatal consequences for him!

6. This sausage-realism in politics was effective as long as there was something else of which the price could be reduced; and we must admit that both our nations [the Czechs and the Slovaks] were quite satisfied with this state of affairs. This realism has been pursued at the expense of economic efficiency; it made possible less and inferior work

(30)

for more money, and it ensured actual legal and economic equality between an unskilled laborer and a university professor. Thanks to this
consensus gentium there has been, in spite of growing economic difficulties, no noticeable political opposition in Czechoslovakia. The country has been slowly dragged into economic collapse with the tacit
agreement of subjugated but thrifty citizens whose aspirations have
not been to seek freedom but to buy a new car.

7. The grave-like quiet of this dictatorship and its truncheon-assured
stability seemed to be unassailable from within. But then all the re-
sources which had been guaranteeing its grand policy, that of bribing
the nation with a higher standard of living, suddenly failed. It was in
fact the economics of a high standard of living itself that failed. The
sudden collapse of the economic structure, by no means incurable, was
enough to shake the precarious stability of this dictatorship and to
evoke a remarkable change of political orientation.

8. The third basic feature of the Czechoslovak totalitarian dictatorship was its extraordinarily conservative character, permanently in conflict with the ineradicable tradition which upheld the existence of elementary human rights in European states. In Poland, they did not execute their Gomulka; in Hungary and Bulgaria they executed one minister apiece; the Czechoslovak sacrificial offering to Stalinism in the
Slanský trial was the richest of all.

9. In every important question concerning the socialist block, Czechoslovak foreign policy has always followed the hardest line. The gradual
emancipation of Yugoslavia, Poland, Hungary, Albania, China, Rumania, and Cuba from the Soviet pattern has always been greeted with
displeasure, and all attempts at emulation have been condemned. This
condemnation has always been done in the same way—by drawing attention to the indisputably lower standard of living in these countries—
that is, by the classical means of drawing Mr. Average Citizen's (Mr.
Novak's) attention to his wallet.

10. The conservative feature of the state's foreign policy has not,
however, been merely platonic, and the sincere statements of devoted
and brotherly support for fascist-like regimes of the Arab Nasserite
type were not empty words. Deliveries of weapons, financed by unlimited credits, directly served the aims of Arab policies.

Thus, if we want to understand the possible further development of this totalitarian dictatorship, we must take into consideration its characteristic features—its specifically Czech pragmatism and conservatism.

IV. Nature of the Present Changes

1. Are we experiencing revolution or revolt? Revolution entails structural social changes in class relations, in economic and political relations, and in the structure of the power mechanisms. Revolt is just a change of the ruling groups and does not affect structural principles and relations. It is up to us to decide which of the two we are witnessing. The game is open.

2. The alternative of revolt is, for us, completely irrelevant. We have no reason to be enthusiastic about a change in personnel. Sociologists and philosophers know that "the institution is stronger than the individual," and that without the control mechanism of public opinion every member of the ruling elite must degenerate. Antonín Novotný started out as an exponent of liberalization. And today, in Poland, students have to barricade themselves in the university against their national hero of 1956.

3. We are on the contrary interested in the possibility of structural change, because it shows the way to an open socialist society, to socialist democracy. However, this is still far off, although it appears now as a national illusion dependent on the resignation of a few people. Students have little reason to support such illusions; on the contrary they have every reason to be on the lookout for the fake cards which will now be played in the game—a game which is to decide the nature of the state in which we are to live.

4. If we observe realistically and critically the results of this three-month-long process of rebirth, we will have to admit that, except for the temporary absence of censorship, nothing has changed in the structure of the totalitarian dictatorship. In Czechoslovakia, the monopoly of one party over political life remains unchanged and, of the processes characteristic of a democracy and essential in the formation and expression of the popular will, so far none exists.

5. The concept of the hierarchic structuring of state bodies manipulated from a single center remains unchanged. It is incompatible with democracy, for which it is essential that the expression of the will of the people be the result of certain social processes, in which the various

elements play relatively independent roles. At the level of ideology, ideological values and political programs must compete with each other; at the level of state power, the legislative, executive, and independent judiciary must check one another; and finally at the level of economic and civic activity, the special interest groups, the bureaucracy, and public opinion must play independent roles.

6. At the present, there is only one fact which justifies hope in the process of democratization—the genuine expression of public opinion; it will be toward this very area that the counterattacks of conservative forces will be directed in the near future. They will call for moderation and will offer new economic programs and fresh personalities instead of fundamental political changes. We, on the contrary, must endeavor fully to exploit the tolerated limits of freedom, in order to press for democratic elections as the next step toward establishing a European socialist state.

7. This progress is possible only if the fundamental conflict of the contemporary Czech socialist state is resolved: this conflict in no way is to be found in the relations of our two nations, but in the mechanisms of the totalitarian dictatorship. . . . We must liquidate this dictatorship, or it will liquidate us.

8. This liquidation of the mechanisms of totalitarian dictatorship and totalitarian thinking is the condition for achieving democratic socialism. Totalitarian dictatorship is our Enemy Number One. We have a sufficiency of brains and hands to realize the program of socialist freedom, but we also have a sufficiency of elements among us trying to stop us. If the question is, "Wherefrom, with whom, and whither?" we could briefly answer: "From Asia to Europe, alone."

9. Characteristic of the present "changes" is the fact that no basic changes have taken place, that the mechanism of totalitarian dictatorship continues unaffected. We are interested in a lasting process of democratization, the permanent transformation of totalitarian dictatorship into a European system with a democratic form of government.

V. Socialist Democracy

1. Democracy is a system of government which can be, and has been, connected with varying state establishments and varying social orders. Democracy is a form of government based on the will of the

people; it is government of the people, by the people, and for the people.

2. People cannot rule directly; they must express their wishes through various ideological and organizational groups, through political parties. The expression of this will takes place in elections whereby a government is constituted. Democracy cannot abolish the reality of government, the difference between the ruled ones and the rulers; it does not even propose to do so.

3. The democratic function of a government is based on a combination of opposing political powers which take turns in government and are under the control of the people. Without this elementary mechanism for the control of power, no democracy is possible.

4. A government in a democracy is a public office, not a ruling establishment. It rests on the principle of the equality of citizens before the law, without being able to abolish the actual differences among people, the inequality of their social positions, and their differences as to material possessions. It postulates the freedom of the individual and is based on the axiom that free thought and personal freedom are inalienable human rights, which provide the foundation of democracy and without which democracy crumbles.

5. The minimal criteria for modern democracy are the following:

a) the existence and assertion of basic civil and human rights;

b) an equilibrium of state powers (including a functioning parliamentarianism);

c) a universal, equal, secret, and alternative voting right.

Democracy is thus a controllable system of power positions, power relationships, and power processes.

6. Modern democracy is a mass democracy which differs from the classic democracy of the nineteenth-century English and French type. The features that distinguish the democratic governmental forms of the present from those of the past have resulted primarily from the formation of large power groups, the bureaucratization of the political apparatus, the concentration of enormous powers in the hands of individuals, and the centralizing tendencies of state bureaucracy.

7. Socialist democracy must fulfill at least the elementary functions of existing democracies; otherwise it becomes a deceptive and misleading slogan, an ideological fraud perpetuated for the purpose of insuring

power changes. Socialist democracy is an optimal connection between socialist goals of social reconstruction and governmental forms suitable to a European, industrially developed society. Socialist democracy therefore cannot be only a change in the leading group of one and the same totalitarian dictatorship.

8. Socialist democracy must, as a first step toward its realization, organize elections and abolish the basic institutions conflicting with the fulfillment of civil rights, that is, with freedom of speech, of the press, of assembly, and of conscience. The democratic axiom that freedom to think is an inalienable human right must find expression as the right of the individual to formulate and express personal opinions, even if these opinions differ from the opinions of the ruling elite.

9. The followers of socialist democracy must demand programmatically the creation of basic mechanisms for the control of the elite, an equilibrium of power, basic civil rights, and the secret ballot. On the other hand, they have no reason to demand personnel changes within the ruling elite. Neither have they any reason to stand in the way of any personnel changes, just as they would have no reason to protest any changes in the tenancy of a strange apartment building.

10. The followers of socialist democracy must insist on a program involving considerable changes to be brought about as a result of a democratizing process through a newly elected national assembly, which would give us a new constitution. Cheering loudly the proposal at a mass meeting that the President of the Republic abdicate is as uncalled for as cheering loudly at his inauguration. Suddenly awakened tolerance, fits of democratization, and the dressing up of old forms in new costumes evoke distrust among the partisans of socialist democracy.

VI. Peculiarities of Present Events

1. In the postwar era every East European state underwent considerable changes through which it satisfied the need to change the original, universal model of revolution and social establishment to a system more suitable to its own historical and social conditions. Czechoslovakia is now undergoing a similar change, with considerable delay, but at the same time going further in the democratization processs than countries

which undertook their emancipation from the Soviet model much earlier. New and previously untried processes emerge from the peculiarities of present events, of which at least three are decisive: the democratization process is directed from the top; it represents a new type of revolutionary process with a new class character; and it opens new possibilities for the role of intellectuals and the middle classes.

2. The democratization process does not take place because of the pressure of a popular movement, but is the result of an intentional move by the power elite. Just as this elite previously liquidated "slice by slice" its political and class enemies (that is, it excluded them group by group from active political participation), it will now perhaps widen the limits of possible active political participation by the same "slice-by-slice" method, and it will broaden civil liberties by means of a certain rationing system. This process is probably necessary and it emanates from the peculiarity of the present establishment—from the specific conditions of the Czechoslovak totalitarian dictatorship.

3. Although the rationing system is by no means ideal, it is nevertheless a realistic move toward a gradual transformation of totalitarian dictatorship in circumstances where real democracy cannot be installed. Directed democracy disrupts the present mechanism of Stalinism without creating the danger that the foundations of socialist social management will themselves be threatened. Therein lies its significance: it is a method which can be used not only by Western Communist parties but primarily to serve the process of further democratization in the states of the Eastern bloc, especially in the Soviet Union.

4. The democratization process so far concerns only the power elite and a small group of intellectuals, students and writers. It appears as a disintegration of the homogeneous, unified political orientation of the leading group, and as a creation of alternative solutions which are the basis of a political struggle manifesting itself in personnel changes among the leading cadres. The remaining strata of the population continue to be manipulated by the same methods as before, and the democratization process only touches their consciousness. Democracy is foisted on the masses in the same manner as dictatorship; that is, without their direct participation.

5. The events of the past three months will represent a new type of revolutionary process, but only under the condition that democratiza-

tion will not stop but instead will reach the social structures themselves. So far, it is not possible to state that the present trend of political changes is championed by a specific class, or that it is an expression of the opinion of a specific social class or stratum; it is, however, certain that it is centered around the intelligentsia and the students—and that it finds more intense support among the middle class than among the workers and the power elite.

6. The process of transforming political life, and possibly also the social structure, rejects in its own way the rigid concepts of Marxist doctrine in the last century. So far, socialist democracy functions in conflict with the Stalin-Khrushchev variant of the theory of class struggle. The leading force behind these changes is not the working class, nor its institutions, its elite, but a small group of Communist intelligentsia relying on the support of wider strata of the population.

7. The process of transformation strives for the unification of freedom and socialism, that is, for the fulfillment of the original meaning of Marx's teaching. It represents a real opportunity for a regeneration of creative Marxism and is an exceptionally important preview of social processes which will take place in the Soviet Union in the seventies. In Czechoslovakia, Marxism proved itself a European, humanistic political strategy suitable for developed countries with a democratic tradition.

8. In this process, which so far is limited to the political sphere and has not touched the socio-economic structure itself, the new role of intellectuals and the middle class takes shape: they become the active, initiating components of the movement supporting democratization. This democratization is carried out within existing institutions and aims at removing past mistakes. However, it has no program of its own and proceeds in a pragmatic way.

9. The goals of the process appear to have been set by a Marxist intelligentsia. The support of the middle class creates the impression that these changes are in its interest. In fact, however, these transformative changes are vitally important to maintain the standard of living of the working class and of the majority of the population of the country, and therefore they have no narrow class goals. The intellectuals do not make "revolutions" for themselves but in the interest of society, and that is an important additional factor in their favor.

10. The labor movement developed most successfully when it was

headed by intellectuals who understood the possibilities of economic development and of workers' organizations. Intellectuals presently trying to bridge the gap between the revolutionary intelligentsia and the working class are reaching back into the thirties—the pre-Stalin phase of Marxism—when this unity was a reality. Stalinism signaled the end of this productive alliance, which had brought forth first-rate values in European culture.

VII. The Role of the Intellectuals

1. At all times—and also in the revolutionary and transformative processes of the present time—the intellectual elite has one central purpose: to understand. The intellectual elite—the only true elite of modern times—must not be one-sided and critical in the name of parochial interests, e.g. the interests of the Union of Writers or those of a student organization. It must understand many aspects of the situation within their context and accurately so, since otherwise it cannot rule. To rule means to understand and direct—not to execute and depose.

2. At all times the intellectual's task is to destroy myths and illusions. His criticism must, therefore, be the more intense the higher the waves of enthusiasm. Mistrust, skepticism, and extreme prudence are justified whenever an apparently all-national intoxication prevents us from seeing clearly and when people can be easily fooled by changes. The illusion of a victory for goodness and freedom over destructive elements is precisely one of the reasons for criticism.

3. At all times an intellectual must concentrate on the meaning of events, which escapes easily in a flood of facts at precisely the moment that history assumes a dynamic character and brings forth many new, partially understood facts. An intellectual confronts the factualism of history with programmed goals. He therefore always asks disturbing questions about the meaning of the resignation of this or that politician, or about the suicide of this or that general, and he must maintain a certain distance from the illusion that a change in personalities is necessarily a change for the better. Working from the opposite assumption is more productive.

4. At all times an intellectual must defend suprapersonal, supraclass, and supranational values of truth, reason, and justice. If he subjects

(38)

them to a functional consideration without regard to the character of this consideration he will degenerate, inevitably, into a manipulatable object of political blackmail. The motives of people who make compromises to the detriment of truth, reason, and justice are, of course, always the best motives.

5. An intellectual of contemporary Czechoslovakia must take into consideration the distinctiveness of Czech thinking, burdened by German culture. While the Germans have thought and now think rationally and accurately in irrational and inaccurate concepts, the Czechs think inaccurately in inaccurate concepts, especially in politics. This they have compensated for by requiring realism in their art.

6. An intellectual is, at all times, prone to succumb to ideologies, to overestimate the function of ideas, and to underestimate the real dynamism of social actions. We must, therefore, remind ourselves of the need to understand historical processes, rather than to translate politics and history into moral terms and be taken in by the extremes of either scientific or utopian thought. Ideologies profit by combining the views of science with those of utopia; therein lies their immense real force, despite their illusory character. An intellectual must be an enemy of ideologies; however, he cannot avoid being confronted with them.

7. The present tasks of an intellectual can change in relation to conditions, but these tasks will always be connected with the basic problems which arose in the early spring of 1968 and with the rotation of the elite. What does this mean in practice? First of all, we must go forward and not believe that it is possible to return to the political system of the pre-Munich Republic. We must create a mechanism of political power for which there is no parallel, which is an attractive and, at the same time, a difficult project. Not even the return to the conditions of 1945–1948 is presently possible, and the scarecrows of old political parties of those years are of no interest to us.

8. The second task is the necessity of liquidating the power monopolies in regular and democratic elections, that is, in the competition of alternative programs and personalities without which there is no growth. Parliamentary elections should bring a radical turnover of all deputies. The intellectuals should not in the next election elect any of the deputies who creatively participated in the downfall of the Czecho-

slovak state and its culture—that is, no one from the present National Assembly. However, who shall nominate the deputies to the National Assembly?

9. The third important task is to create an alternative program—a minimum program of defense of civil and human rights. Not even the writers were able to build such a program. We cannot approve of their cooperation in compromising individual persons. This is especially valid when such maneuvers were agreed upon ahead of time with the purpose of creating the illusion that writers can change presidents.

10. The forms the struggle of young intellectuals will take probably will be the same as those forms taken by the struggle of their Western colleagues. Their strength is in ideas, in "heads." They must use their heads to break through the walls that surround us and cut us off from Europe, since there is no other way to break through. The only policy, therefore, that is worthy of a student and an intellectual is the policy of "heads against the wall."

VIII. Praxis

1. In the era of dictatorships, do not think of politics in terms of classical liberalism and its ideology. In the present wave of democratization, do not think in terms of totalitarian dictatorship and its ideology. Think about reality in terms capable of expressing reality itself. Thus, do not erect before your actions new barriers of an ideological character; instead try to understand reality. Only in this way will you understand what is happening and only then will you be able to act effectively.

2. Remove your political thinking from the area of passions, ideals, and illusions. Rationalize your thinking and understand politics as a matter of reason, interest, and purposefulness. Let no emotions carry you away; instead, calculate coldly the optimal variant of behavior, following the theory of strategic games.

3. Live in productive tension with the times, not in conformity with the times. You are responsible for your world and that responsibility demands of you a continuous nonconformism of free, rational, and dialectic thinking that always reflects the real motion of the world, lasting changes, and permanent transformations. Do not repeat journalistic clichés about democracy, regeneration, and deformations. The so-

called deformations are no deformations at all, but the normal, necessary, common phenomena of totalitarian dictatorship. They are not surgically removable tumors on the peaceful body of socialism, but a blight that spreads through the entire governmental system. Totalitarian dictatorship itself is a deformation, and to remove this deformation means to remove totalitarian dictatorship.

4. Do not believe in theories which excuse past mistakes and deformations by pointing to the common praxis of the era. These theories consider totalitarian dictatorship as a necessity, as an expression of the objective law of history, as an expression of the non-existent lawfulness of historical movements. Politics is not a question of the application of *a priori*-valid general laws and prefabricated models to a social establishment, but a matter of creative subjectivity, of struggle. The theories of the historical inevitability of dictatorship eliminate individual responsibility and replace it with objective laws, class interests, racial views, the power of the apparatus, or "reasons of state."

5. Do not excuse past reality by present baseness, and never exclude the individual responsibility of a man for what he does. Thus, do not see in the historical personalities of the last twenty years people who acted under the pressure of a personality cult, or people who were disappointed, or victims of circumstance. Consider them as unpunished criminals, willing collaborators with those in power, individuals who failed as human beings, as examples of character, as persons of integrity—but judge them always according to their real behavior and their measure of responsibility for the devastating operations carried out under their leadership.

6. Beware of attempts to reproduce utopian plans. Utopia resists contact with reality and with history and therefore it fails in the same way as terror. Under the pretext of broadening freedom, freedom can easily be limited. The liquidation of civil rights and rational politics was always accomplished in the name of higher freedom and higher rationality.

7. Be critical disciples of Karl Marx, the Copernicus of social sciences and modern politics. Do not forget that this man never defended the role of any one party or any apparatus over the working class, but, instead, created his politics in agreement with the basic interests of this most important class of modern history. The concept of the role of the Party as the instrument by which a decision-making elite brings its

ideas to the masses, is an idea of Russian nationalists and Lenin, already criticized by many Marxists at the time it was first conceived.

8. Do not forget that Marx wanted to broaden the civil rights of man, to make formal rights real, not to abolish them. The idea that the Party leads the working class and the people, that the Party implants its ideas in the people, is a concept in which the Party itself plays the role of the working class, the Party apparatus plays the role of the Party, and the individual plays the role of the Central Committee. An ideology based on this foundation has nothing in common with Marx but has very much in common with the constant blotting out of critical thinking and of human freedoms through the hypnotic monotony of the followers of the Dzhugashvili cult. If they are Marxists, then we are not; if we are Marxists, then they are not.

9. Do not permit yourselves to be brainwashed through the mass communications media and their slogans, and do not accept any language of non-thought. The monotonous drill of propaganda can now work with different markings but with an identically aggressive stupidity, which presents further errors as a final accounting with errors. There are and will be many propagandists and missionaries of false ideologies interested in you in order to convert you to their beliefs. Convert to yourselves.

10. Believe in IDEAS, do not believe in IDEOLOGIES.

REASON	ILLUSIONS
CONCRETE MAN	ANONYMOUS MASSES
LOVE	POWER
SOCIALIST DEMOCRACY	TOTALITARIAN DICTATORSHIP
INTELLIGENCE	APPARATUS
PARADOXES	CERTAINTIES
COINCIDENCES	PLANS
FREEDOMS	NECESSITIES
YOURSELF	AUTHORITY

Young people, believe in yourselves!

Dedicated to the students of the Philosophical Faculty of Charles University in Prague, on the eve of the windy spring of 1968.

The Rules of the Game * ~~~~~~~~~~

Face the Facts.

T. G. MASARYK

1. When the nation is silent, the artist, scientist, or intellectual must speak. When the nation speaks, what should the artist, scientist, or intellectual do? He must think, since under all circumstances his central task in culture is to think. Every culture is the result of an action originating in ideas, in reason; it is the fruit of the mind. The measure of the rationality of a society is also a measure of its culture. A functioning reason is a prerequisite for a functioning culture. There is no culture without reason.

2. The central question in every culture in every era is the number of civil rights, the existence or nonexistence of civil rights, and not art alone. Any culture which tolerates the limitation of freedom of thought and of human rights in the name of power-political interests is qualitatively different from a culture in which a citizen acts, performs, and creates as an equal, free citizen, as a creator and recipient of cultural values. Therefore, the determining factor for us is not the enthroning of a president but the enthroning of civil rights, the enthroning of civil freedoms. An incidental historical "play on words" taking place these days is perhaps a favorable sign that we shall be given real freedom and not an emperor.**

3. The process of democratizing culture is related to the central question of human rights. In the present state, the bureaucratic-power apparatus played a decisive part in cultural politics. Its members made decisions erroneously, incompetently, and, what is worse, without having the cultural jurisdiction to do so. The notion that values, culture,

* Contribution to a discussion at the Union of Film and Television Artists Conference, March 29, 1968; published in the weekly, *Filmové a televizní noviny* [Film and television news], Prague, in 1968.

** Reference to President Svoboda and to the other candidate in the recent presidential election, Čestmír Císař. *Svoboda* means "freedom". *Císař* means "Caesar" or "Emperor."—Ed.

art, social relations should in any way be tied to institutions and authority is only another version of totalitarian thinking. The conflict between culture and the ideologies of the power apparatus is inevitable, since every culture, and *a fortiori* humanistic culture, assumes an objectively conflicting stance toward the contemporary state. Thus, the process of democratization is not possible without overcoming totalitarian thinking in culture.

4. The present political changes are, so far, changes in the power elite, changes of persons, individuals; they are, so far, not changes in structure. The bureaucracy of a totalitarian dictatorship will reconcile itself easily with personnel changes, while it is afraid of structural changes and will fight them with all its power. Therefore we must ask for structural changes and not be satisfied with personnel changes.

5. The present political changes are, so far, a change in the ideology of one and the same power elite, they are an exchange of the ideology of bureaucratic functionalism for that of pragmatism. Values of good and evil are replaced by pure expediency and by not too large a measure of tolerance toward the standpoint of nonmembers of the Party, a standpoint which cannot, at the present time, be suppressed. Concrete, real humanism, however, is unacceptable to the bureaucracy of the power apparatus. We do not want to liquidate only the ideology of Stalinism, but its power structure as well. Therefore, we must ask for the liquidation of the heritage of Stalinism and its power structure, not a mere exchange of ideologies within the power apparatus.

6. The democratization process, so far, is directed from above, by the power elite which itself is extremely antidemocratic and is not directly interested in democracy. Its maximum program of democratization is our minimum program of true democracy. Democratization only makes sense as a road toward democracy. We do not ask for democratization but for democracy—which is an enormous difference.

7. Our effort should be directed toward the liquidation of the power monopoly through regular elections, not through changes in personnel and in ideology. I do not consider as correct any policy put forth by intellectuals or organizations of artists, if it focuses the attention of the nation on secondary questions. Our endeavor cannot be to change persons and ideologies. In the area of cultural politics we must demand the end of the policy of brandishing a cultural whip over artists, the end

of the administration of "nationalized" brains. The cultural terrorists of the past era cannot, under any circumstances, be democratized, for the same reason that no one is able to square the circle. Totalitarian dictatorships and their mechanisms are and will remain incompatible with the notions of democracy, with the government of free people.

8. One of the most serious questions of democratization is that of the leading role of the Communist Party. As long as this requirement does not originate from the reality of social and political life, it is, in itself, antidemocratic. The requirement of a leading role for the Communist Party has no theoretical support in the works of Karl Marx. It is a result of Lenin's reflections, which once upon a time—in a very logical and theoretically correct manner—stemmed from the fact that in Russia the working class was an insignificant fragment in the illiterate sea, in the midst of tsarist despotism. The leading role of the Party was institutionalized into Stalinism, which is unsuitable for democratic countries where there are no illiterate people—in spite of the concentrated efforts of Comrade Hendrych * and his collaborators.

9. The artist, scientist, or member of the intelligentsia must, under all circumstances and in all historical situations, pose the question of the meaning of the recent changes, the meaning of the social process, the meaning of political events. Under all circumstances they must understand and destroy myths, not only the old ones but also those which are being born. They must know what is a myth and what is the truth. An intellectual can best serve his time if he identifies the truth as truth, and illusions as illusions, in a given historical moment.

10. An artist, scientist, film producer, intellectual, does not render accounts to any office or organization, regardless of whether it is democratic, democratized, or totalitarian. The discipline of truth is the hardest of all the disciplines that must be followed by artists and scientists. The discipline of truth is superordinated to the discipline of institution. This great idea, which was propagated by Karl Marx, can now be not only expressed, but also defended.

11. We cannot sacrifice critical thinking on anybody's altar, neither that of an individual, nor that of an institution, nor that of the Party, nor that of democracy. Artistic freedom is an axiom of culture, not

* Reference to Jiři Hendrych, second-in-command in the Novotný government hierarchy.—Ed.

because the artist is somewhat different from others, but because the same civil freedoms apply to him as to anyone else. The interest of an artist is, under present conditions, identical with the interest of the population of Czechoslovakia; it is, at present, as much opposed as it always was to the interests of the power elite.

12. Intellectuals, artists and scientists, on the one hand, and workers and working people on the other, have had, and continue to have, a common enemy: the bureaucratic dictatorship of which they want to rid themselves. Rejecting the conflict between social groups encouraged by the apparatus to prove its apparent usefulness, we, the artists, scientists, and intellectuals must reach a point where we can tell the workers: "We do not defend our own professional interests, but the interests of the great majority of people living in this state. Through a dramatic historical movement we are back at the turn of the spiral that we left twenty years ago. Today we can formulate our goal by this slogan: "Long live the unity of working hands and working brains."

Second Act: Collision

PROBLEMS OF WORKERS

In its rational form, dialectics . . . is, for
a doctrinaire, a scandal and an infamy, because in its positive conception of being
it includes also the conception of its negation, of its necessary destruction; it
conceives every form that arises as being
in a state of flux, that is, it sees it in its
ephemeral aspect, it does not allow itself
to be impressed by anything; it is essentially critical and revolutionary.

KARL MARX

Contents

Chronology

April 2

Student published open letter demanding an investigation of Foreign Minister Jan Masaryk's "suicide."

April 3

Commission set up to inquire into Masaryk's death.

April 4

First mass meeting demanding unity of workers and intellectuals held in Doubrava mine, Ostrava-Karviná.

April 5

Discussion club KAN (*Klub angažovaných nestraníků,* or Club of Committed Non-Party Members), founded in Prague.
The Central Committee approved the Communist Party "action program."

April 6

Oldrich Černík entrusted with the formation of a new government.

April 10

The Central Committee of the Slovak Communist Party demanded federalization of the republic and equality between the Czechs and the Slovaks.

April 11

Club of Independent Writers founded.

April 18

First public political discussion organized by the newly founded Club of Committed Non-Party Members (KAN).

May 3

Minister of National Defense General Dzur confirmed that during the recent visit to Prague of Marshal Yakubovsky, supreme commander of the armed forces of the Warsaw Pact countries, maneuvers on Czechoslovak territory were discussed.
First spontaneous meeting of young people at the Jan Hus Monument, Old-Town Square, Prague—KAN manifesto read at the rally.

May 3 (continued)

Lecture, "The Genius and the Apparatus," given at Charles University on the anniversary of Marx's 150th birthday.

May 5–7

General Secretary Luigi Longo of the Italian Communist Party visited Prague.

May 14

Club of Non-Party Members founded in Ostrava. [The clubs for non-Party members founded around this time had various names. KAN was the original club, founded in Prague, but some clubs in district towns had other names, like "Club of the Young," or "Political Club." None had legal recognition and all were forbidden immediately after the occupation, in accordance with the secret clauses of the Čierná-Bratislava conferences.—Ed.]

May 17–22

A delegation of the Soviet armed forces headed by Minister of Defense Marshal Grechko visited Prague.

May 18

Mass meetings of KAN in Prague, Žofín.

May 29

General Kazakov and representatives of the armed forces of other Warsaw Pact countries arrived in Prague to prepare for June staff exercises in Czechoslovakia.

June 27

Publication of the *Two Thousand Words* manifesto.

Dubček depicted as Jánošík, a legendary Slovak "Robin Hood," dancing over a time bomb.

Open Letter to the Workers and Technicians of the Doubrava Mine in Ostrava* ～～～～

Dear comrades, communists and trade unionists of the Doubrava mine:

Some technicians from your mine have published, in *Nová svoboda*, a comprehensive account of their reaction to my contribution to the inquiry run by *Literární listy* and have invited me to reply. I am addressing my answer not only to the technicians, but also, and above all, to you, the workers. For as I see it, the best guarantee that our process of regeneration will be socialist and democratic in nature lies in the alliance of workers and intellectuals, that is to say in you, the working class of the Ostrava district and of socialist Czechoslovakia, and not in the signatures that some smart conservative *apparatchik* promptly collected in the complicated situation in Ostrava at the beginning of March. He could not come out into the open, so he had to take cover behind the pretense of a democratic expression of the technicians' views, as the intelligentsia of your plant. I agree with the underlying intention of the technicians' resolution, which is to get the technical intelligentsia to act together with the workers and to put their whole weight behind the common demands of both. But at the same time I consider that they are wrong on all three of the main topics dealt with in the article.**

* Speech, March 29, 1968, at a special meeting of miners from Doubrava; published in the Ostrava daily, *Nová svoboda* [New freedom]. [See " 'Wherefrom, with Whom, and Whither?' " in the previous section of this volume. This "Open Letter" is Sviták's reply to "Our Voice in the Discussion," a resolution issued on March 12, 1968, a week after the March 5 publication in *Literární listy* of " 'Wherefrom. . . .' " The sixty-two signers of the resolution wished to "make it clear" as "members of the technical intelligentsia," that the views expressed in Sviták's *Literární listy* statement, and in statements by others that "bore the mark of nervousness," did not have "the silent approval of the whole intelligentsia as a social group."—Ed.]

** "Our Voice in the Discussion" objects to Sviták's use of the term *totalitarian dictatorship* rather than *proletarian dictatorship* in describing the post-1948 era in Czechoslovakia, and distinguishes *totalitarian dictatorship* as "the term we have

Comrade technicians, don't you feel today, now that it is the end of March, that you let yourselves be tricked into giving your signatures, that you were fooled by some *apparatchiks* who were afraid for their positions at a time when the position of the chief *apparatchik* at the head of the state was so precarious and shaky that, bankrupt politician that he was, he thought of calling up the army and the people's militia to help him attain his personal goals? Why do you argue against ten lines by an unknown philosopher, instead of taking the initiative and adopting resolutions in favor of the regeneration movement? Why do you not denounce the fact that one of the victims of Antonín Novotný, Rudolf Barák, is still being held in the Opava jail, not far from you? Why do you not ask yourselves if the leadership of the Ostrava district are not taking a strangely equivocal stand in the midst of the crisis? Why do you keep silent about the fact that a delegate to the district conference in Ostrava and an executive member of the Olomouc District Committee of the Czechoslovak Communist

---

become accustomed to reserving . . . for fascist Germany." Conceding that "the proletarian dictatorship to some extent went astray," starting with the "infamous trials," the resolution contends that "the democratic discussions now going on prove that it . . . did not reach the stage of totalitarian dictatorship." Criticism is also made of Sviták's demand, in "Wherefrom . . . ," for "the observance of fundamental human rights, at least to the same extent as in the Czechoslovakia of bourgeois democracy." Recalling the restrictions imposed upon the labor movement and the Communist Party by earlier Czechoslovak republics, "Our Voice . . ." calls for a democracy that will "defend freedom and human rights not just to the same extent as the bourgeois-democratic republic, but to a much greater extent, for it will include all working people." While admitting the need for reforms in the Party apparatus, "Our Voice . . ." also questions Sviták's apparently pejorative use of the term *apparatchik*. The Party, according to the resolution, "has always, at all stages, had a group of professional revolutionaries, its secretaries and active politicians, whom Ivan Sviták today calls its *apparatchiks*." Hence the "apparatus" is merely "a group which handles political activity and its organization on a full-time basis," and "to do away with this apparatus means doing away with the party." "To that, of course," the resolution continues, "we do not agree, because the working class . . . must necessarily have a political organization of its own, to fight for a policy . . . which . . . can bring about swift advances in the scientific and technological revolution, so that each worker may develop his personality more and more and take full advantage of the level of civilization and culture that mankind has now attained." "Our Voice . . ." concludes with an endorsement of "wide-ranging discussion," through which the principle formulated as "the right people in the right places" should quickly be "put into effect."—Ed.

Party, the newly-elected (!!) Karel Zorek, is openly threatening Alexander Dubček and the intellectuals with the militia?

Karel Zorek, as chairman of the Communist Party Committee for the Uničov machine-building plant, said precisely this:

Further, I should like to speak about the attitude of another intellectual by the name of Sviták, who after being thrown out of Olomouc is teaching at Charles University and spreading his demagogical opinions about the existence of thugs in the Party through his lectures. And the Central Committee is putting the means of Party agitation into the hands of the reaction, which is belittling everything that we have done, in the Party, for society in the last twenty years. A great deal could be said about that; but all I want to do is warn those who are sharpening their teeth and getting ready to seize power, that for the time being it is we who have the weapons in the factories and that we are good at using them. (*Nova svoboda*, March 24, 1968)

Why are you silent about that? Why do you prefer to dwell on the ten lines of my contribution to an inquiry in a literary magazine and, what is more, in the process to attribute to me thoughts which I do not share? Don't you find it strange that someone is leading the technicians of the Doubrava mine in the peculiar direction which is being talked about as the Ostrava faction? Who was it in the Doubrava mine who organized the political events of the exciting days at the beginning of March in such a way that an unknown philosopher became the target of verbal attacks, while the way was left open for Karel Zorek to make threats with the militia, and while the question of the meaning and aims of the regeneration in the Communist Party and in the Czechoslovak Socialist Republic was so curiously neglected? I frankly say to the authors of the resolution that I distrust them, while in the signatures I see only the temporary error of the technicians, who once again allowed some conservative *apparatchik* to use them for a bad purpose; it is neither the first nor the last time that this has happened. At the same time I affirm my complete faith in the communists and trade unionists and in the workers and technicians of the Doubrava mine, and my faith in the movement for the revival of socialist democracy.

The technicians' statement deals with three important questions: dictatorship, human rights, and the apparatus. It is surprising that the authors of the resolution, who are speaking for the technicians, have so extensive a knowledge of political, scientific, and sociological problems that they can positively say what dictatorship, human rights, and the apparatus are, without feeling at all uneasy about the more complicated aspects of the matter. One can recognize the hand of the apparatus, with its bureaucratic reasoning, behind their approach and their language just as clearly as the teacher can see at first glance when an adult has guided a child's hand in his homework. Technicians and workers, surely you do not need the *apparatchiks* to lead you by the hand, to tell you what you ought to think and to organize a collection of your signatures in support of a bad cause. Let every man speak for himself, then we shall easily understand one another, and the discredited apparatus will have no one to hide behind.

The *apparatchiks* have got used to treating the people, the working class, and the intellectuals as if they were children or things to be manipulated. They have mismanaged our work, our thinking, our trust, and our money, and they are still doing so. They have put themselves in the position of people who have the right to make decisions concerning us, of people who know what we should do, what we should think, how we should manage our affairs; we have only to give them their mandate and sign an occasional resolution. They are playing at being conscientious parents, who give their children everything they need, and want nothing in return except that the children be good and thrifty. They magnanimously give them a piggy-bank, but when it is full they empty it and take the children's money to buy them cod-liver oil and castor oil. The *apparatchiks* have been emptying our piggy-bank long enough to feed us with cod-liver oil and castor oil. We know them, and we say, "That's enough!"

The term *totalitarian dictatorship* which appears in the article in *Literárni listy* is a precise technical term with a definite scientific content. It cannot be changed simply because the authors of the resolution associate it exclusively with fascism; the meaning of a scientific term does not change with what someone may think, but according to reality itself. Totalitarian dictatorship may be exercised to promote different aims and for the benefit of different social classes, so that it has been equally possible to rule through totalitarian dictatorship in a fascist country like Nazi Germany, in a Catholic country such as Franco's Spain, in Communist China, and in a people's democracy. Though the aims of each of these regimes are different, their structure is similar, just as coal is mined in more or less the same way in Communist countries as it was mined in Nazi Germany, and in Fascist Italy. What is different are the social relations in the various countries, the ownership of the coal or of the means of production, but not the process of extraction, which is almost identical.

The term *totalitarian dictatorship* designates a certain form of government, not the class structure of a state or society; it designates the manner in which one class dominates another. In the same way, democracy is a specific form of government; it had already come into existence long ago, independently of the character of social relations, in slave-owning societies and in the feudal city republics, and even before the emergence of capitalists and workers. It was, of course, a different democracy than that of today, but the basic principles, the forms of government, were the same. If the authors of the technicians' resolution call the last twenty years a proletarian dictatorship, they part company with reality; current events alone suffice to prove that it is the apparatus which has ruled over the workers, over the intellectuals, and over the people. Whether we like it or not, for the last twenty years we have lived in a totalitarian dictatorship, exercised by a constantly narrowing circle of persons directly connected with the apparatus based on the police and the bureaucracy.

The reliance of the executive power on the police and the bureaucracy—that is, on rule through the state apparatus or through a political apparatus—is the distinguishing feature of modern totalitarian dictatorship. It does not have much in common with the splendid democratic idea of proletarian revolution as Marx and Lenin understood it. While I have always defended the thought of Marx and Lenin, I cannot conceal the fact that the fake, pseudo-humanistic values of totalitarian dictatorship and of its apparatus-bureaucracy fill me with the same disgust and nausea that they evoke in the immense majority of the people of this country.

How to replace totalitarian dictatorship with a socialist democracy, or, in other words, how to change the way power is exercised, without giving up the conquests of socialism, especially the social ownership of the means of production—that is the basic problem of today. But it cannot be solved unless entirely different forms of government are

adopted and unless the respect of human and civil rights can be ensured *"at least* to the same extent as under bourgeois democracy." This
point aroused the indignation of the authors of the resolution and led
them to protest that I am calling for a return to the conditions of the
First Czechoslovak Republic [1918–1938]. But the police persecution
of the workers [during that period] was an infringement and a violation of fundamental civil rights, because to shoot at peaceful demon-
strators is a crime everywhere and always, in a bourgeois republic no
less than in a socialist country, in Ostrava under the First Republic as
much as in Poznan in 1956. So if somebody demands that fundamental
civil rights be respected, at least to the extent provided for by the earlier constitution, it does not mean that he is calling for police persecution; on the contrary it means, in this case, that he is demanding that
the Ostrava miners be granted at least the right to strike, the right to
demonstrate, the right to elect their own representatives freely, and the
right to form their own political associations freely.

Why then do the *apparatchiks* try to blacken in your eyes someone
who is demanding precisely what you will need most in the coming
months? Why? Because here someone is demanding those very rights
that the *apparatchiks* have taken from you in the last twenty years,
the rights that they will never voluntarily give back to you, because,
once you have these rights, you will drive them out of their jobs; and
the sooner the better.

The authors of the resolution also make no bones about their total
solidarity with the interests of these *apparatchiks* and they openly tell
you that the labor movement cannot manage without them, the *apparatchiks*. They claim that to do away with the apparatus means doing
away with the Party. They are lying. The Party is you, real people,
not the apparatus. The labor movement, this glorious movement which
is of paramount importance in modern history, was created by miners,
metalworkers, and factoryhands long before the first *apparatchik* came
to sit on its neck. The movement was born, grew, and developed in the
political struggles of the people, of social groups and classes, who were
not a compliant mass manipulated by apparatuses, but the bearers of
historical progress, the active makers of history. Of course, every
movement also creates its apparatus, but the key question is whether
you control the apparatus or the apparatus controls you. And that is

precisely the point at issue now. No one is calling for the liquidation of the apparatus, because that is senseless and impossible, but what the spokesmen of the movement for regeneration—unlike the centrists— are openly demanding today is the liquidation of the overwhelming influence that the apparatus-bureaucracy has assumed in the life of the state and of the Party. And that is no longer a senseless or an impossible demand; it is the reasonable and attainable goal of today's labor movement, a goal which of course infuriates the *apparatchiks* and drives them mad, because it means the end of their prerogatives and their privileges, the end of their absolute rule over the workers, the technicians, and the intellectuals.

Your *apparatchiks* make a show of aiming their guns at an unknown philosopher in Prague, and of doing so not with their own hands but by using the technicians of your plant as cats'-paws; in fact their gunfire is very carefully directed at you, the workers, the miners. They are doing just what they have done for the last twenty years, but now their time is running out and their powder is wet. Nevertheless they are still as dangerous as they ever were, especially for you, the workers and technicians of industrial plants, and connections with them are still just as profitable for people who are flexible and who can be bought. So whoever wants to help the workers and the technicians must support the labor movement without its *apparatchiks*.

In full solidarity with the Communists' movement for regeneration, with comradely greetings to the miners and technicians of Ostrava, but at the same time with undiminished distrust of the *apparatchiks* in the Doubrava mine, in Ostrava, and anywhere else,

Yours,
Ivan Sviták

Your Present Crisis * ᥒᥒᥒᥒᥒᥒᥒᥒᥒᥒᥒ

The time is out of joint—O cursed spite,
That ever I was born to set it right!—
Hamlet, Act I, Scene v

I. Problem of Crisis

1. The time is out of joint. Each one of us is in the situation of Hamlet, whom fate had given the task of correcting a wrong. Just as Hamlet had to act regardless of the consequences, so must we.

2. A three-month intermezzo between totalitarian dictatorship and socialist democracy ended with the Communist Party's acceptance of the democratization program. It was not until now that the second stage of the democratization process started. It is a stage which is much more essential than the first one, a stage in which a decision will be made concerning the nature of future political relations. The second stage will be decisively influenced by the answer given to the central political question, which is far more significant than the troublesome events of recent months.

3. The question, formulated in various ways, is: Should six million non-Party citizens of this state have the same political rights as the members of the Communist Party, or should they be granted only a larger dose of freedom which does not endanger the privileges of the Party members? Are we facing democratic, free, and secret elections, or an old game with new people? Are we going to live in a sovereign European state with a polycentric political system, or in a nonsovereign state structure whose leadership is most afraid of the troops of their allies?

4. Assuming that the progressive wing of the Communist Party is taking its promises about civil rights seriously, it may be able to win the confidence of the basic strata of the population and bring about

* Lecture at the KAN Club, Prague, April 18, 1968; published in the weekly, *Student*, Prague, in April, 1968.

a unique synthesis of socialist and humanist thought which would probably be followed in one form or another by a considerable majority of both the Czech and the Slovak nations. If this progressive wing does not manage to carry out the promises of the program, with all its consequences—including the existence of additional parties—then perhaps we are about to get a greater abundance of bread from the outside, but certainly much less freedom.

5. And so we must start from the conflicting character of the forces in the Communist Party, in state institutions, and in special-interest organizations, and we must proceed as follows: a) we should implement our own demands of consistent democracy for the benefit of non-Party people, including the opportunity of founding a political party which would have equal rights; b) we should not place obstacles in the way of the progressive current in the Communist Party, to the extent that the Party wants to implement a demanding program of socialist democratization (we should not weaken this wing of the Party by taking ill-advised steps); and c) we should limit the prestige and power of conservative politicians as much as we can.

6. Politics is not only a game for power, it is also a game for power in terms of time. Time is the most dramatic and most demoniac category not only in the history of philosophy but also in politics. Time works in our favor, but only to the extent that we are active and realize that certain steps can be taken only now or never. What steps?

7. We do not want to take a step into darkness. However, wherever we go we are confronted with the question of founding a second party. The first step must be to clarify the problems, the situation, the opposition, and the prospects. One collective formulated the matter realistically as follows:

8. "We are considering the question as to whether it is appropriate in the present situation to start a new political force directly and to constitute it officially, or whether we should merely prepare the legal and political facilities for its creation and work out a clear and effective method for our future work. . . . We are considering the question of how all such activities can be coordinated as fast as possible and before a new political party can be formed."

9. We can immediately found a political party which would fall apart before the elections, during the elections, or after the elections,

or we can found a political party which would lose all the way as soon as the excited mood of criticism was gone. A newly founded political party cannot operate effectively today against the apparatuses of the existing political parties and mass organizations. Should we then give up such an idea? But we know that without an equal partner of the Communist Party which would have equal rights we cannot have either elections or democracy, and that the time of the spring and the time of the autumn are not, and will not be, the same. What can we do? A provisional answer to that question is our club. We are not in a crisis, comrades, not us.

10. Norbert Wiener once tried to determine exactly why the mongoose, a tiny animal the size of a badger, is the winner when it fights snakes which are many times stronger. He studied in detail the records of such fights on film and found out that the mongoose wins because its type of signal system is of a higher order than the signal system of the snake, that it maneuvers continuously in the fight, retreats, and attacks in the same single situation. Then it makes a deadly attack on the vulnerable spot of the snake and thus takes advantage of its own short reaction period, its "intelligence." We have a good signal system, we manage to retreat before the snake of dictatorship, and so far we have not lost anything.

II. Prague in Springtime

1. What happened during the first stage of democratization which has just been completed? There were two types of changes: seemingly significant personnel changes, which were structurally insignificant, and much more important structural changes sometimes even brought about by people of the old political configuration. The first type of change brought about mass excitement, because such changes were accompanied by well-channeled demagogy against the lambs which were and are supposed to remove sins; the second type of change brought about an unusual, unique political reversal carried out with precision and improvisation; in the final analysis, however, this was a political reversal unwanted by the Party elite.

2. Personal, structurally insignificant changes were made for the time being only at the top levels. Totalitarian dictatorship carried out the

change of personnel, publicly announcing its crisis and its will to bring about a new form of political life.

3. At the same time, it left untouched all its mechanisms and did not deprive any of the representatives of the old force even of their mandates as deputies in the parliament, nor did it deprive them of their positions as members of the Central Committee of the Communist Party. The progressives and the conservatives made a temporary compromise which is bound to fall apart soon, because it is impossible to continue the demagogical search for culprits who are bound by absurd ties to their own victims.

4. Personnel changes have been completed among Communists holding leading posts. Non-Party people had no say in these changes, although the government purports to be the government of all the people. If you want to hear our word, then expand the government by including representatives of six million adults who are non-Party members. We have candidates as good if not better than those proposed by the Communist Party.

5. In addition to the changes in personnel, there were also several basic structural changes which are a much more significant guarantee of democracy than the new persons: a) *de facto*, not only *de jure* freedom of the press, and limited freedom of assembly; b) a spontaneous wave of political demands that the citizens themselves addressed to the government, among which the most important is the demand for the rehabilitation of political victims; and c) the creation of clubs, discussion groups, and new organs of existing institutions offering by their very creation an alternative to the existing policy.

6. The value of these structural changes is very high. However, we must anticipate that pressure will develop precisely against those values, in the sense that they will gradually be limited and controlled. So we must develop civil rights among the masses of non-Party people without demagogy against the Communists, relentlessly, rapidly, energetically, consciously—here and now.

7. In addition to these two types of changes, we must also note changes which did not take place. Nothing has changed so far in the mechanism of totalitarian dictatorship and its heritage. Intelligent and able politicians at the head of a monopolist apparatus of power are

much more dangerous than simple-minded daddies who are unable even to choose capable generals for their coups d'état.

8. The National Front is being revived artificially, so that the old game can continue within it. The idea of the National Front, which represents broader, supra-Party interests, is not alien to us. However, we must say openly that non-Communist parties and organizations in the present form represent everything under the sun except the nation, ideals, or democracy.

9. No political group has been formed, or could as yet be formed, so as to be capable of creating a political party or organization with an openly political goal. A return to the pre-February [1948] structure of the National Front and to the political configuration of those days is not a step forward, while the creation of at least two new parties on a Christian and social democratic basis is indispensable.

III. Opposition

1. Political activity originates both in an organized manner in certain institutions, such as political parties, and in special-interest organizations, and spontaneously outside of the framework of the given institutions in the form of demonstrations, strikes, discussions. Under normal political conditions in democratic states, there exists the ruling party and its opposition in parliament. This basic type of division of labor and competition for political power is also projected in the special-interest organizations and in cultural life.

2. The model of democratic competition for power is not ideal, but it is the best existing model. In the history of political theories and in the constitutions of states, proposals have been made, on many occasions, to establish mechanisms of executive power which were theoretically better. But these mechanisms were not put into effect, or they collapsed into much worse systems, endangering human freedom more than the imperfect, vulnerable, but functioning democracy. We will welcome and want a democracy better than Western democracy, but we do not want a worse democracy. We are absolutely unyielding on this point.

3. The present conditions of political life in Czechoslovakia require

that we have a healthy opposition to the Communist program. Not an anti-Communist party which would see its goal in a change of economic relations and of the overall orientation of the state, but rather a political party or parties which would strive to establish a joint rule and partnership with Communists as representatives of voters with full rights.

4. If the Communist Party is consistently in favor of freedom of assembly, then it must recognize that within the limits of the present constitution every party which acts in harmony with the declaration of human rights has the right to exist. Therefore, as far as we are concerned, there is no question as to whether it is permissible to found such a political party; the only question is how to found it, when to found it, with whom, and with what program. We want to take part in the life of the political institutions of this state.

5. We shall determine which way is the most passable and whether there is any purpose in posing the question of oppositions. An opposition and a political party are not the same thing. We must distinguish between the political party of totalitarian dictatorship with a monopoly of power; political parties of the classic Western democracies which compete for power but have bureaucratic machineries similar to those of the totalitarian parties; political parties as parliamentary groups of deputies which represent a certain professional, national, or class interest; and finally parties in the form of political clubs (the original form for modern political parties during the French Revolution). A real political opposition can exist even without such organizational forms. It may operate spontaneously as an opposition outside parliament, as a student movement, or in some other way.

6. As a result of some irony of history, there exists at the present time a conglomerate of political forms which has no parallel: next to a Communist Party with a monopoly of power there exist two political parties which are relics of the former democracy, but which in the past represented institutionalized collaboration, and not a political program, and which do not represent a political alternative even today.

7. Under these circumstances, we cannot have any confidence in the institutions of the existing non-Communist political parties. However, it is possible that they will pass rapidly through a strong process of change. Changes can be enforced through the existing apparatus at

(64)

their disposal. For the time being, these parties have an organization but no members. Social democracy is missing among the existing parties.

8. Potential voters in the next elections would like to see new representatives of political life who have not been discredited, that is, representatives of "the other party." But such a party cannot be established on the negative program of opposition. It needs a specific program and organizational and personnel preparation, not to speak of the fact that we assume that there will be regular secret elections with several candidates. This is still uncertain at the present time. The decision will be made soon.

9. Regardless of temporary complications which will be solved quickly through an open exchange of views and attitudes, a spontaneous movement of clubs of committed non-Party members has appeared. This movement is an extremely important phenomenon. As of today, the clubs are already a political platform, and in view of their different viewpoints, they represent a real political power—an "opposition." We must expand the clubs of committed non-Party people and unite them in such a way that the polarization of views would stimulate the natural trend to form new political parties.

10. Regardless of the formation of other parties—their admission procedures, to be exact—the clubs have considerable opportunities right now. They can become the tribunes of political thinking and stimuli for public activity, which by itself is more important than the act of election. To say it figuratively with Ludvík Vaculík: "It is up to us to decide which whores we can afford."

IV. Prospects for the Clubs

1. The main issue of the second stage of the process of democratization is the elections. They must be secret elections with independent candidates, and with separate lists of candidates, unless the process of democratization is to become a fraud from the very first. The nomination of independent candidates proposed by nonpolitical organizations—for example, by clubs of non-Party members—must be legalized in the electoral law. The method of elections and the wording of the electoral law are the most important issues of this spring.

2. We can let the president and the government be forced upon us,

but we will not allow having the electoral law and the rules of the democratic game forced upon us. The clubs should declare openly that they want to have an effective influence on the nomination of the candidates, on the actual course of the elections, that they want to nominate independent deputies. We will not elect anyone who was a deputy in the present National Assembly. Nobody, without any exception.

3. In the first place, we do not agree with the trend toward making future elections objects of political trading with the existing parties of the National Front—for example, trading an increase in the number of the deputies of the existing non-Communist parties for the concession of limiting the choice of candidates to a single list. We want to elect personalities and separate programs of various political parties, we do not want any mock elections with concessions of any sort. Elections without an alternative are a fraud.

4. At the present time, the clubs represent various political views of non-Party people. They also constitute the basis for activities of non-Party people in special-interest organizations, particularly in trade unions and youth movements. We cannot for the time being anticipate the organizational forms of the clubs and their future characteristics, which will necessarily become more definite from the political viewpoint.

5. We should appear soon before the general public with a certain political concept, with some sort of minimum program of civil rights in Czechoslovakia. There is no need to dream up the most radical demands. Instead, we should openly obligate ourselves, the candidates of non-Party people and the possible future representatives of the state power, to agree to the principal demands on the basis of which we are willing to support certain deputies.

6. Such a program of non-Party people can become the political foundation of the electoral contest between persons, parties, and institutions. We do not want to elect merely new people, we also want to elect new thoughts and to obtain certain guarantees. The program of the Communist Party reflects certain views which are close to us, but the program does not represent our starting point or our goal.

7. The Clubs of non-Party members should be formed quickly on the base of mass organizations and unions. They should guarantee a

basic program of human rights. I am saying openly that we are not enemies of the Communists, that we shall keep away from an anti-Communist policy. We are adult, politically thinking citizens of a socialist state who have full legal rights, citizens who have grown out of the tutorship of a police-bureaucratic regime and want freedom under socialism.

8. We are striving to bring about parliamentary opposition as an alternative to the present implementation of state power, because we are afraid that an opposition outside of parliament would be much more dangerous. Unless the political activities of the people are purposefully integrated in the creation of socialist democracy, they will unavoidably assume forms which would be much more problematic, forms which it would be difficult to prevent them from assuming, and which could endanger the state, as well as its two nations.

9. We know from an old fairy tale that the wolf can change its voice in order to get hold of the lambs. We know the voice of the wolves, the voice which was as dangerous to the Communists as it was to the non-Party people. We shall not open the door when the wolf tries to convince us by changing his voice, because only fairy tales end well. We do not distrust the Communists *a priori*, but our answer to mutating Stalinists is an unequivocal no.

10. The victory of little David over the giant Goliath is a myth. But the descendants of David's people, whom Hitler's fascist dictatorship cremated by the millions in concentration camp gas chambers, are a reality. These are the young Israelis who tell us: *"Never again like sheep! Never again like sheep!"*

The Meaning of Our Regeneration Movement * ～～～～～～～～～～～～～～～～～～～

> The working conditions that we have to-
> day, even in the newest plants, are not as
> good as those that workers have won in
> some advanced capitalist states. And the
> average living standards of the working
> class are lower in our country than in
> some West European countries whose
> starting point after the war was the same,
> if not lower, than ours.
>
> JOSEF SMRKOVSKÝ, 1968

Workers and Intellectuals in Alliance

1. In the middle of this beautiful windy spring, the meaning of our regeneration movement is still unclear, to the workers and the intellectuals alike. Intellectuals and workers still have the same enemy as yesterday—the police dictatorship and its apparatus. The apparatus is still trying, and indeed will go on trying, to drive a wedge between the two groups.

2. The working class and the labor movement have always won their greatest victories when the revolutionary intellectuals have stood at the head of the movement, when the enormous power of human thought and the strength of labor and its free organizations have joined forces. It was on this basis that young Marx, a hundred years ago, shaped his conception of the working class and its political organizations.

3. The relationship between intellectuals and workers as conceived by Marx was destroyed by the Stalinist power-apparatuses, which created and have systematically fostered the rift between these two social groups. For, made up as they are of the police and the bureau-

* Lecture at an opening meeting of KAN, Gottwaldov and Olomouc, April 28, 1968, published in the Prague Trade Union daily, *Práce* [Work], May 19, 1968.

cracy, these apparatuses can rule over these groups and over the whole of society only once they have managed to make the intellectual look ugly to the workers, and the worker to the intellectuals. Both workers and intellectuals must see the ugliness where it really is, in the apparatuses of police and bureaucracy, which have left the citizen fewer rights than he had under the Emperor Franz Josef.

4. The working class includes the majority of the population in Czechoslovakia; it is the principal class of this country and it will play a decisive political role regardless of the personal or political composition of the government. The leading role of the working class is a political reality; it is an unchangeable and permanent basic fact of political life, whether anybody likes it or not. The position of Czechoslovak labor more or less corresponds to what Karl Marx had in mind when he spoke of the historical mission of the working class in the emancipation of mankind. This mission is in total conflict with Stalinism, which sentenced all sections of the population equally, not excepting the workers, to loss of freedom.

5. The working class has no reason to be afraid of the rule of the people, which is what the word *democracy* means. The people who do have reasons to fear it are those who have become accustomed to speaking in the name of the working class, the *apparatchiks* of all kinds in the various organizations; these people know very well that today's working class has no confidence in them and that in a free election it will not keep them as its leaders. That is why they feel they must create the illusion that the labor movement is the force which could, or might want to, change the course of the process of regeneration, and that it will impose its policy by force of arms. But they are generals without an army, and the working class itself will deal with them.

6. The leading role of the Communist Party in political life is also a reality. It is a political fact of life which in no way depends on whether anyone likes it, nor, indeed, on whether it is written into the constitution or not. Today, the Communist Party clearly recognizes that the six million people of working age who are not party members cannot be permanently excluded from political decision-making. It intends to submit its leading role to the test of public competition and secret elections, so that the people themselves can say what they want.

7. The historical role of the working class and the leading role of

the Communist Party are two different things. The political forms of the working-class struggle may change, but its emancipating role in modern history endures, regardless of the immediate configurations of power. Any political current that tries to bypass the reality of the working class and the labor movement will fail, whether it is defended by the progressive wing of the party or by the opposition. The workers themselves will see to it, and that is as it should be.

8. The form that the leading role of the Communist Party has taken in East European countries in the last twenty years is entirely unsuitable. . . . Lenin's conception of the Communist Party and its function in the revolution, once inevitable, can no longer be maintained in advanced countries.

9. If goverment is to be exercised democratically, it is essential in the first place that other political currents be given the possibility of forming their own political organizations. By permitting this, neither the working class nor the Communist Party would betray even Lenin; on the contrary, they would make it possible for political life to develop in a country which no longer knows class conflicts of the old type. This follows from the fact that they are dealing with a country whose labor movement has a hundred-year-old tradition, a country where there was no mass illiteracy at the time that the Communist Party came into being and where even then the working class represented a third of the population.

10. The first act of state sovereignty of the Czechoslovak Socialist Republic and the first act of a policy that is independent, Czechoslovak, national, socialist, and European must be the acceptance of the plurality of the political system, the admission of other political parties to real power through free elections.

Workers' Rights

1. Civil rights are the same for all citizens of the state, but the demand that they should be respected and observed has a different sound among the workers than at the university. The writers whose wit scintillated in the Congress Palace forgot to tell the workers the elementary thing: that is, what civil rights mean for the principal class of our society—the workers themselves.

2. They mean something much more important for the workers than the arsenals of the militia; they mean: a) the right to strike; b) the election of the managers by the community of producers; c) the defense of workers' rights by free trade unions. In short, they mean the end of the rule of the *apparatchiks* over the working class; they mean that those who work in industrial plants should have a direct influence on production and on management. These rights, which the worker-president Antonín Zápotocký never wanted to give up, are the most powerful weapons that the working class can have anywhere in the world; they are more important than the machine-guns and cannons of the militias.

3. Comrades, if you have these rights, what do you need machine-guns and cannons for? Against whom will you use them, since you are the majority of the nation? Is it not somebody else who needs the militias more than you? And what does he need them for? Are the militias not needed by those very *apparatchiks* who are afraid of only one force—your own—and who will never stop trying to stir you up against the intellectuals?

4. Do not put weapons in the hands of the middle classes or of the intellectuals; give them back to the National Assembly and to the Communist Party in exchange for the best weapons to be found in the political arsenals of the working classes of all countries and all nations: the right to strike, the right to elect management, the right to choose trade-union officers by secret ballot. In this way you will win one of the hardest battles for socialism.

5. The fundamental rights of the labor movement are just as important for workers as freedom of the press is for intellectuals. The two demands are still being kept apart because so far neither the intellectuals nor the workers fully realize how much their interests overlap. That is why today the intellectual must openly say to the worker, "If anyone tries to infringe upon your right to strike, I shall defend it just as resolutely as the right to free speech for myself." In the same way the worker should openly say to the intellectual, "If anyone touches your right to freedom of expression, I shall strike." This is the only way in which socialist democracy can begin; there is no other.

6. Novotný, Mamula, and Šejna used the threat of workers' weapons not only against the Communist Party but also against all representa-

tives of the regeneration movement. Today they cannot do it overtly, but they are still speculating on weapons. They have the effrontery to profess their allegiance to the regeneration movement in public, as, for example Antonín Novotný did. He, of course, no longer has power. But other, smaller dictators still have it, and they are still threatening; they are threatening in the name of the workers.

7. At the conference in Karviná, Rakszewski, a member of the local District Committee of the Communist Party, said: "What are we afraid of? Of a few clowns in Prague who are talking a lot of nonsense on television? They will have to let us speak too, and if they do not, the dictatorship will have to start again, so that they will give us a chance to talk too." That is the unambiguous speech of an *apparatchik*, who wants to go on in the Stalinist way and utterly loathes everything that is new. It is not what the workers say. Their view was expressed by Comrade Buřičin, a hewer of the Doubrava mine in the Ostrava district, when he said, "I wish the process of regeneration would go on forever."

8. One of the most dangerous of the ideas that are today menacing the socialist and democratic character of the labor movement is the technocratic conception, according to which society should be ruled by technicians (so as to secure the greatest possible production). This idea has nothing to do with Marx and Lenin, but it has a lot to do with Stalin and Khrushchev. Technocrats are today of the opinion that the government should have full jurisdiction with regard to technical questions and that the role of the labor movement and of political parties in political decision-making is to be left as it is—delegated to the present power elite. This is unacceptable.

9. Modern technocrats claim that man is only a functional object for manipulation, that the division of society into the rulers and the ruled is eternal and that the elite understands the interests of the people better than the people themselves do, so that it is undesirable and wrong for people to be politically active. Socialists and democrats, on the contrary, think that real people, social groups, and classes are the active makers of history, that the division into rulers and ruled can be limited by mutual control and that the interests of the people, classes, and groups are understood by the people, classes, and groups at least as well as by the power elite, if not a good deal better.

10. The technocrats do not consider that man, the working class or any other group, is an active historical force, an agent of history and politics; they see them all as puppets to be manipulated. The whole technology of totalitarian power is based on this assumption. The technocrats have completely given up the original aim of the socialist movement—the freedom of man in a classless society. They are striving for a more efficient elite, which will have greater skill in production; they are making no effort to obtain a program of humanist values for the freedom of man.

The Unions

1. If the working class were satisfied with replacing the private owners of industrial plants with state officials, it would not need to have its own organizations and trade unions under socialism. But the standard of living does not depend on the kind of managers that run the plants. It depends on the productivity of labor, whose growth must be organized and ensured by the growing efficiency of the worker.

2. That is why the basic class of producers—the workers—must be protected by their own trade union organizations. Without this protection there is no guarantee that the producers themselves will derive any real benefit from the growth of productivity and that the workers will not unilaterally bear its cost. So the trade-union movement must go on defending the interests of the producers against the apparatuses, the manipulators, the technicians, and the managers, because the change of social ownership alone does not guarantee that under the socialized ownership of the means of production the workers will not be exploited as much as before, or even more.

3. The system of bureaucratic despotism abolished the fundamental rights of the working class, together with the rights of all citizens, and replaced them with arbitrary rule. If it is true that ideas and people are no longer under martial law, then the workers have no more important and urgent duty, now that the Stalinist power-structure is falling to pieces, than to revive the trade unions to their full strength, as a movement for the defense of the workers' own fundamental rights.

4. For the time being, the unions are not the equal partners of the employers, but it can be assumed that great possibilities are opening be-

fore them, since the monopoly of ideology and power has been abolished. It may even soon become absolutely indispensable for the trade-union movement loudly and emphatically to defend the interests of the principal class of producers. For, if the working class gave them a free hand, the technocrats would ruthlessly introduce measures detrimental to the workers' standard of living. Any attack on the living standard must be repulsed.

5. The trade unions lost their fundamental rights because, instead of the real guarantees and rights of free association and free defense of social objectives, they accepted promises of much more extensive rights and freedoms. But these have never materialized. The liquidation of real rights is always carried out under the pretext that these rights are to be expanded, because people would not allow their real freedom to be restricted if the restrictions were not presented as a *temporary* sacrifice on the road to greater freedom.

6. The revival of the trade-union movement as a true reflection of the interests of the working class is not easy, because the working class itself has greatly changed. When using the term *working class* we must recognize that even social science has a very poor knowledge of its real face, hidden as it is behind ideological delusions and self-deceptions. The working class of today is greatly diversified politically as well as in its social status and wage-levels. The assumption that this class is homogeneous and morally and politically united is just as wrong as the comparable assumption that the intelligentsia is equally united and undiversified in its politics or interests.

7. The revival of the trade union movement has started in several places independently, through spontaneous efforts to expand the unions' influence on management, through wage-demands, through criticism, and through the first signs of open support for fundamental civil rights. The fact that the manager of the Dukla mine in the Ostrava region was elected to his function by the employees, in perhaps the first such case in the history of socialism in our country, is one of the most important events of recent months.

8. Similarly, the rise in the Ostrava district of workers' committees for the defense of freedom of the press is a clear sign that the movement of democratization has reached a new phase in which the workers and the middle classes (the intelligentsia) are beginning to form a com-

mon front on the basis of their political aims and interests; in other words, to form that alliance of working hands and brains which alone can ensure true democracy in a socialist society.

9. The trade-union movement of the working class has essentially the same interest in the destruction of the power structure of Stalinism as the spontaneous tendencies in the movement of writers, scientists, and artists. As citizens, workers, and intellectuals rid themselves of their own inhibitions, which had been fostered by the former regime of fear and group interests, so there arises the wider awareness that every attack on the freedom of the press would lead to an attack on the workers' standard of living and vice versa. The stronger the awareness of the common interests of workers and intellectuals is, the more irreversible will the road to socialist democracy be.

10. Workers and the intelligentsia have a common enemy—the bureaucratic dictatorship of the apparatus, which equally despises manual labor and intellectual work, and for whom workers are only an obedient militia, just as the intelligentsia are only executors of power. That is why, for the sake of socialist democracy, we must strengthen the unity of working hands and working brains against the apparatuses of the power-elite, which have been, are, and will be the most formidable obstacle to our nation's unique experiment in socialist democracy.

Forbidden Horizons * ᷼᷼᷼᷼᷼᷼᷼᷼᷼᷼

Let us suppose that I live in a large
apartment building and I am attacked by
thieves; I am allowed to defend myself
and, if necessary, even to shoot; but I am
not under any circumstances allowed to
blow the building up. It would, of course,
be an effective defense against the thieves,
but the evil it would cause would be
greater than any that I could suffer. But
what if the thieves have explosives which
can destroy the whole building? Then I
shall leave them the responsibility for the
evil that is committed and I shall not add
to it myself.

MAX VON LAUE

I. Illusions and Realities

1. If you strike a match in the bathroom in order to light the gas
water-heater, nothing extraordinary will usually happen. But if the
equipment is faulty and the bathroom contains a mixture of air and
gas, then you have struck your last match. And people around you,
who were not careless and who did not even know that there was any
danger, will be blown up with you.

2. The explosive mixture consists of such perfectly ordinary, common, and even useful substances as air and cooking-gas. In politics, the
explosive mixture is a certain blend of illusion and reality, which may
be quite harmless in themselves but which can become extremely dangerous when combined; this is true in many spheres, but particularly in
politics. Politics is the constantly renewed struggle of illusion against
reality and of reality against illusion; it is in other words the interaction
of people's longings with inflexible facts, the conflict of utopia and
science.

* Speech at an opening meeting of KAN, Ostrava, May 14, 1968; published in
Student, May 29, 1968.

3. The politician's greatest skill is to decide what is realistic at a given moment and what is utopian. The people who acquire this skill are rare, because they must have a very high degree of education and, at the same time, a sensitive understanding of the simplest things of everyday life. But in a situation of crisis, only politicians of this kind are capable of leading, of drawing up a program and preventing an explosion, of grasping the illusions and realities of the era in which they work and think.

4. The first basic reality of today is the fact that we have lived and will go on living in a socialist order of society. However many negative elements the last twenty years may have brought, there nevertheless remains the great positive side, to which history will probably attribute much greater importance than to the mistakes, and that is the reality of socialist transformations. Whatever reasons may be found to justify, or on the contrary to reject, the socialist type of ownership of the means of production and its chief consequences for the future, the socialist society will endure even if it changes its doctrine, its culture, and the way in which it controls political power.

5. The second basic reality is the Warsaw Pact, which creates the "legal possibility" of intervention. If it were merely a by-product of the cold-war years and an answer to NATO, this reality might eventually be open to change. But the Pact reflects a much more essential reality, that is, that *every* government of the Czechs and Slovaks will have to rely on an alliance with the Soviet Union. This is not due to reasons that depend on ideology (and may therefore change with it), but to dominant national interests, which correspond to the age-old friendship of the Czechs for the Russians and of the Russians for the Czechs; it is far more than the fellow-feeling that the bureaucratic apparatuses of the two countries have for each other.

6. The third basic reality is the leading role of the Communist Party, which may be questioned as a prospect for the future, but which for the time being and in spite of the present crisis remains unchanged. We do not think that this reality is unchangeable, but unless we take it as our starting point at the present time, our appreciation of the fundamental elements of the current situation will be wrong. The personalities that are the objects of a cult may change, but the granite blocks of the pedestal and the concrete injections holding up the monument

of Stalinism (for here the earth itself protested against Stalinism and had to be artificially reinforced to make it bear the monumental weight of violence) remain embedded in the soil of our country and prevent the natural landslide.*

7. At least three principal illusions stand against these three realities. The most widespread at the moment is the illusion of the intelligentsia. It is wrong to assume that the aims of the progressive wing of the Communist Party, more precisely of the party intelligentsia, have a wide backing among the masses. The projection of the aims and interests of a given social group (or class) on to another social group (or class) is always the source of the biggest political mistakes, and this holds true even when the projected interests, aims, programs, and ideas are absolutely justified, logical, and universally beneficial.

8. The second basic political illusion is the assumption that the atmosphere of Prague, which is in fact exceptional, extends to the provincial towns and villages as well; but the conservatives are very well aware that this is not so. The political structure of power in the towns and villages has remained almost untouched by the recent changes. The woman reader from a provincial town near Prague was quite right when she wrote: "If we did not have the press, radio, and television, no one here would know that any process of regeneration is going on."

9. Finally, the third illusion lies in the false assumption that in the vital matter of the process of democratization the Czechs and the Slovaks have the same interests. This process embraces two different programs, federalization in Slovakia and democracy in the Czech lands; some of the interests are intertwined and interrelated, but not to the extent of combining to form one minimal program supported in the whole country. The process of democratization is a compromise that brings under one roof the program of federalization and the program of democracy; it is a useful, good, and convenient roof, but it is only temporary.

10. The illusion of the intelligentsia, the illusion of Prague, and the

---

* Stalin's monumental statue, built on a hill overlooking Prague and subsequently demolished, was so heavy that the soil had to be reinforced with injections of concrete into the side of the hill, and the pedestal could not be removed after the statue itself had been torn down.—Translator.

illusion of the Czechs clash not only with fundamental realities but also with the illusions of other social groups, of other regions, and of the Slovaks. If a way out of complicated and intricate social configurations is to be found, illusions must be recognized as illusions and realities as realities. This is how social science approaches our present situation.

II. Social Democrats

1. It seems to me, with my limited information, that this is more or less the same approach as that of social democracy, which represents the most important, though repeatedly forbidden, horizon of our time. This socialist, democratic and working-class party is being forbidden even before it has again come into being, perhaps because one wing of the Communist Party has taken over wholesale all the principles of the 1945–1948 social democratic program; though naturally it has not dared to confess this sin, which is mortal from the point of view of its own ideology.

2. The social democratic movement in our country has existed for almost a hundred years and its tradition is not rooted in the ideology of some *apparatchiks* but in the real struggles of Czechoslovak workers for a democratic and humanist socialism and against the totalitarian tendency of capitalism, fascism, and Stalinism to manipulate people through bureaucracy. It fought heroically against nazism during the war—a fact that is passed over in silence to this day in official historiography; through its policy of nationalization in the years of 1945–1948 it laid firm economic foundations for socialism; and, it was bitterly persecuted in the twenty years that followed. Now there lies before it an open horizon—the hope that the aims of the program of democratic socialism will be realized.

3. At present, social democrats are filled with true enthusiasm at the prospect that the Czechoslovak experiment may actually create democratic socialism and thus make a contribution to the world socialist movement. As in the past, their first political consideration is not political prestige and personal ambition but the real issue, that is, how best to uphold democratic socialism and its chief representatives. Whatever detours history may have made, and however we may in the

future judge the forms that relations between Communists and social democrats have taken in the critical situations of the past, the fact remains that the Czechoslovak working class and society as a whole now stand at a crossroads in history; before them lies the road along which the social democrats above all have always wanted to travel as independent partners of the Communists.

4. For a clear-sighted politician there can be no problem as to whether the Social Democratic Party can or cannot be recognized, because the fact is that it actually exists. But the problem does arise for the short-sighted *apparatchiks* who want to protect their monopoly of power over the workers, and they rightly view such a recognition as a threat to themselves. If the social democrats have not revived the party so far, it is because they want to help their Communist comrades, who regard freedom under socialism as their own particular perspective, compatible with Communism. The sooner the *apparatchiks* realize this, the sooner they will get out of the habit of trying to solve the question which was unacceptable even at the time of Emperor Franz Josef, the sovereign of a world power, and is much less acceptable at present coming from one of the secretaries of the power-apparatus, however ominous his name.*

5. Social democrats have proved many times in their history that they are capable of sacrificing their prestige and their organization for the sake of the real interests of the working class, for broader freedom and democracy. In the same way they have proved that prisons cannot stop them, because they rely on the true interests of the population of this country and that is an invincible strength. The only way to make their program obsolete is to put it into effect. Their strength does not lie in a political party apparatus—they have no such apparatus; it derives from the actual condtions which now govern this country.

6. If the Communists take their own promises seriously, they cannot shut out from the prospect of democratic socialism those very social democrats who can guarantee support for this program in the broadest sections of the population, and who have clean hands and a clean slate. The social democrats, who were recently still serving their ten-year sentences, are not returning now with thoughts of revenge but with a stubborn faith that a synthesis of democracy and socialism can be

* Reference to Čestmír Císař, whose name (Císař) means "Emperor."—Ed.

created in a state whose security is really assured, perhaps for the first time in history, by its alliance with the USSR.

7. It must not be overlooked that not only some wing of the Communist Party but even the idea of socialism itself may one day become isolated. For a long time to come, and even if the former prisoners do not say a word about politics, the program of rehabilitation will go on creating a situation in which the very fact that it was possible to commit such crimes in Central Europe, and in the name of socialism, will have a shattering effect on young and adult voters alike. The Communist Party cannot stand up to this pressure alone, unless it is ready to resort to repression, which would mean going back to the old ways. Comrades, look for allies! They are among the representatives of democratic socialism who yesterday were still in jail. At least you are much more likely to find them there than among the shadowy parties which you are maintaining in the government and in the National Front.

8. In the life of every political party there are critical situations which are judged far more competently by history than by the decisions of authoritarian office holders. Social democrats have themselves lived through many such crises, so they know what it is to be suddenly excluded from the nation or, on the contrary, to live up to the responsibility of holding power. Neither the working class nor the Communist Party, which was its real representative, is to blame for the past; the responsibility for specific acts must be borne by the specific persons who committed them. It was tragedy of a great idea that it came up against the system of totalitarian power.

9. The tragedy of great ideas is best understood by those who were the victims of a tragedy in which they themselves played a part, by those who, in the midst of sunshine, saw the cloud heralding the storm. This could be confirmed by those Communists who found themselves in jail, where the social democrats offered them the hand of friendship and human understanding. They do understand the crises of history, because they learned socialism from Marx, not from Stalin, from the activity of the trade-union movement, not from the practices of the apparatus of manipulation, and also from the realities of Leopoldov and Mirov * rather than from the grandstands at May Day parades.

10. Social democrats are not alone in the world; they have many

* Concentration camps—Translator.

friends in Europe and elsewhere. It is up to the Communists to decide if they will recognize them as a real force in the sphere of ideas and a potential force in the sphere of action, or if they will regard them only as a suitable new subject for hidden, or even open, threats. Social democrats will go on observing certain principles in politics: a) to speak the truth; b) to keep their word; c) to operate on the basis of ideas and not of naked power.

III. The Mystery of the Independents

1. Besides the social democrats and the Catholics, the most significant force at present resides in the six million non-Party members. Several organizations of political importance have spontaneously arisen among them, the most advanced so far being the Prague discussion club called the Club of Committed Non-Party Members [Klub angažovaných nestraníků or KAN], which has drawn up a specific political program.

2. The members have proclaimed their adherence to the ideas out of which our state and national independence were born fifty years ago. They believe—as the founder of this state did—that states survive through their fidelity to the ideals from which they arose. They profess these ideals in their contemporary, modern form, laying stress on at least three fundamental principles which have now become the backbone of the club's thinking.

3. First of all, they consider that the basis of all modern European politics is the idea of human and civil liberties and of the equality of all citizens, which was once expressed in the revolutionary Declaration of the Rights of Man and which is now incorporated in the Universal Declaration of Human Rights adopted by the United Nations. They regard the defense of these rights against the dehumanizing forces of capitalism, fascism and Stalinism as the continuation of the unbroken tradition of the struggle of the Czech and Slovak nations for democracy. They openly proclaim their allegiance to it, for in their view it constitutes the solid base of the Czech nation and the central idea of the Czechoslovak state.

4. The second starting point of KAN's political effort is the humanist tradition of Czechoslovak culture. It believes that our nations found

the most significant incentives for their development not on the battle-field, in the struggle for world domination, or merely for consumption, but in the spheres of science, art, religion, ethics, and philosophy. In accordance with this international humanist tradition of solidarity between men and peace and cooperation between nations, KAN considers that the decisive value can not be found in the nation, the class, or the race because the true meaning of human existence is determined by the personality of man, his unique role in life, and his creative activity.

5. Finally, the third starting point is the impressive idea behind the Czechoslovak experiment: combining democratic socialism with a far-reaching program of personal liberty. The socialist order of society, the democratic exercise of power and the freedom of the individual are the points from which KAN starts in its political thinking, as well as the goals for which it is striving in the current reconstruction of political life. As the atmosphere of fear changes to one of trust and good will, and as the structure of political thinking is transformed, hundreds of thousands of personal revolutions are taking place in the hearts of people who have realized that it is unworthy of a man's human dignity to go through life simply trying to sneak through without getting caught in the totalitarian clutches of a small group of people who have seized power.

6. KAN believes that in the newly emerging structure of our political life, which cannot yet be discerned more precisely or in greater detail, there are certain elements that bring all non-Party members together, in spite of any differences in their opinions or political attitudes; it considers that these elements represent a potential base for the non-Party members' political activity, both within the club and outside it. The club has so far deliberately concentrated its political activity on promoting only this minimal program, incorporating the demands common to all non-Party members, because it is convinced that further normalization of social life will lead to the next stage—the creation or reshaping of political parties on the basis of principles and of a consistent and forward-looking philosophy. For the time being, the club does not aspire to this role, because it does not yet have the legal, organizational, material, and personal means to carry it out. But it feels that now is the time to bring the key issues to the attention of the

public outside the parties and to take the proper steps to ensure that the fundamental rules for the democratic shaping of political life and state power will be observed and respected. All non-Party members now have an interest in such a program, independent of what present or future political parties may put in their programs; this question will have to be dealt with later, in connection with the elections.

7. These minimal rules of the democratic game, which inspire the political activity of the club, include first of all the defense of fundamental civil rights, especially the equality of Party members and non-Party members. Unless this principle is accepted, it will be impossible to correct the defects of public life in any significant way or to overcome the crisis in our economy; the six million non-Party members of working age cannot go on forever being dominated by methods which gave them even less opportunity to lead an independent political life than was permitted under the Austrian Empire in the years 1905–1914. Apart from this equality of the two principal groups in our public life, the main issue of the coming months, in the club's opinion, is the democratic elections. The only way it is prepared to imagine this is as a secret balloting for separate lists of candidates put forward by several political parties, as well as by independents. The election law must contain at least these elementary provisons for the free participation of the citizen in the formation of the political organs of the state; it must provide the citizens with really genuine alternatives if the process of democratization is not to be paralyzed at the very outset.

8. Finally the club proposes to form alternative platforms, not only in connection with the elections but also in discussion of the serious political issues of the day. It intends to be the independent political power behind independent candidates representing the interests and opinions of non-Party members. It is not anti-Communist, and it does not formulate its view *in opposition to* the Communist Party. Its members are committed citizens, independent non-Party members, and they are forming their platform *by the side of* the Communists; the goals at which they are aiming are of a kind to unite Party members and non-Party members, in so far as the Czechs' and Slovaks' national program is the same as it was in the time of the man who founded our state on the basis of humanism, democracy, and social justice.

(84)

9. KAN itself includes the most varied trends and of course it will not be able to play the role of a political party until it manages to define itself more precisely, to draw up a program and to provide an alternative. But it can already help to sort out non-Party members' views about political life, to coordinate the various currents of the independent stream and to stimulate the kind of political discussion that is good for the process of democratization. For the time being, KAN describes itself as "a free platform where the Czechoslovak citizen without Party membership can form his political opinions about both fundamental and current questions of public life." It professes the ideals of freedom, democracy and socialism, it strives for tolerance and equality for non-Party members, and it opposes discrimination between citizens.

10. The main political activity of the club is centered on the rules governing elections, while the question of working out a program and a general philosophy still remains in the background. At present the demand for democratic elections raises such issues as the nature of the electoral law, the participation of several political parties, their admission to power, separate lists of candidates, the independent candidacy of non-Party members, the principle of the secret ballot, the rejection of crossing out names as a method of selecting candidates, the publication of the costs of each party's election campaigns, equal access to mass information media and the press. The elections will crystallize people's views, but they need not mean the end of KAN.

IV. The Specter of the Opposition

1. "He who fears the opposition is afraid for his position," proclaimed one of the wittiest of KAN's banners in the May Day parade, as if to prove once again that however complicated the political process may be, it can be reduced to certain elementary truths that can be grasped by any man of good sense. This is being denied by the manipulators of power, because they want to transform politics into a functionally technocratic machinery which could be run only by experts in "politology," who would therefore naturally appoint themselves man-

agers of the "lonely crowd," of an amorphous herd, or of group interests. The real object of these technocrats of power is now to confuse the issue of the opposition. They are enthusiastic about some kind of functional freedom, which is to produce a higher form of democracy, but without recognizing basic democratic rights; for minds trained in dialectical acrobatics this raises no problems.

2. "The views expressed from time to time about the need to create a new political party whose mission it would be to act as the opposition, and thus provide a mass counter-weight to our party, are not, in our opinion, correct. A plurality of political parties fighting for power in such a way that the very essence of socialism would be at stake is contrary to the needs and interests of the people; it opens the way to a possible relapse into capitalism and thus creates the danger of a violent conflict and a need to defend socialism by force. The rise of an opposition party with an antisocialist program would mean the end of the Czechoslovak experiment in creating a model of democratic socialism. As against this, it is perfectly feasible to transform the National Front into the political base for the fruitful cooperation of all the parties and other bodies in the Front, fulfilling all the functions of socialist democracy and representing a new model of the internal political articulation of a society without antagonistic classes." (Čestmír Císař in Pilsen, *Rudé Pravo*, April 27, 1968)

3. So this representative of the Czechoslovak Communist Party apparatus refers to the opposition as an antisocialist party which must be resisted by force. This kind of talk may help to accelerate the accumulation of personal power, but it does not solve anything. Besides, in his threat to use force the author is not bothered by the fact that within one single paragraph he uses the term *opposition* in several different senses. In the first sentence the opposition is a mass political party confronting the Communist Party. In the second, it becomes any plurality of political parties striving for power (and what else do all political parties in the world do, including your own?). In the third sentence, the opposition is a party with an antisocialist program, though we are not told who is to decide which program is socialist; *opposition* thus becomes a concept which extends the promise of violence even to the hitherto devotedly cooperative People's Party.

4. This jargon, which strikingly recalls the *Tass* statement,* ignores the fact that we see the opposition differently according to *where we stand politically*, and that it is not possible to speak about opposition in general but only about opposition to something, because we cannot disregard *what* is being opposed. If for Čestmír Císař the dangerous opposition is whatever goes against the policy of Communist Party, a social democrat, for instance, sees a dangerous opposition in the ranks of the Communist Party apparatus which is trying to delay the program of democratization; a typical representative of this apparatus is Čestmír Císař himself, a man who has introduced himself to the political scene in the last three months by open threats of violence, perhaps specifically in order to rid youth of the illusions which it has had about him.

5. Opposition to the socialist order and political opposition are, moreover, different things; a man, let us say a social democrat, who is unreservedly in favor of political opposition to the Communist Party may be just as unreservedly in favor of the socialist order of society and prepared to accept no other. No one has any interest in threatening a political force of this kind with violence, unless he happens to be an enemy of democratization who is drifting with the tide and hoping with the centrists that it will turn. *There is no democracy without political opposition*, but a given social order may last for centuries without a program for an alternative social order being put forward. No political statement has appeared in recent months which might suggest that the opposition exists in any form that could call for threats of violence. But many such threats have been made by conservatives, even apart from Císař.

6. Opposition in the sense of a platform alternative to the policy of the Communist Party is a reality, whether we recognize it or not. The center of this opposition was a wing of the Communist Party, which brought about a shift in political power relations; so Čestmír Císař's pronouncements should apply to himself, in so far as he belonged to this opposition and played a more serious part than that attributed to him by youth, when with their usual love of puns they shouted, "We

* This statement on T. G. Masaryk described the first Czechoslovak president in most unfavorable and impolite terms.—Ed.

want the Emperor (Císař) on the throne!" If he were to reread the passage about the use of force against the opposition in this context, he would see it in a different light, in the light in which it is read by the six million non-Communist voters at whom the threat is directed.

7. Opposition is today a reality, a political fact, but it is not embodied in any political party. If it is impossible to suppress and forbid opposition—which it is, at the moment—then the apparatus at least intends, by its threats, to prevent it from becoming a political institution. Real opposition to the past—which is not the same thing as opposition to the Communist Party or to socialism—has penetrated into the center of power, the Communist Party itself, as well as into the organizations that are spontaneously springing up, and into the National Front. The attempt to prevent the normalization of political forces by threats of violence is so bad a mistake and so grave a provocation of the potential allies of democratic socialism that not even Antonín Novotný would have to be ashamed of it.

8. If we give problems their right names, then we shall realize that the groups that offer alternatives to the Communist program, that is, the social democrats, the independent clubs, and the groups with Christian tendencies, constitute a political opposition, but that they do not represent organizations of a kind to justify threats of violence being made against them even before they have been properly set up—though the threats may serve to underline the controversial side of democracy. Political opposition is not a danger, it is not an anarchist negation, and it has nothing to do with the anti-Communism which is being attributed to it. The opposition is a necessary alternative, without which there is no civil liberty.

9. For the time being it is not the thinking about the opposition, restricted as it is to essays in literary magazines, that creates the risk that the Czechoslovak experiment will come to an end and that there will be a violent conflict; it is the far more dangerous latent force of two types of extremism. The first, and most absolutely dangerous of these, is the force exerted by the conservatives inside the Communist Party, who would like to paralyze the process of democratization and who, if they do not have the backing of classes, groups, people, and ideas, still hold in their hands the apparatuses with their considerable potential strength. The outcome of the Czechoslovak experiment de-

pends on whether the progressive Communists, with the help of other elements of political life, will be able to resist this strength; they can get such support because every clear-sighted man knows that the fate of this country at the present time depends not on the social democrats, nor on KAN, nor on an opposition party, but on the Communists.

10. The other grave danger lies of course in mindless anti-Communism which, however, in this country—unlike Hungary—is being rejected not only by Communists but also by democratic socialists and Catholics. So long as the Communist Party pursues its program of democratization and goes on normalizing political life along parliamentary and generally acceptable lines, the social base for anti-Communism as well as for the conservatism of the apparatuses will grow narrower and narrower. The dangerous concentration of the explosive mixture of illusions and reality will again be replaced by the air of freedom and the apparatuses will function as they should, so that they will be able to deal with the potential dynamite of political problems without running the danger of blowing everything up.

What Next?* ~~~~~~~~~~~~~~~~~~

Quieta non movere.
[Whatever is quiet should not be moved.]
Metternich's principle

1. The issue in the first phase of democratization was one of personnel changes and of raising demands. In the second phase, last month, the issue became one of how these demands are to be met. This is an entirely different matter. The first attempts to implement democratic liberties encountered exceptional difficulties. Only now has the real opposition begun to raise its head and only now have the difficulties begun to increase. Only now has the apparatus begun to raise its voice openly, threatening to use force.

2. We cannot ignore the fact that it was Čestmír Císař who was the first to threaten to use force, when he spoke in Pilsen at the end of April. It does not matter whether he was expressing his personal opinion or the opinion of a larger group. I believe that, in a situation in which arms are to be used or the potential danger or threat of their use exists, we find ourselves in a new phase in which, as happens so often, the former exponents of critical tendencies change their standpoints.

3. There are two basic dangers. First, there are the conservative forces, which still bank on the use of arms and on the people's militias, believing that the chances are good for a turn of events or for events to be suddenly arrested in their course. These people are wrong. The workers would not go against the intellectuals. Perhaps some officials of the people's militias and the apparatus would like to have a go at "putting things in order," but not even those in the militias would oppose the democratization process.

4. Potential anti-Communism is the second main danger. It would be illusory to deny that there are people who would like to see a radical

---

* Speech at the Union of Film and Television Artists Conference, May 18, 1968; published in the weekly, *Filmové a televizní noviny* [Film and television news], Prague, May 29, 1968.

turn in our current situation, including the liquidation of Czechoslovakia's membership in the Warsaw Pact. This is a latent danger. On the other hand, it seems to me that, today, almost every other person who advocates equality for members and nonmembers of the Party alike, that is, whoever wants an elementary program of civil rights is accused of anti-Communism. *Anti-Communism* is a term that is ambiguous, unclear and ill-defined. I do not know of anyone who has demanded a return to capitalism or who has propagated anti-Communism, speaking in the press, on the radio or television.

5. I am not aware of anyone having advocated in public that Czechoslovakia ought to abandon the Warsaw Pact. Therefore, warnings of this kind, referring to anti-Communism, are uncalled for. Indeed, it is articles of the type that appeared in *Sovietskaya Rossiya*, the first to spread the idea of the existence of anti-Communist views, which serve as the most effective instruments of anti-Communism, in the sense that articles that represent Masaryk as a blackguard are apt to affect the whole nation and to generate really hostile moods.

6. One might say that two alternatives are possible now: reconciliation, or further strife. These alternatives were suggested in *Literární listy*. I myself do not believe that we can tolerate criminals, but that we must expect strife. It would certainly be desirable for the exceptional atmosphere of the past three months to be consolidated in a manner preventing explosive situations, but this can only be done if the government creates the conditions under which elections are to be held—free, democratic elections. This is what Czechoslovak citizens await. In my opinion, situations of conflict cannot be solved by attempts to reconcile that which is irreconcilable; they can only be solved if channeled through democratic procedures.

7. The question of how to tackle the political heritage of the past—not so much the economic aftermath, but the political lacuna which has opened up in the past twenty years—is one of the most difficult tasks. This hiatus brought about immense apathy and indifference, overcome, until now, in only one social stratum, that of the intelligentsia, and still holding broad sections of the people in its grip. It is precisely in the working class and in the industrial plants that there exists an enormous potential of possibilities, which can be utilized if the intellectuals grasp that it is not enough to be brilliant, witty, and

humorous before television cameras, but that the issue is to formulate political rights for the workers.

8. To date, neither we, the intellectuals, nor any one else has said that the program also includes the right to strike, to free association in trade unions, and to the secret election of managers. It is precisely these elementary rights which interest the workers and which are just as important and attractive to them as the demand for freedom of the press or freedom of information is to us.

9. The critical question facing us, facing the intellectuals, the intelligentsia, the artists, is the question of how we can justify our saying to the workers: "Should someone touch your standard of living, we shall protest!" Then, the workers will be quick to grasp—and some of them in the Ostrava region have already grasped this—that they themselves must protect freedom of the press, freedom of information, and of television, and that they must say: "Should someone touch freedom of the press, we shall strike!" And, at the moment, strikes, political strikes, are feared most by those who are not afraid of anything and who always have their arms at the ready. This unity of intellectuals and workers, or at least this identity of interests, can be created and propagated because, latently, it does exist.

10. The rehabilitation of reason, justice, truth, and conscience is another of the specific tasks of the intelligentsia. Indeed, because of the former prostitution of these great words, the rehabilitation of elementary values is one of our most important tasks. At the same time, we must tear down taboos, we must enter prohibited territory, and, willy-nilly, provoke thought. Our task indisputably is to provoke thought and to remove existing taboos in situations in which up to now we had become accustomed to refrain from being specific, and from formulating certain thoughts at a time when distortions of thinking had gone so far as to allow us to move only within a circumscribed area, and when criticism was expressed only at the risk of one's life.

11. The intellectuals are not alone, nor is Czechoslovakia alone. The intellectuals have allies and so has Czechoslovakia. These allies are the European Left, people to whom the symbiosis of socialism and democracy is just as topical as it is to us. These supporters of ours can be found in Western and in Eastern Europe. We are not alone. Therefore, if we, the non-Communists, may give some advice to the Com-

munist Party and to its progressive wing, we would like to say something like this.

12. "Comrades, look for allies among socialists and democrats. You are certain to find these allies. Look for allies even there where you were not used to looking for them. You will be surprised to find that, let us say, people who were released from prison where they had been sent for so-called political crimes, or people who were persecuted because of their ideas on socialism and democracy, will be quite willing and glad now to cooperate in the program of democratization and to be your allies, rather than your enemies."

It Is Not We Who Are Afraid * ᘓᘓᘓᘓᘓ

1. The democratization process initiated by the Communist Party of Czechoslovakia enters its second, decisive, phase in which civil rights are to be put into effect as proclaimed. We are therefore greatly disturbed by the noticeable slowdown in the democratization process. We are disturbed especially by the unfounded accusations against some democratization forces as being anti-Communist and extremist while a benevolent neutrality is being maintained toward leaflet campaigning and appeals to overthrow the "government of revisionists."

2. We are also troubled by signs of the return of the leadership of the Communist Party to a closed-door policy. Fundamental civil rights, especially democratic elections, are a national concern of all Czech and Slovak citizens and cannot be regarded as a merely internal problem of the Communist Party. To deal with these state and national interests within constricted top-level governmental and Party circles means that the basic subject of every democratic policy—the people—is *de facto* left out in regard to important decisions.

3. We regard the leading role of the Communist Party as a binding political reality and this is why we see in its measures important acts of our national policy. Any attempt to stop the democratization process, "to keep things in one's own hands," and once again to solve political problems through power would be fatal to the prestige of the Communist Party, in which we see the guarantee for developing a Czechoslovak socialist democracy, and whose progressive orientation we shall support.

4. We regard the national sovereignty of Czechoslovakia as an inalienable value. We think there should be no doubt about this matter, and this is why we and the millions of our citizens have raised pressing questions concerning the practical problems of this sovereignty. We

* Resolution presented at the Union of Film and Television Artists Conference, May 18, 1968; published in the Prague Socialist Party daily, *Svobodné slovo* [Free word], May 22, 1968. This text differs slightly from the original draft. Point 6 has been added and certain points reformulated.

regard it as inadmissible for domestic problems of our state and national life to be permitted to become the subject of negotiations in foreign countries and institutions, without the full knowledge of the Czechoslovak people.

5. We give our full support to our government in its defense of Czechoslovak state sovereignty, but we also ask that it consult the Czechoslovak people on its important decisions; the people trust it and therefore should be trusted in return. It would be improper if our government interfered in the domestic affairs of other states, but we also demand in a resolute way that any attempt to interfere in our domestic affairs be rejected uncompromisingly. The policy of friendship with the Soviet Union and other socialist states, the policy of socialist internationalism, cannot have positive results if it is not based on the principle of independence and equality for all partners.

6. Our point of departure is our belief that a federative arrangement of our republic, as a highly democratic requirement, is not only in the interest of the Slovak nation, but in the interest of the Czech nation as well. This is true because only a federation is in a position to preserve both the loyalty and the participation of the Slovak nation in formulating ideas and in solving practical problems of Czechoslovak statehood. We appeal to the National Assembly to proclaim the federative order of Czechoslovakia through a special constitutional measure immediately and without delay. Only such a measure will provide us with a legal basis for the establishment of Czech national organs and make possible their dialogue with the Slovak national organs. A nationwide discussion has proved that the idea of federation is ripe enough and that any delay is unfounded and even undesirable. The importance of this task within the democratization process is clear, especially in regard to the planned elections, which should already be based on the new system of regional and national elective organs.

7. With regard to the democratic traditions of both our nations, we believe that one of the most important present problems is equal civil rights for all members of our state regardless of their party affiliation. We are disturbed about the fact that equal rights for our nations are a generally recognized requirement, but the requirement of equal civil rights gave rise to doubt, and even suspicion, in some places, that it was anti-Communistic. We are convinced that the majority of the citizens

of our country, whether organized in non-Communist parties or without party affiliation, are not anti-Communistic or anti-Soviet, but want to be regarded as a force with equal rights; these people want to be partners of the Communist Party, ready for positive cooperation in implementing the socialist and democratic program. We therefore think that an equality of political rights for all citizens, and the abolition of the privileged status of some, are indispensable conditions for democracy and guarantees for the free development of our society. This equality of rights should take the form of the opportunity and the right to express opinions on public affairs and of participation in decision making at all levels of the social structure.

8. Many times in history, Czech and Slovak artists have expressed the most important political problems of our nations. In continuing this tradition we, as part of the Czechoslovak intelligentsia, once more advocate an alliance of workers and intellectuals striving for the implementation of democratic socialism. We are aware that ideas on civil rights have been formulated in an incomplete manner in terms of the requirements for freedom of the press, of assembly, and of conscience; rights of workers and other working people to strike, to enjoy self-rule, and to have free trade unions in accordance with the above rights. In their totality they represent, in practical form, a guarantee for the standard of living of all working people.

9. We welcome the Ostrava workers' committees for the protection of the freedom of the press as the beginning of a direct link between workers and the intelligentsia, the only means to safeguard the indivisibility of all civil rights and freedoms vis-à-vis bureaucratic attempts to limit them. We, the workers in Czechoslovak films and television, reply to any attempt to lower the standard of living or limit the civil rights of workers with the same resolution with which the working class responds to attacks against freedom of the press, of thought, and of information.

10. Any attempt to limit freedom of information would make the working class defenseless against an attack on its standard of living and against complications which will be the necessary result of the new economic system. It means that the mere threat of using the workers' militia "to restore order in radio and television" can harm workers in the first place. The attempt to avert their attention from

their rightful discontent with their standard of living by attacking "intellectuals in television" is a transparent ruse on the part of those who have always tried to find a scapegoat for their own shortcomings, in order to protect the guilty ones. We who work in television and film would like to assure those who inspire such tendencies that we feel strong in our consciousness that we are struggling for a great and just cause. Today it is not we who are afraid.

The Genius and the Apparatus* 〜〜〜〜〜

> Master Chuang once dreamt that he
> was a butterfly, fluttering hither and
> thither. The butterfly felt like a butter-
> fly, and lacked nothing—it did not know
> that it was Chuang! Suddenly Chuang
> awoke and was amazed—he was Chuang!
> And he did not know if Chuang dreamt
> that he was a butterfly or if the butterfly
> was now dreaming that it was Chuang.
> Chuang or butterfly—surely there must
> be some difference!
>
> CHUANG-TSE (Chinese philosopher,
> Fourth Century B.C.)

The Truth of Paradox

1. If Marx came to life and wished to define himself in relation to the image of Marx that has been built up since his death, he would find himself in Chuang's situation. Like the Chinese philosopher more than 2,000 years ago, Marx, too, would have to master the problem of the truth of paradox. He would do so through the antinomies and paradoxes of reality, for his genius is his clear and precise consciousness of the self in the world and the world in the self; it is the transparent reflection of contemporary society in the consciousness of the individual. The more universal genius is, the more it unites within itself scientific truth, the message of freedom, and, unfortunately, authority for weaklings.

2. Marx the scholar is the Copernicus of social sciences; he brought about a transformation of the sciences dealing with man, a transformation similar to that which marked the move from astrology to astronomy. In speaking of Marx as the Copernicus of social sciences, we are not implying that the founder of modern astronomy was infallible. It

---

*Lecture at Charles University, May 3, 1968, to commemorate the 150th anniversary of Karl Marx's birth; published in *Student* in 1968.

was Galileo who discovered that the orbit of planets around the sun is elliptical and not circular, as Copernicus himself believed. Similarly, modern social science reinterprets the functioning of man in the modern world, but Marx's anthropocentric standpoint still holds true.

3. Marx was not, is not, and will never be the discoverer and theoretician of totalitarian dictatorship that he appears to be today. . . . Marx strove for a wider humanism than that of the bourgeois democracies he knew, and for wider civil rights, not for the establishment of the dictatorship of one class and one political party. What is today thought to be the Marxist theory of the state and Marxist social science is simply an ideological forgery, a false, contemporary conception, as wrong as the idea that the orbits of heavenly bodies are circular.

4. To understand Marx truly we must be aware how much he was conditioned by his time, determine his theoretical place and not confuse his thought with the later interpretations by Lenin, Stalin, and Mao. A true picture of Marx depends on an awareness of his historicity; the ideological conceptions of "Marxism," "Marxism-Leninism" or "Maoism," however, are functional ideological tools used by apparatuses to manipulate the masses, not objective, truthful, and historically valid interpretations. Just as it was necessary to separate Stalin from Lenin, so Lenin must be separated from Marx, not in order to oppose one with the other but so that both may be understood as real historical personalities.

5. If we approach the writings of Marx and Lenin in this historical, truthful, and objective manner, we must distinguish Marx's great thought as to the liberating role of the working class in modern history from Lenin's specifically Russian thought on the leading role of the Communist Party. Broadly speaking, Marx defended the leading role of the *working class;* he defended its historical mission and its workers' activity, but he never imagined that this class itself might be dominated by a political party—and especially by the apparatus of this party. According to him, the dictatorship of the proletariat was to be the *temporary* rule of the *majority* over the minority, not the *permanent* terror of a *minority* against the people.

6. Marx relies on man, on the working class, on the people as the driving force of history, not on the manipulation of people. For him, man is the subject of the historical process, not an object to be manipu-

lated by apparatuses. Lenin's concept of the Bolshevik party is fundamentally different. . . .

7. Putting Leninism into effect in Russia led to the political success of the working class, to a victorious revolution and to the founding of a socialist state. Putting the same pattern into effect in Czechoslovakia, where the literate working class was already the strongest political force at the time the Communist Party came into being, and where it represented the majority of the population, even at the very beginning of the process of building socialism, has led to clear failure. It was, and is, just as inappropriate that the Party should dominate the working class as that the Party apparatus should dominate the state. And it is so not because we are against Marx or Lenin, but precisely because we are for Marx and for an understanding of the historical context in which Lenin specifically adapted Marx's heritage to Russia—not to Europe.

8. If we think of Marx the scholar historically, bearing in mind the time in which he lived, the question of the timeless truth of his individual statements and attitudes does not arise and we can appreciate the real worth of Marx's valid and still applicable methodology; moreover, we can turn it against his apparent disciples—the ideologists. To see how right this approach is, one has only to notice how violently the very people who claim to be Marxists hate the ruthless search for truth which is their master's methodology. The power apparatus has won all along the line against the real Marx, but in this it has only confirmed the genius's paradoxical truth that institutions are stronger than people, a truth the genius had already arrived at in his high school essay, whereas it took the apparatus a whole century to get there.

9. Because of its mass diffusion, the false image of Marx, as forged by ideologists of all shades in order to justify totalitarian dictatorship, cannot be changed all at once. At the moment it is enough to say that the present process of democratization is being hampered not by Marx but by individuals with much smaller intellectual capacities. We can hope to defeat them, because reason alone can permanently overcome power.

10. The ideological caricature of Marx can perhaps be adequately conveyed by the absurdly surrealistic metaphor of one sociologist for whom Marx, perverted and deformed in the consciousness of society, is a monster with two heads which are trying to shout each other down,

one with Soviet and one with Chinese slogans. By contrast, the faithful, historical picture of the real Marx shows the scholar, the European, the democrat, the socialist, the tribune of the people, the humanist, the revolutionary, the internationalist, the giant personality, and the messenger of freedom. This true picture of the man Marx really was has been transformed by the apparatuses of the movement and by history itself into an absolute labyrinth of contradictions.

The Message of Freedom

1. Marx was a scholar of genius. But scientific knowledge continues to develop. Insofar as this means that the limits of knowledge are constantly expanding, Marx's scholarship is being outstripped by the evolution of the very social science that he founded. In discovering a valid methodology of social science, Marx discovered a weapon against himself as a fetish-idol, against ideological authority, and against the perversion of his own message of freedom.

2. Marx was an earnest European, with deep roots in the European culture based on antiquity, Christianity, the Renaissance and the Enlightenment. But his teaching was taken over in the east of Europe and in Asia, where there was not only no Enlightenment but also no Renaissance. The core of Marx's discoveries—his criticism—had to be transformed into a bigoted orthodox faith in the unity of church and state, which took the shape of a monopoly of power irreconcilable with European cultural tradition, with criticism and with science.

3. Marx was one of the greatest democrats of history. He stood for human and civil rights as the basis of political life. But the rise of the giant bureaucratic apparatus of the modern state, of industrial societies, and of political machines, as well as the practical impossibility of following democratic procedures in tsarist Russia and then in a land of semiliteracy, has obstructed the development of those features of democracy which Marx took for granted, convinced as he was that "one form of freedom depends upon another. . . . Whenever a specific freedom is questioned, freedom itself becomes questionable."

4. Marx was a socialist; he worked to change production relations in order to emancipate the working class, humanity, and man as an individual. But the narrow interpretation of his program in purely economic terms, as a program of future prosperity, has led to the techno-

cratic effort to create a consumer society. The *means* to the emancipation of mankind have become ends, contrary to Marx's original intentions; for him, economic demands were only a means of emancipating man, and not ends in themselves.

5. Marx was a tribune of the workers' movement in which he saw a guarantee that mankind would be emancipated. But eventually organizations, apparatuses, and even state apparatuses acquired power over the movement itself and stifled every spontaneous expression of the workers' will as treason against Marx. The greatest treason against Marx, however, is the very existence of these power apparatuses, dominating the political movement of the working class.

6. Marx was a humanist, for whom the meaning of human life lay in creation, in the development of man as a many-sided personality, in people's participation in the historical process, and in the growth of human freedom. But these original aims, through which Marx hoped to achieve a revolutionary transformation, have, in the apparatus version of Marxism, been completely subordinated to the functional conception of man as a mere object to be manipulated. In the vocabulary of the apparatus, his central postulate, the freedom of man, has become a reactionary slogan; this is the most brutal castration that Marx has had to suffer.

7. Marx was a revolutionary fully aware of his goal. Being a radical humanist in the middle of the nineteenth century meant trying to bring about a revolutionary change in the political and economic structure of society. But the transformation of the industrial countries of Europe that was brought about by the organized strength of the workers' movement set in motion processes which changed the social position of the working class, its opinions, its political goals, and even the very character of the revolution. The original conception of the proletarian revolution as a means of winning power is being changed by the radical transformation of science and technology; this is the true revolution, which is bringing mankind, and the working class, much closer to freedom than any fighting on the barricades.

8. Marx was an internationalist, for whom national frontiers were barriers to understanding between nations and between the working classes. But the doctrine of socialism in one country, which is incompatible with Marx's appeal to the workers of the world, has created a nationalistic pattern of cooperation between unequal nations. The

ploughed-up stretches of land and the barbed wire between European countries are most flagrant violations of the idea of internationalism. It is *against his idea* that the armed units stand on guard along the frontiers of socialist countries.

9. Marx was a great and many-sided personality. But he became the refuge of nonentities who knew, and know, that they cannot hope to turn the zeros that they are into a number except by hiding behind his great figure. We need only compare the personality of Marx with that of today's leaders to become convinced that history has a sense of comedy as cruel as it is malicious.

10. Marx was a messenger of the freedom of man. That is why he attracted the hatred of apparatuses of all colors. And inasmuch as progress is the growth of human freedom, the living Marx will go on attracting their hatred. In the same way, the embalmed corpse of the ideology connected with his name will go on and on being exhumed in the solemn discourses of the official spokesmen of the apparatuses, who, in the name of the very working class whom they would like to use as an alibi before the judgment of history, shower their decorations upon the dead genius only because he does not have the strength to throw the medals back in their faces.

The Lie of Salvation

1. The ideological interpretation of Marx is a perversion of the real Marx, used to justify the domination of apparatuses over the workers' movement. Marx is at the same time turned into a myth, an irrational authority, into the guarantor of faith in the messianic role of the working class in modern history, into the focal point of the prophetically foretold workings of the laws of history. But Marx is not a savior.

2. As the social function of his teaching has changed, Marx has been made a prophet, a visionary, and a messiah; this was the outcome of the historical process in which, after his death, Marx's various scientific views became norms of behavior with absolute validity for the workers' movement. In this way, scientific analysis of capitalism gradually grew to be a stereotype of ideological formulas; for quite a long time these could reflect the reality of capitalism, but nevertheless they lost their scientific character. Marx is not an earthly messiah.

3. As the discrepancies grew between Marx's analysis—perfectly ac-

curate as regards the capitalism of his own time—and reality at the turn of the century, and then reality in the period between the wars, so the giant of critical thought had to be smothered in thicker and thicker clouds of the incense of faith and turned into the impotent dummy of May Day parades. The gap between dogma and reality can be bridged only by faith—by faith in a leader, the secular god of a mass movement, or by faith in the institution, the secular church which guarantees salvation to man. But Marx cannot be an object of faith, for he is not a secular god.

4. As soon as the lie of salvation, that is, faith in the revolutionary liberating mission of the Communist Party, was substituted as a principle for the discipline of truth, the problem of faith and of the decline of faith emerged as the central issue. There came the break with the intellectuals who were unwilling to lay down their own intellect on the altar of the Party, of the nation, or of the movement. The famous statement "Believe the Party, comrades," * and the endless discussions on whether the Party is always right revealed the total bankruptcy of critical thought, which was all the more absurd for being brought about in the name of Marx.

5. At the same time, the absurd statement that the Party was the guarantor of truth and the focus of faith reflects the deep crisis in the consciousness of the left-wing intellectuals of the 1950's. It reflects the tragic confusion in thought and practice which accompanied not only the trials but also the establishment, in the heart of Europe, of a measure of barbarity such as Czechs and Slovaks had hitherto experienced only at the hands of foreign invaders but never at the hands of representatives of their own nations. To this day, textbooks quote, as a warning example to school children of the inhumanity of a system based on slavery, the killing, 2,000 years ago, of the woman mathematician Hypatia by the mob of Alexandria, held fully responsible by history for the murder. Yet the present apparatuses are just as fully responsible for an act which is a unique performance in modern world history— the execution of a woman, Milada Horáková, for her political activity

* In a speech after the executions that followed the Slanský trial, Czechoslovak President and Communist Party Boss Klement Gottwald said that many comrades were asking, if so many Party leaders had been traitors, whom they were to believe. His answer, as reported in this speech, was "believe the Party, comrades."—Translator

in time of peace. It is to be hoped at least that she will not be covered with the filth of rehabilitation by alibi-seekers, but rather that she will be revealed in her true character to the same school children, whose mental hygiene is so dear to those concerned with the political education of youth and, at the college level, with the so-called social sciences.

6. Faith in the Party was a defense against the appalling absurdities of life, which appeared totally incomprehensible and incompatible with the humanist goal that the ideology proclaimed in words and destroyed in practice. The psychological mechanisms, both individual and collective, of faith and despair, frustration and salvation, explain why, in a situation in which critical thought had totally ceased to function, attitudes toward the trials, toward the USSR or toward Stalin became the "touchstone." Once those premises were accepted, by which the discipline of truth in regard to reality is subordinated to Party discipline and to faith in salvation through the Party, all that remained was to believe—to believe even beyond the grave, like those imprisoned Communists who died with Stalin's name on their lips. It is precisely those who provoke the deepest disgust.

7. The problem of faith—in the trials, in the Party, and in Stalin—also reflected the central issue, that is, the conviction that one has to accept guilt in order to save the meaning of one's former commitment to the cause of socialism, the meaning of the fight against fascism, the meaning of the building of socialism. The greater the doubts that arose, the higher did the flame of faith have to rise, the showier did the auto-da-fé have to be. And the readier was the average man to accept the stereotyped resolution of his doubts, presenting them *before his own conscience* as a narrow, inessential kind of consideration, insignificant in comparison with cheering crowds, with the building of new plants, and with the undoubtedly noble aim of helping the people, constantly put forward as reality by the agile ideologists, though in practice this aim did not exist.

8. Neither Marx nor the working class accepts the ghastly game of pinning medals on the breasts of corpses in the name of their murderers. Neither Marx nor the working class, nor indeed history, recognizes the rehabilitation of corpses, for, unlike the alibi-seekers of the apparatuses, they know very well what justice is. The working class, as Marx's heir, has a clean slate; it did not murder and persecute freedom, so it does not

need the alibi and the farce of the sinister ceremonies in which decorations are solemnly returned to corpses which gave thanks for their executions, accepting the appalling sacrifice as a logical service to the same apparatuses which executed them and to which, during their lives, they had themselves belonged. The working class, like the intellectuals, looks with horror upon this senseless performance which is meant to exculpate the apparatus against common sense, especially if these acts are performed in the name of the process of rebirth, on Workers' Day, on May 1, 1968.

9. The baser the goals that are aimed at, the nobler must be the ideology that is used to justify them, for people do not normally have the courage to do evil, to hurt others, or to spread suffering unless the institutions of salvation, the Church or the Party, offer them sedatives to calm their conscience. Man cannot save himself through faith in a leader, an ideology or an institution; he cannot, through his emotions, win heaven, or reason, or happiness, which is a more civilian term for salvation. But he can understand himself as a free, active, responsible being, with his own reason and feelings. Then he will not be deaf to the heritage of the genius, whose last will and testament, translated into the language of today, might sound something like this:

YES to INTERNATIONALISM	NO to NATIONALISM
EUROPE	ASIA
SOVEREIGN CZECHOSLOVAKIA	NEOCOLONIALISM
SOCIALISM	STATE CAPITALISM
DIRECT DEMOCRACY	DICTATORSHIP
PARLIAMENTARIANISM	MONOPOLY OF POWER
CULTURE	APPARATUSES
HUMANISM	MANIPULATION
CRITICAL INQUIRY	AUTHORITARIANISM
THE PEOPLE	THE MASSES
THE INDIVIDUAL	THE ELITE
FREEDOM	ANARCHY

YES TO OPEN SOCIETY. NO TO TOTALITARIAN MECHANISMS. PEOPLE OF THE WORLD, UNITE AGAINST THE RATS OF THE WORLD. MARX IS DEAD. LONG LIVE MARX.

Third Act: Crisis

PROBLEMS OF POWER ELITES

℘

Material force can only be overthrown
by material force; but theory itself becomes a material force when it has seized
the masses.

KARL MARX

Contents

Chronology

July 14–15

Russian, Polish, Bulgarian, Hungarian, and East German leaders met in Warsaw and drafted the stiff Warsaw Letter.

July 18

Dubček asked the Czechs and the Slovaks, in a television appearance, for their support. The reply to the Warsaw Letter dispatched.

July 29

Meeting between the Czech and the Soviet leaders in Čierná opened and continued for four days.

August 3

Bratislava Agreement signed by the leaders of the six Warsaw Pact countries.

August 9

President Tito arrived in Prague.

August 20–21

Invasion of Czechoslovakia by the five Warsaw Pact armies.
Dubček and other Czech and Slovak leaders arrested in the name of the "revolutionary government of the workers and peasants."

August 23

President Svoboda's delegation arrived in Moscow.

August 26

Moscow agreement concluded. Dubček was to carry on as First Secretary; the invasion forces were to be gradually withdrawn, but a part of them were to remain on Czechoslovakia's western frontier; censorship was to be reintroduced, and the Party was to strengthen its leading position in the state.

[The caption for this *Literární listy* cartoon parodies the heavy-handed vitupera-
tion of Soviet-style political satire; Ludvík Vaculík, as a reformist writer, is
linked here with the *Two Thousand Words* manifesto and the "Moral Terror"
supposedly unleashed by journalists upon the Novotnýites. He is also, absurdly,
blamed for a wide assortment of governmental blunders and natural mishaps.—Ed.]

Kdo je Ludvík Vaculík?

Ludvík Vaculík se narodil ve dnech podepsání hanebného Kellogova paktu. Již ve čtyřech letech netajil se před svým „oblíbencem" místní římskokatolický farář svými neskrývanými sympatiemi k proradné japonské intervenci v Mandžursku.

Záhy se naučil psát, aby mohl snáze ostouzet dělnickou třídu.

Na velkostatku svého „moravského" strýčka nadšeně uvítali pokořující mnichovský diktát, se špatně utajovanými sympatiemi k sudetoněmeckým landsmanšaftům.

A jak se choval za války? O tom by mohly mnohé vyprávět bedny z Černého jezera.

V Únoru 1948 poznal, že mu pšenice nepokvete. Už tehdy zakopal na zahradě rodné „usedlosti" v kompostu Hitlerův obraz a dva páry gumových rukavic. „Na později," jak se tehdy cynicky vyjádřil.

A po lednu? Nu, to ví přece každé malé dítě.

Kdo zapálil Suchánkovu stodolu? Kdo vyřadil z provozu hrudkovnu v Ejpovicích? Kdo způsobil nízkou dojivost skotu na Tachovsku? Kdo rozpoutal bestiální morální teror? Kdo potajmu sepsal s různými Procházky, Svitáky a Goldštjukery smutně proslulý pamflet 2000 slov?

To je on!

Ne ne, Ludvíku Vaculíku, takhle ne!

(THIS IS HE

Who actually is Ludvík Vaculík?

Ludvík Vaculík was born when the infamous Kellog Pact was signed. Already by the time he was four he did not conceal from his favorite, the local Roman-Catholic priest, his open sympathy for the treacherous Japanese intervention in Manchuria.

He learned to write at an early age so he could sling easier mud at the working class.

On the estate of his "Moravian" uncle he greeted the Munich diktat with enthusiasm and with a badly concealed sympathy for the Sudeten-German *Landsmannschaften* [a Sudeten-German Nazi organization].

And how did he behave during the war? Boxes at the bottom of the Black Lake could tell much about it.

In February 1948 he realized his good time was over. He therefore buried a picture of Hitler and two pairs of rubber gloves in a compost in the garden of his native "farm." "Good for some future time," declared he with a cynical smile.

And after January? Well, every little child knows.

Who set afire Suchanek's barn? Who put the ore-processing plant in Ejpovice out of business? Who caused the low milk yield in the cattle of the Táchov District? Who unleashed the heinous Moral Terror? Who with Procházkas, Svitáks and Goldštückers secretly produced the ill-famed *Two Thousand Words* pamphlet?

This is he!

No, no, Ludvík Vaculík, not this way!)

Ten Commandments for an Adult Intellectual* ～～～～～～～～～～～～～～～

> If you're not part of the solution, you're
> part of the problem.
>
> *Familiar Slogan*

1. Speak the truth regardless of tactical considerations, since concessions to tactics are concessions to truth. If you cannot speak the truth, be silent. The discipline of truth is the hardest of all disciplines.

2. Rely on your own common sense and do not believe in the revealed certainty of any churches, parties, or messiahs. The specialists will always tell you that "things are more complicated," although the basic questions of human rights, of the fate of man, and of personal freedom are open to all, to every sound reason.

3. Rely on the strength of thought, do not trust power. Only ideas win in the long run over power. Ideas corrode power.

4. Ask disturbing questions which transcend the conventional horizon. In this manner you test the freedom which always lies in exceeding given limits. If you give in to conventions and given limits, you are abandoning the principal mission of an intellectual.

5. Respect facts and the purity of basic notions—the instruments of thinking. Prevent the substitution of stereotyped slogans for the analysis of facts and concepts. Stereotypes of ideas used in slogans are the manipulative means of the apparatus in the play for power, the instruments of false consciousness of society about itself.

6. Concentrate on the political nerve—the group interests. The function of an intellectual does not lie in playing the game of a politician with these interests but in understanding them. Thus, he knows that the power elite has under all circumstances one overriding interest—to maintain itself in power.

7. Trust people as the source of power in the state, since this source

* Contribution to a discussion launched by *Literární listy*, June 20, 1968; published in the weekly *Student*, Prague, in July, 1968.

of power is a more reliable basis for politics than any ideology. Believe in the genius of people, do not believe in "the conscience of the party," in institutions, or in apparatuses, since apparatuses have neither conscience nor reason, which are the privilege of people. Apparatuses have been, are, and will remain nonreasoning and devoid of conscience, whereas people have been, are, and will remain superior to apparatuses, ideologies and institutions, regardless of monarchs, tyrants, social elites, totalitarian dictatorships, and political parties, which have claimed and now claim for themselves the right to lead people.

8. The final institution of appeal in politics is neither science nor institutions but the sovereign people. Neither the "conscience of the party," nor the reason of intellectuals, nor the privileges of elites are judges of people. It is the people who are judges of political institutions and individuals.

9. Consider it an irrefutable axiom that freedom is your inalienable human right. The freedom of thought includes the right to disagree with the power elites. The limitation of this freedom is an ancient method of enslaving man without regard to motivations and ideologies, which cover up this praxis, and without regard to the fact that the newer dictatorships consider precisely this limitation of man's freedom as a triumph of progress.

10. Commit yourselves to the cause of human freedom as the highest value of mankind. Individuals, movements, states, and blocs that wish to create a new culture of society based on other foundations than human freedom are merely modern forms of slavery. The theory and praxis of totalitarian dictatorships are the worst threat to mankind in the entire history of man on this planet. Remember this: "Man can be destroyed, but not defeated."

Truth as a Provocation to Power ∾∾∾∾

> "Oh," said the mouse, "the world is get-
> ting narrower every day. At first it was
> so wide that I was afraid, I ran and ran
> and finally I was happy when I saw walls,
> left and right, in the distance; but these
> long walls converge so quickly that al-
> ready I am in the last room and here, in
> the corner, stands a mousetrap and I am
> running into it."
> "You just have to change your course,"
> said the cat—and ate the mouse.
>
> FRANZ KAFKA, A Small Fable

The Lesson of the Fable

1. A mouse who knows that it is running toward its trap will not be happy to see the walls in the distance, but will change its course before the walls appear. The walls are an indication of the limits of freedom, toward which trained mice will gladly run only when they do not know what follows. Neither mice nor people can run the road of knowledge twice, first as uneducated beings and then as wise ones. They are wise either always or never.

2. The cat is not an ally of the mice, not even when it tells the truth to a mouse, because a smart mouse knows that a cat will tell it the truth only if the mouse cannot use the truth to save itself. A cat is interested in eating the mouse, not in chasing it into the trap. There-fore, it advises the mouse correctly to change its course, but only because the cat itself has an interest in this solution. The mouse would quite certainly choose the trap and a postponement of its end, rather than an instantaneous death in the cat's mouth.

3. If the mouse has hitherto overlooked the danger of the narrow-ing walls, it no longer has any choice, since the trap is just as destruc-tive an alternative for the mouse as are the jaws of the cat. If the

* Article in *Student*, in June, 1968.

players of a structurally similar game get as far as the mouse, they are then bound to lose under all circumstances, and the manner in which they lose the game remains the only question. In other words, they lose at the very moment it seems to them that the walls converging upon their freedom facilitate their course, as they continue their approach to the trap and the truth of their destruction.

4. The trap appears to the mouse as a better alternative than death, since it offers a certain hope of postponing destruction. However, this hope is fictitious since without a change in course there is no hope for rescue. If the mouse is so stupid as to be pleased by the signs of lost freedom, by the walls which narrow the space of its free movement, then it does not deserve anything but its own death. The absurd mouse is itself guilty of its own destruction, because its awareness comes too late.

5. From this closed situation there is no escape for Kafka's mouse; because it was naive it lost, through its own failure, every chance of escape. The truth—that the mouse needed to change the direction in which it was running—had always existed; it was always within the mouse's capacity to understand this truth. The decisive factor in the critical situation of Kafka's mouse is its own knowledge of the situation in which it finds itself at a certain time—in other words, its recognition of danger.

6. If the mouse knows that, after the walls and the narrowing space, only the cat and the trap remain, then it is saved. If it does not know it and continues in an orderly manner on its course, then it is lost. At a certain moment the mouse loses the alternative of salvation and the chance to change its course as it runs. This can appear to its naive disposition as a happy moment in which the limitless space of freedom is overcome.

7. In old cartoons clever Mickey Mouse triumphs over cats by somehow always outsmarting them. He evokes enthusiasm in children and adults, not by pondering over his destruction but by acting cleverly, by being skillful and having good ideas. Mickey Mouse elicits sympathy because he resists force and most people have a sense of fair play; they root for the weak against the strong.

8. A smart Mickey Mouse would thus not be pleased by the walls, as was Kafka's absurd mouse. He would instead change the course of

his run in time or he would escape the cat by using a ruse, since he knows very well, as Heinrich Heine knew, that rascals must be treated with cunning, otherwise one is lost.

9. We must protect the little mouse of absurdity against the interpreters who would explain its course into the trap as antisocialist orientation. Unfortunately, though, the mouse runs into the trap in an orderly manner, and does not even talk back.

10. In science there exists a so-called homology of structures, according to which—roughly speaking—the basic relationships are valid, regardless of the subject they pertain to—We can learn from the mouse if we understand that we are all mice, that the trap is the structure of monopolistic power, the cat is the police dictatorship and the walls are the limitations of civil rights. Only certain generals do not fit the fable, since not even Kafka could imagine that the cat could accuse the mouse of counterrevolution only because the mouse refuses to remain orderly while it is being eaten.

The Consequences of Words* ~~~~~~~

—Don't you know that no force can
tame the spirit of freedom?

MACHIAVELLI

In the play which has just opened, the Communist Party is faced with
a critical dilemma: to win over millions of people to their perspective
of democratic socialism, or to retain 100,000 persons in their· official
posts. Will the Communists regard the Party as a political party of the
people and of the principal strata of our society? Or will they regard
it as a power apparatus designed to use any means at its disposal in
order to uphold naked power over the masses that have no rights? Almost everything—the future of the nation and the existence of liberty—hinges upon this question.

The Communist Party still has a good chance to win in regular,
secret, and free elections, if it chooses the first alternative and if it asks
for confirmation of its mandate to lead the people of Czechoslovakia.
A party identified with a victorious democratization process is certain
to win such elections, just as a party identified with abortive democratization is certain never to permit elections of this kind. And this alternative frightens politicians of the Indra, Kolder, Švestka type, just as
it is apt to prompt the best brains in this country to give their enthusiastic support to the progressive wing.

However, is the Communist Party able in the final analysis to change
from a military-bureaucratic organization into a civilian party that re-
spects fundamental human rights? The importance of this question
transcends national frontiers; it is the cardinal question of the world
workers' and socialist movement, on which depends the chances of
peace, and of containing the conflicts in Europe and in the world.

In other words: Is the Communist Party still able to resolve questions
concerning the state and the nation in accordance with the ground
rules of European politics that have been valid since the French Revo-

---

* Article in the weekly *Literární listy*, Prague, July 18, 1968.

lution? That is to say, Is it still able, first, to ascertain the will of the people and to respect the sovereignty of the people as the source of all power in the state, standing above personalities and institutions, the Communist Party itself not excluded? If it is not able to do so, it must give up its intention of preparing constitutional and other radical changes in advance within the old power mechanism; it must, on the contrary, consult the people on the ground rules of the democratic game and must provide the opportunity to elect legitimate representatives of the people.

However, it is not possible to resolve this problem at all unless the conservative forces of the old power-bureaucratic apparatus are suppressed, and unless there is a popular movement headed by progressive Communists. The progressives must understand this key question, or this problem will again raise its head with incomprehensible and destructive severity—even as the omissions of the Polish October have been visited upon its very originators. This holds true even though, as leading politicians have repeatedly declared, the progressives will certainly be able to cut off extremists from the right as well as from the left, and to ensure a passable standard of living for a few years. History is as implacable as nature.

The road toward power, and toward the leading role in this nation of ours, travelled by the Czechoslovak Communist Party's Central Committee can be travelled only via a properly elected parliament; today everything else is compromised as fraud. The strenuous efforts made by the centralist politicians again to settle state policies and questions of national interest without the people, to settle them in advance within the Party and to have them approved in a formal and meaningless procedure, is a mistaken political gambit which cannot succeed. This policy is fatal because it relies on the acquiescence of defeated politicians who are supposed to resign; however, those who believe in such utopian ideas do not realize that no power elite has ever voluntarily committed suicide in order to make room for its critics.

The leadership of the Communist Party cannot repeatedly overlook the fact that the program of democratization cannot be furthered or implemented by means of neo-Stalinist methods, and that only new and expeditiously elected representatives of the *people, not only of the*

Party, can lead the nation out of the crisis. Repeated threats to use force can only lead to a tragedy. The endeavor to settle state policies without genuine elected representatives of the people is a tragic error on the part of the progressives, and they must either extricate themselves from it in the coming period, or be defeated by the neo-Stalinists.

Today, the conservative wing of the Communist Party likes to be described as the center, although its supporters would be more aptly described as "orphans" bereft of Antonín Novotný. The Novotný supporters without Novotný would like to stop the regeneration process which they heartily detest. None of them has ever wanted anything more than a personal change in the leading post of first secretary of the Communist Party's Central Committee; and none of them has tried to conceal his hostility toward structural changes.

The progressive wing cannot play the game of politicking and factional tussles at the Castle [Hradčany Castle, seat of the national government] with these people, because it would lose this game. The leaders of the progressives must realize that their strength lies in their allies, or they must desert and join the center.

The final decision must therefore come from the Extraordinary Congress, which may mean a thorough transformation of the Communist Party and a rupture with the Stalinists and the neo-Stalinist technocrats. Let us hope that a nonviolent, prudent solution will prevail; however, to believe that the "orphans" will give up without a fight is sheer illusion. Therefore the polarization of contradictions and the situations of conflict that will arise during the summer are not and will not be an expression of the personal wishes of "extremists"—as some of the leading figures in both factions maintain, trying to forget the ABCs of Marxism—but are and will be the mirrored likeness of real conflicts in social relations and in sectors of the population.

A ballot, which will be the expression of a secret decision of the voters—if such a ballot takes place—will rid the Communist Party of the ideologically obsessive belief that on the Party alone depends the future of the state and socialism. This unwarranted obsession regarding the importance of one political party, ideology or personality is as old as humanity itself, and is always repeated with the same monotonous instrumentation whenever the old set retires, convinced that its disappearance is the beginning of the end of the world. Living ideologies, parties, and people survive exactly because they are not guided by obsessions.

An obsession with their own indispensability is the only significant idea of some politicians. They base their thinking on the defeatist conviction that Communist policy will collapse without the apparatus of violence. In this they resemble Novotný. As a matter of fact, Novotný was no worse than they—on the contrary. The centralistic neo-Stalinists are mistaken when they connect the future of socialism with the apparatus of repression. On the contrary, the wider the Communist Party opens the doors to freedom the more firmly will the power of socialism be anchored, not only in the apparatus of the institutions but in the people themselves. The present has opened a new perspective, in which the Communists may proceed side by side with the non-Communists and win the elections on a ticket acceptable to an overwhelming majority of the nation, assuming that the candidates will be new people for whom non-Communists also will be able to vote in all good faith. It is as easy for the writer Ludvík Vaculík and the authors of the Declaration * to win the support of non-Communists as it is impossible for the Indras and Kolders. It does not matter if the new people have little experience in politics. Even if they wished to they could not, considering their intelligence, make as many grave errors as were committed by the professional politicians of the preceding era. The victory of socialist democracy is more important than the existing structures, habits, and mechanisms. If the Communists are capable of leadership—and they have again proved in these days that they are—let them lead. If the professional politicians are only able to place new and yet newer obstacles in the way of democratization, let them go.

Truth may appear as provocation when it comes after years of the rule of lies. Truth is annoying to falsehood. Truth is as pitiless, ruthless and sure as the x-ray picture confirming malignancy. A doctor must be tactful and must not tell his incurably ill patient the truth, for that is his duty. But he must not himself believe lies or half-truths, for the only chance of healing a malignant process is to know that it is malignant and whether there is a metastasis.

* The *Two Thousand Words* manifesto—Ed.

Truth provokes power, not because someone wants to provoke the power elite, but because a mere mental reproduction of the existing conditions is prosecuted by the power elite as a personal offense to the powerful. In all social orders and political regimes, the basic truth has been met by scoffing, and persecuted as high treason, but, whatever the circumstances, the truth prevailed in the end, or at least it remained when everything else had been squandered. Truth provokes power because it is stronger than power.

The old rule of politics used to be that one cannot sit on bayonets. The modern totalitarian dictatorships have proved that one can sit on bayonets, provided that one possesses, as the modern political fakirs do, one essential requisite—the well-known "lead bottom." * So they can sit; their balance is not too stable, however, because truth may kick the bayonets out from under their bottoms. We must succeed in doing this during the summer, for otherwise a new generation of bureaucrats will suffocate us.

* Allusion to Trotsky's metaphorical description of Stalin's bureaucracy—Ed.

The Seasons, 1968 * ᴖᴖᴖᴖᴖᴖᴖᴖᴖᴖᴖ

Revolutions for Human Rights

1. Totalitarian dictatorships deprecate human life by considering it nothing more than a means to state power and by acting on the conviction that man is the means to the goals pursued by the state, party, class, or leader. This degradation of man's unique personality is all the deeper, the more perfectly the dictatorships function and the closer they come to reaching their goals, whether those goals be those of the "nation," of material welfare, or of class interest. People who are considered as a means to state goals and not as goals in themselves are all the more ready for desperate revolt as they realize that to be the means of a state is to witness the gradual dying away of all human values. From such an absurd human condition a revolt is born.

2. The European or world revolution for human rights was introduced by a series of student revolts in the West and the East. This revolution is first of all a revolt against the absurd alienation of men in industrial society, against the dictatorship imposed on man by the false values of a consumer economy. How can we explain the inexplicable wave of force in the Western democracies [in late spring, 1968] or the silent, calm and moderate revolt now taking place in Czechoslovakia, a country that spent its last twenty years under a dictatorship? Of highest significance among the events that took place in Paris and Prague in May 1968 are the completely new motivations for political actions— protests against the fate of man in industrial society.

3. Policy has become applied anthropology, the practical philosophy of human existence, an attempt to solve the crisis of the human situation and of present values. Therefore, the main force behind this policy is that of the intellectuals, who do not follow material or power aims, but who try to realize or extend basic human rights. The transforma-

* Lecture at Students' Conference in Ljubljana, Yugoslavia, July 6, 1968; German translation published under the title "Menetekel 1968," in the monthly *Wort und Wahrheit*, Freiburg, September, 1968.

tive process which changes the economic face of industrial societies leads to a movement for human rights, to a revolt against absurd alienation in the midst of prosperity. This is a new type of revolutionary process. Without this precondition one cannot understand anything that has taken place in Czechoslovakia nor anything that has taken place in Paris, because without this understanding, the Czechoslovak Spring appears like a series of personnel changes, or at best as simply the failure of dictatorship.

4. Socialism may be defined by various trends of revolutionary and democratic socialism; however, there is a basic agreement on the conception of the socialist society as a society of high production and high consumption, as a society which owns its main means of production. The basic disagreements, on the other hand, have always centered around the question of how to reach such a state of society and to what extent the political party, government, or movement can sacrifice civil freedoms and democratic control of the ruling power elite in order to achieve their programmatic economic aims. Various social trends differ from each other by providing differently for civil rights.

5. The position of the citizen in the structure of political life and the structure of the governing power is of great importance, because it reflects a basic orientation toward either the democratic or the totalitarian conception of socialism: either to respect human uniqueness and therefore to conceive of the freedom of man as superior to policy, power, welfare; or, on the contrary, to put the economic or power interests of the society above those of the individual. Human-oriented values are central to European society, as are certain beliefs concerning human existence in the world and the universe.

6. What is involved basically in the democratization process is an attempt, which now in various forms characterizes society in both East and West, to introduce human rights into modern technocratically manipulated civilization; to apply the findings of modern science and contemporary wisdom to the process of social change caused by technology in every modern society. This revolution for human rights is carried out by a strong movement for civil freedoms which puts back in the center of events the rights of man as against the dogma of ideology. It is in this sense that policy has become applied anthropology. The contemporary contradictions in Czechoslovakia are not only con-

tradictions involving individuals or involving conceptions of socialism, they are contradictions concerning the structure of industrial society, the emerging European socialist transformation, the emergence of an international revolution of human rights.

7. Such a conception of our contradictions requires a solution going deeper than a set of practical political actions to be included in the party's program. The central demand must be to exceed the horizon of the consumer society. As long as on the horizon of the politicians' imagination there appears no program for overcoming the alienation of man in industrialized society; as long as man does not enter the historical scene as the subject and executor of civil rights and liberties; as long as the equal rights of nations are not based on the equal rights of man, all solutions proposed by politicians must seem to people with any historical knowledge and imagination as no more than a perversion of the humanistic aims of Marx's socialism.

8. At present, a politician who may want to look beyond this consumer society may find himself in isolation, just as he will be hailed as farsighted in ten years' time. At that point, on some student barricade in Prague, some people will realize that the consumer society did not provide a solution to the conflicts of industrial society, but only brought them to a head, despite the profusion of consumer goods under which human freedom in fact only smothers.

9. It is a cruel fact that in no "authoritative" speech did any "authoritative" spokesmen of any wing offer a realistic program for socialist humanism. Socialist humanism is for all those in power alien and impossible to understand. It is considered utopian, extremist, and unacceptable, like everything else which tends to transcend the established system. The solution to the problem of the growth of human freedom in the socialism of tomorrow's consumer society is the weakest link in the democratization concept, if indeed it is a link at all in the series of technocratic formulas, political promises, and proclamations which constitute the "ersatz" for a theory of international socialist democracy.

10. In this technocratic conception, socialist democracy is not based on electors, producers, man, but on the fictional alliance of institutions, drawn together only to strengthen the control of the unsteady establishment over the unruly citizen, and to prevent elections. These men lack statesmanship and do not understand that the democratic system

cannot be founded on institutions, but only on men. The Czechoslovak intelligentsia has an unfulfilled ideological task—to work in the area of problems connected with the future consumer society, human freedom, and socialist democracy. Unfortunately, neither the writers, nor the scientists, philosophers, artists—much less, their organizations—have tried to formulate an alternative program to the projected technocratic-consumer solution to our present problems. Opposition to discredited politicians is much easier than opposition to the limits by which the uncompromised politicians are now trying to delineate the horizon of the future.

11. The task of the intellectuals is to question these limits on the freedom of tomorrow, to go beyond the horizon set by a politician's practical imagination, to introduce into immediate practice those problems which are, for the majority, beyond the horizon. We are to decide whether, in the contradictions of the summer and the near future, we shall be able to solve only personal and national difficulties caused by a local economic crisis, or whether by resolving these contradictions we shall have created through peaceful means an experiment in socialist humanism which will have contributed to expanding the concepts of democratic socialism throughout Europe—East and West. Let us hope that a nation which during the last fifty years has tried all state systems, from liberal democracy and monarchy to fascism and Stalinism, will have sufficient political wisdom to create a regime able to continue its history as a European country, to find the thread in its interrupted tradition of humanism and to experiment with the most important matter—with socialist democracy.

12. It is not certain that the peaceful transition to democracy and the process of liberalization will remain a purely local phenomenon, whether it will become the first expression of a movement for the freedom of man, for human rights and equality for all citizens, or whether it will stop at the horizon of the consumer society, the efficient technocracy. If the latter, then the alienation of man in industrialized civilization will not be overcome and we will produce cheap cars for the children of tomorrow, who will burn these symbols of wealth under the banner of Mao Tse-tung, cursing the society of prosperity as inhuman. This is perhaps the only argument that can shake the materialistic realism of our politicians. To force upon them for

one moment this improper thought—which they will immediately reject: a program of authentic Marxism as a humanist doctrine of freedom. Marxism for all free people—what a horrendous thought for the united apparatuses of all countries!

The Contradictions of Summer

1. Politics is the resolution of social contradictions. Therefore, to understand the contradictions of the given moment means to understand the opposite forces as well. A few months of democratization uncovered at least three basic contradictions: 1) a contradiction between the power apparatus and the democratic rights of the citizens; 2) a contradiction between the conservatives in the Communist Party and the people of this country; and 3) a contradiction between the economic basis of socialism and individual freedom. The structural, suprapersonal contradictions can never be resolved by force, arms and power; on the contrary, they *can* be resolved by democratic procedures. While the members of the Communist Party—particularly the Party intelligentsia—realize this quite clearly, the apparatus of that same Party stubbornly refuses to take any notice of this and tries to create the illusion that the district secretaries reflect the opinions of the Party.

2. The basic contradiction is the actual and still unlimited power of the Party apparatus compared to that held by the supreme bodies of state power—parliament, government, and courts of law. The power apparatus of the monopoly political party disregards the opinion of the masses of millions of non-Party members; some of the *apparatchiks* even openly threaten these masses with the arms of the people's militia, and the apparatus reacts with demagogic rhetoric about alleged "antisocialism" whenever this crucial question is raised. The ideological and personal appearance of the dictatorship has changed, but the old game continues, now all the more dangerous when Novotný-like arguments about the use of the militia come from the former representatives of the democratization process.

3. The power tendency of the state and Party apparatus is faced by a movement for civil freedoms, which emerges in the various forms of

the newly established organizations and clubs. Even though, for the moment, the new organizations have only very limited political significance, the potentiality for a strong movement, incompatible with the idea of a manipulative political apparatus, stands behind them. The more the apparatus continues in its policy of attempting to resolve contradictions within the existing power system, the more pressing will become the problems within the new movement, which will become radicalized at the moment that people realize the incompatibility between their own program of freedom and the apparatus' goals in manipulating the masses.

4. The second main contradiction arises from the conflict between the tendencies of the conservatives and the democratic tendency of the people. The Communist Party is not united in its evaluation of the contemporary situation. It has so far not been able to rid itself of its military bureaucratic structure and change into a civilian party, basing itself on the voices of its electorate and not on naked force. Is the Communist Party at all able to change into a civilian party?

5. If it is, then the Communist Party must give up the idea that it will be capable of creating within the existing bodies the new system of the state and that it will continue to manipulate the elected organizations of the people. Then, however, it must necessarily ask the opinion of the people in free elections, respect it, and not confuse the solution of its internal problems with the crises of the state. If, on the other hand, the Communist Party will not give up its idea that its bodies express the will of the people and of the working class—without asking the people or the working class for a confirmation—then unavoidably the division between the sole political organization and the people will only increase. Democratization will prove to have been a fraud in the play of power factions inside the monopoly party.

6. The third contradiction—the least discussed, but the most crucial—is the contradiction between the economic activity of the state and the meaning of socialism. A state traditionally understood to represent a class force is now introducing itself as an "all-peoples' state" (an old piece of nonsense criticized by Marx), as the personification of the idea of a nation or class. However, the only idea that this state publicly advances, with the taciturn agreement of the huge majority, is raising the standard of living regardless of ideology—and that is all.

The state is understood as an industrial entrepreneur; it is, however, a very bad one.

7. Among both the working class and the population at large the idea is not dead that human freedom, and not the standard of living, is the basis of socialism. People are today no longer satisfied with monotonous litanies about the untouchability of the power elite; they understand that trends that do not lead to wider freedoms for real people are deeply reactionary, regardless of whether they are called liberalism, Christianity, or socialism. The worst antisocialist aspects, i.e., aspects limiting personal freedom, are being proclaimed as a danger to freedom by the representatives of monopoly power-elite.

8. We, who are for the Czechoslovak experiment and for the ideals of socialism and democracy, must say quite openly that the conservatives in the Communist Party are the worst antisocialists those who are threatening the new freedom and have nothing to do with socialism. These people have also nothing to do with democracy, nor with the European Left, nor with the beautiful ideals of socialism which were and still are synonymous with the greater freedom of man. We have to ask those annoyed militia members who are writing resolutions against the television programs on prisons whether they are not also the ones who signed the resolutions demanding murder.

9. The contradictions between the Party and the people, between the power apparatus and the democratic rights of citizens, between the economics of living standards and human freedoms, are *contradictions that can be resolved*. Historically, they arose under conditions of bureaucratic dictatorship, and they can be overcome—if the area for citizens' activity is made broader, not narrower. A regime that, on the other hand, would arise from the defeat of the working class by the right or the left would be just as bad and would again drag the lonely masses toward the same contradictions, by then made unresolvable. The contradictions of the power elite must leave us completely indifferent; at the same time, however, we cannot but insist as effectively as possible that there should be democratic elections which would put an end to this base game of power elites.

10. The contemporary contradictions of the democratization process are resolvable contradictions, which can not, however, be postponed without increasing risk. The contradiction between the power ap-

paratus and the democratic rights of the citizens can be resolved by introducing civil rights in such a way that the power apparatus will be submitted to democratic control. The contradiction between the conservative wing of the Communists and the people can be overcome only by direct democracy, including parliamentarism, not only by the possible defeat of the conservatives at an extraordinary congress. Finally, the contradiction between the economic foundation of socialism and the program of human freedom can only be solved in the long run by the development of self-administration and by adequate support for the transformation of the style of living along the lines of socialist humanism.

11. If these contradictions are not resolved, they will be brought to a critical point, and hopes of a peaceful, forceless solution of antagonistic tendencies will then become less and less. The growth of extremism in the two opposite wings and the narrowing of room at the center are not work of spiteful individuals, but the result of the objective growth of conflicting situations. Extremism can grow only if the conflict grows; on the other hand, it organically recedes as soon as the conflict situation is resolved.

12. The three above-mentioned contradictions are contradictions of a socialist system. The solution of these contradictions does not concern the economic foundations of socialism—social ownership of the means of production remains untouched—but affects the political structure of the society. At the same time, the realization of formerly nonexistent civil rights has deep structural consequences for the power elite and the social system. Therefore the members of the power elite—regardless of whether they are conservative or progressive—try in unison to discredit every criticism of the political system as an attack against socialism, with which they feel personally identified, just as Antonín Novotný identified himself with his system of personal power.

13. While the former progressives realized very well that the removal of the political system based on personal power did not mean the destruction of socialism, but on the contrary, its new lease on life, yet now they willingly forget this and present as inviolable the new power apparatus drawn from a somewhat reshuffled elite. The basic demagogy of the centrist wing is revealed by this shift in terms and aims, by the intensive spreading of the rumors about a potential danger to so-

cialism, though they know that an extension of civil rights can only be beneficial to socialism and can endanger only the position of the centrists. A democratic political system based on a socialist economy is neither counterrevolutionary nor an expression of antisocialist tendencies; it is the fulfillment of the constitutional rights of the citizens in a socialist state.

14. Any speculation other than the development of democratic freedoms would be fateful for Czechoslovakia, for the ideals of socialism and the conservative forces as well. And here again we encounter Lenin in the year 1918, in the crucial situation of mid-civil war, again advising the Presidium of the Communist Party of Czechoslovakia: "The people must have the right responsibly to elect their leaders. The people must have the right to change them. The people must have the right to know about and test every single step in their leaders' work." The people, yes, the people.

[Editor's note, in *Student,* August 29, 1968: "At the beginning of last August, Professor Ivan Sviták had brought to our editors an article analyzing the reasons which, in his opinion, would be instrumental in leading to an intervention by force into the affairs of our republic. There was no time to include it in the regular issue of *Student.* The editors have decided to print the article now—not only because it documents Professor Sviták's foresight, but because it offers an explanation of the reasons for Soviet neo-imperialism."]

Prologue to Intervention* ～～～～～～～

> No objective requiring wrong means for
> its implementation can be a right one.
> KARL MARX

I. The Power Rationale of Intervention

1. The 1956 Hungarian Revolution offers proof that Soviet leaders consider intervention in the internal affairs of a sovereign allied state not only a justified act, but also their fraternal duty. Nineteen Soviet armored divisions drowned in blood a spontaneous uprising of Hungarian workers, who, however, continued their resistance for another month after the Soviet occupation. Budapest was shot up by Soviet tanks in the name of fraternal assistance to class brothers—the Stalinist bureaucratic elite of the repressive police apparatus. The working class, as it did once before during the days of the Paris Commune, proved itself capable of marshaling its forces in quest of a paradise on earth, without any need for a totalitarian apparatus.

2. In spite of solemn proclamations guaranteeing the sovereignty of the people, independence of the state, and self-determination of the Communist parties, the Soviet Union has held, now as before, that mere ideological diversity entitles a stronger party to interfere in the

---

* Article written after the Čierná-Bratislava Conference of August 4, 1968, and published in the last, illegal issue of *Student,* August 29, 1968; parts published in German in the Vienna daily, *Die Presse,* August 24, 1968, under the title "Die Angst vor der Infektion durch Freiheit."

internal affairs of another socialist country. As long as the representatives of the Soviet Union consider all that does not conform to their orthodoxy as hostile ideology, they either have to excommunicate the dissidents or intervene militarily. The cases in point are Yugoslavia in 1948, Hungary in 1956 and China in 1960. Chinese intervention in the USSR will be—or already is—readied on the basis of the same argumentation.

3. National egoism—called proletarian internationalism—rules today's neo-Stalinism, just as it did during the Stalin era. The national interest of the USSR supersedes all other considerations and is interpreted so as to provide justification for aggression against a sovereign state. The Russians have gotten rid of Stalin, but the isolationist heritage of Holy Russia lingers on in the form of the myth of "socialism in one country," a country surrounded by the enemy. The Stalinists have helped bring about the downfall of revolutionary tendencies whenever these tendencies have interfered with the interests and objectives of Soviet policy (the Shanghai Commune, the pact with Hitler, Soviet policy toward Western Europe between 1945 and 1948, Yugoslavia, Hungary).

4. The overriding reasons for intervening in the internal affairs of sovereign Czechoslovakia are not of the power-military variety, but rest on ideological and prestige considerations. In the Soviet monolithic system of bureaucratic elitism, the basic function of ideology is to direct policy. For this reason, ideological deviations are viewed as potential political acts. The dispute between the USSR and Czechoslovakia thus far is an ideological contention over what socialism is or what it should be, and a contention over the ideological primacy of the USSR. In this context, Soviet tank maneuvers are but a manifestation of the integration of theory with practice—according to the philosophical concepts of Soviet bureaucracy.

5. The ideological import of planned intervention may not be openly acknowledged by the Soviet leadership, but it forms the basis of its principal apprehensions. The immediate arguments in favor of intervention—spelled out in the [Soviet-inspired] Warsaw Letter—deal only with internal Czechoslovak affairs and, no matter how clumsy, are not the type of arguments that would be decisive in ordering the Soviet columns in the Ukraine readied to move in. Immediate reasons for an intervention are of a military, power-imperialistic character.

6. The decisive reason is well-founded fear of [Czechoslovakia's] infection of other [socialist] countries with the ideas of a socialist democracy. Assertion of the fundamental rights of the citizen is considered by Soviet leaders a threat to freedom (whose?) and to socialism (what type?), on the correct assumption that the political systems of police-bureaucratic regimes cannot survive public criticism. Socialist democracy, with its respect for the will of the people, is therefore *a priori* unacceptable as a system of government—just as the neo-Stalinist system was and is unacceptable to Eastern Europe.

7. Socialist democracy is therefore dengerous even as mere ideology. If we awaken public awareness to the fact that socialist democracy represents a real alternative, then—though the problems connected with practicing a socialist democracy may well be postponed—they cannot be permanently tabled, since the awareness of a new potential is irreversible and cannot be rolled back. The worst kind of oppression is that of the intellect, of spirit and thought—the attempt to compel people to accept their status as permanent, to accept the idea that *they have* to be oppressed. Conversely, the act of liberating one's awareness is irreversible.

8. The Soviet leaders are willing to tolerate, in Eastern Europe, any kind of benevolent dictatorship, but not political freedom based on respect for fundamental human rights. They do not espouse the idea of sovereignty of the people, nor the idea of sovereignty of states. Their conceptual approach to the Communist parties and the discipline of the Communist movement is not at all different from that of Stalin. Thus, should the Czechoslovak Party try to assert its right to self-determination, it must be excommunicated or isolated; for what if the Soviet republics in the USSR were to demand the same?

9. The Czechoslovak example already stimulates, and will continue stimulating, internal conflicts within the USSR—the struggle between the doves and the hawks and the struggle between the bureaucratic and the more liberal-oriented factions within the Soviet power elite. The Czechoslovak example is not only a localized weakening in the link of a *cordon sanitaire* forged by allied countries. It also attests to the crisis of the neo-Stalinist system, the disintegration of Soviet domination in Eastern Europe, and the intensity of the quest for independence from the Soviet power system. The Czechoslovak crisis is a crisis of the future of the neo-Stalinist system in the USSR! It mirrors the forthcoming

crisis of the Soviet empire and reveals to Soviet statesmen the shape of things to come in their own future. Hence their dread of the Czechoslovak heresy; the Politburo must have goosebumps just thinking of it!

10. A paramount reason for intervention is the Czechoslovak attempt to subordinate the power elite of technocrats, ideologists, bureaucrats, and manipulators to some sort of mechanism on which they themselves would be dependent. A power structure selected and elected on its merits represents a frontal attack on the key principle of every totalitarian dictatorship—the uncontrolled supplementation of the ranks of the elite by the elite itself. The neo-Stalinist bureaucracy damns this deadly deviation from the bottom of its heart, since "Communism's bogeyman" is only a benign bugbear compared to the nightmarish threat of liquidating the absolute power of the bureaucratic caste. This caste is getting ready right now to chase the nightmare away with the help of intervention, so that it can sleep in peace.

II. The Ideological Meaning of Intervention

> Errors committed by a genuinely revolutionary workers' movement are far more fruitful and historically valuable than the infallibility of the best Central Committee.
> ROSA LUXEMBURG

1. The contention between the Czechoslovak and Soviet Politburos is basically a contention over the meaning of socialism, a dispute in which the Czechoslovak Party to date represents a variant closer to Marx—at least in as far as it espouses the principle of sovereignty of the people. The decisive difference is whether the society is administered from above by the ruling elite (Stalin, Mao, Castro) or whether socialism is regarded as a social framework established through a struggle for liberation by the working class—from below.

2. The only policy in tune with Karl Marx's original conception of socialism is one that considers socialism an act of liberation by the working class itself—not a gift from an enlightened elite, nor a well-meaning progressive dictatorship, not a Messianic quest of philanthropists. On this point Marx is one with Babeuf, Weitling, Proudhon, Lassalle, Saint-Simon, Bernstein, and all the followers of socialism, and he

cannot be reconciled with the "socialism from above" practiced by Stalin, Mao, Castro, Nasser, Tito, Nkrumah, or Sukarno. An authentic conception of socialism is only the one in which the decisive role is played by the people, the working class, the majority of modern industrial society—not by some sort of elite or by individuals who speak in the name of the working class or the majority, without acknowledging its fundamental civil and human rights.

3. The present-day reality of socialist social structure is far from Marx's original idea, which calls for the people to work out their own liberation and to give reality to the socialist idea during the struggle for their liberation. Marx flatly rejected all utopian, elite-oriented, anti-democratic, and technocratic concepts of a future society. He equally rejected vulgar communism that negates the very personality of man, since socialism to Marx was a full-fledged bloom of humanism and man's individuality—a program not only of social, but also of individual freedom. Marx understood the truth (still valid today) that in an industrial society—in the capitalism of his time—the majority should be and is interested in changing the system, in changing the capitalism of the monopolies as well as state capitalism, whatever its shape or form.

4. Defense of Marx's ideas is correctly considered to be the greatest peril to the elites, since, in analyzing Marx, persistent questions come to the fore. The state owns the means of production; but who owns the state? If the state is dominated by a bureaucratic elite, not controlled "from below" by the workers, is this bureaucratically administered collectivism actually socialism? Is it not in fact merely state capitalism under a misleading ideological label?

5. Behind these questions is hidden the great problem of modern industrial society of the East as well as the West—the problem of how to bring the elite under democratic control. The system of parliamentary democracy in the West produces consequences and an end product beyond such direct control, as does the system of the monopoly of power practiced by the East's dictatorships. The most important political activity therefore lies in searching for a way out of this, through direct democracy of the producers and through direct action. From these endeavors, there can evolve socialist democracy in the form of a government of and by a classless society.

6. The perspective of "socialism from below" is being rejected as an

unrealistically visionary form of utopian-idealistic quixotism by the same advocates of "socialism from above" who today, under new slogans and new leadership, want to introduce the theoretically anti-Marx concept of a new technocratic elite that would lead the nations into the promised land of a consumer society of tomorrow. Theoretically, these representatives of "progressive" forces lean on an ancient iron precept of the oligarchy buttressed by the belief that elites exist and will continue to exist and that to trust the people, the working class, with governing is misplaced utopian thinking. The inevitability of change generated from above is too obvious to them to warrant further discussion.

7. The representatives of the intelligentsia have often dreamed of enlightened dictatorships, in which the rule of reason would replace that of money or naked power and the intelligentsia would be free of proprietary pressure and could control the owners from below. Today these systems go by such names as meritocracy, managerism, technocracy, industrialism. In Czechoslovakia, too, they are being disseminated under various labels. The advocates of these concepts (which today can be presented quite decorously and appetizingly) thus in fact become apologists for authoritarian regimes. Well-meaning despotism never draws back from destroying autonomous organizations of the working class and the workers' movement—under the pretext that "someone has to govern."

8. Even in this case we again face the basic question of the meaning of socialism. Either we accept the arguments of the elites about the inevitability of the rule of some people over others or, the same as Marx, we consider the people, the working class, capable of governing and controlling society, having learned by experience how to do so, in the struggle against oppression and the newest class, the managers.

9. In these critical days and hours when the representatives of the Czechoslovak state are in direct political conflict with the representatives of "socialism from above," it is necessary to stress that for the working class of this country the illusions of the technocrats are and will be unacceptable, since they only want to modify the economic makeup of our society. Neither the progressive faction, which flirts with the efficiency of the West's industrial society, nor the conservative faction, which ogles the arms of the militia, can speak for the working

class. Soon the working class will have spokesmen of its own, and they will once again defend the abandoned program of Marx—socialism from below, a road to a democratic process of self-liberation and the liberation of the entire society. The quarrel between two Politburos has evolved into a dispute about the meaning of socialism. Our chances for building socialism from below are right now being determined. But as to the shape or form of this socialism, it will be determined by us, the workers and the intelligentsia. Yet without such an alliance there can be no moving forward to a classless society, in which there shall be no political elites.

III. The Prelude to Intervention

> The hawk does not have to show himself at the top of the hill. When his shriek is heard, he may be in hiding but his young one will hear his voice, will recognize it and answer.
>
> I Ching *Book of Changes*
> (a collection of old Chinese proverbs)

1. The shriek of the hawk has sounded in Warsaw, and the question arises whether his young one will answer it.* Amidst the political problems of searching for a way toward socialist democracy, there suddenly arose the question of national independence, of state sovereignty. Democracy has entered a period of stifling summer.

2. All political factions in the Czechoslovak Socialist Republic have so far tried to handle with utmost tact the basic problem—the Warsaw Pact, the country's relationship to the Soviet Union, and the Soviet Union's version of socialism. Now these problems have been presented from an outside source, in the form of an open attempt to intervene in the internal affairs of a sovereign state. While for the politicians it was hardly news that the USSR was claiming the right to interfere in the internal affairs of its allies, it was a radical warning to the

---

* In this Aesopian metaphor, the old hawk is Brezhnev. The young one is a representation of the Czechoslovak "hawks," not yet identified at the time this article was written (the first week in August, 1968). Two weeks later, their answer identified them as the leading collaborators, Bilak, Indra, Kolder, and Švestka.—Ed.

people concerning the restrictions and the injustices with which the people and the statesmen were faced.

3. The Warsaw Letter of the Communist parties was a political ultimatum, and is accompanied by open preparations for military intervention by Soviet tank divisions. The Soviet armies are to remain on Czechoslovak territory even after the maneuvers are ended, in order to encourage the centrists and the followers of Novotný to stage a coup. Propaganda campaigns describe Czechoslovak conditions as "creeping counterrevolution" or "a counterrevolution of a peaceful type." In so doing, they create the prerequisites for justifying military intervention in a foreign country.

4. The fateful moments of this stifling July are new only in appearance. In reality, this is already the third Soviet attempt to change Czechoslovak conditions from the outside. Aside from Kosygin's May visit, we see that the first critical situation arose at the end of May. While the session of the Central Committee of the Communist Party was in progress, Soviet armies had entered the territory of Czechoslovakia with the obvious aim of helping the centrists and the Novotnýites to stop democratization. As a result of the army movements, the followers of Novotný did not resign but waited for an opportunity to attack.

5. The followers of Novotný and the centrists, people like Bilák, Indra, Kolder, Švestka, and others, believed and still believe that an opportunity will arise to effect a reversal, with the aid of the Soviet army and the militia, because it would suffice—at the right moment—to ask for the help of the Soviet army for them to thwart an attempt at a "counterrevolutionary coup." Key communications are in Soviet hands. Although the maneuvers ended on July 4, the Soviet army remains on Czechoslovak soil for the seventh week. 16,000 Russian soldiers, 5,000 vehicles, 2 armies, and 2 additional airplane staff units can achieve a total military occupation of the country within hours.

6. A second attempt to create a situation which would justify armed intervention was made at the end of June, on the occasion of the publication of the *Two Thousand Words* manifesto. The centrists and the Novotnýites openly went over to the attack, and their principal man, Indra, described the manifesto as an appeal for counterrevolution. The same was done in the parliament by General Kodaj and—to the

astonishment of the nation—also by the leader of the Czech progressives, Josef Smrkovský. Further astonishing changes will be comprehended by the nation only after it understands that it is projecting on the representatives of the progressive wing only its own illusions, in reality not at all matched by the acts of these men.

7. The wide support received by the *Two Thousand Words* manifesto made the initiation of full intervention impossible. The Central Committee of the Czechoslovak Communist Party condemned the appeal of the scientists and writers just as unanimously as did the parliament and the government, with this positive, for us, effect: that it made it impossible for Kolder, Indra, Švestka, and Bilák to pose as fighters against counterrevolution. Thus the centrists and the followers of Novotný lost the last opportunity to stop democratization by the force of the militia and the apparatus, simply because public opinion in the factories had unanimously backed the *Two Thousand Words* manifesto. The second attempt at intervention was therefore thwarted not by the progressives in the Communist Party Presidium, who all voted against the "counterrevolutionary manifesto," but by the *movement for civil rights which was and is the decisive driving force of democratization.*

8. A critical situation thus arose because the district conferences of the Communist Party of Czechoslovakia had proven that, if the Extraordinary Congress of the Party were held in September, not only the Novotnýites but also the centrists would be beaten. The main representative of the center, Drahomir Kolder, failed to be elected in his own district as a delegate to the congress, and the second chief centrist, Aloís Indra, had to be maneuvered into the congress later. The centrists and the Novotnýites thus found themselves fighting for time and had to begin acting. At this moment came the Warsaw Letter.

9. This third attempt at a reversal so ideally synchronized the Soviet tanks and the Czechoslovak centrists that a defeat seemed impossible. The Soviet units were still on Czechoslovak soil, and they were now under the command of leading Soviet politicians, rather than the Warsaw Pact military staff, so that their recall was, as a matter of fact, a controversial political question. Everything was perfectly prepared for intervention at the moment that a new Kadar, for whose role there were several willing potential candidates, could be found in Czechoslovakia.

Everything was prepared, except for the help of the people themselves.

10. The Soviet leadership did not perceive that since March it had lost all its domestic political allies, and that it could not repeat in July what it could still do in May. The forces which had backed the Novotnýites and the center in March, and were still backing them in May, were not backing them now, in July. It was in these circumstances that the Soviet leaders made their appraisal of the situation as counter-revolutionary, requiring forceful intervention. The reaction to Soviet pressure was exactly the opposite of what the Soviets had expected, since it had managed to unite the wavering part of the working class with the progressives. The progressives, who were to have been isolated under the triple pressure of Soviet help, centrist maneuvers and Novotný's militia, found themselves, on the contrary, backed by a unified nation. Under these circumstances came the publication of the Warsaw Letter.

11. The Warsaw Letter depicted the situation as absolutely unacceptable, as the beginning of a counterrevolution, and claimed the right to intervene in the internal affairs of a sovereign state, something which had not happened since the era of Stalin and the excommunication of Yugoslavia. The letter demanded: a) an offensive against the anti-socialist forces; b) the suppression of their political organizations; c) the takeover of the mass communications media by the Party; d) the adherence to the principle of democratic centralism (i.e., the liquidation of democratization); e) support for the centrist forces, so as to enable them to defeat the "antisocialist forces."

12. The Soviet Letter via Warsaw resulted from an absolute misunderstanding of the internal situation, because its effect was exactly contrary to the reaction expected. The spontaneous resistance against the criticism from Warsaw made it impossible for the centrists to exploit the situation; they were even forced to vote, in the Central Committee of the Communist Party of Czechoslovakia, in favor of the negative standpoint, because the progressives had, on their side, the option of convoking the Extraordinary Congress at once and thus preparing the legal defeat of the centrists. The Central Committee session—composed mainly of centrists—was forced to accept the standpoint of the progressives and to reject the letter. It was now possible

to change the power relationship of the domestic forces only by occupying Czechoslovakia, and thus repeating Hungary.

13. The Soviet Warsaw Letter failed because of the political ineffectiveness of the guard whom the Soviets themselves had considered dependable politicians. The Stalinists of the conservative wing were paralyzed because of the spontaneous support the people gave their opponents, even though for the time being the people still have to accept that the results of this movement are being used by exactly that faction of the Communist Party which looks upon this independent, spontaneous *movement* with distrust.

14. It was now possible to proceed only by using crude force, through military intervention. At the time that the Politburos of both sides were meeting at Čierná, the armies of the Warsaw Pact were prepared for the largest land maneuvers since World War II. The USSR would have had to use armed intervention without any pretext that it had support in the country itself.

15. In this situation, the Russians found allies where they least expected them—in the Presidium of the Central Committee of the Communist Party of Czechoslovakia. The apparatuses will in the end always agree. The result is the Bratislava Statement. The young one has heard the shriek of the hawk.

IV. An Absolutely Unacceptable Situation

Let's be realistic! Let's want the impossible!
Inscription on the wall of the Sorbonne, May, 1968

1. The Bratislava Statement is a neo-Stalinist pact against the sovereignty of the people. It is a statement of which no orthodox Stalinist would have to be ashamed. If the Czechoslovak Communist politicians are able to present this document as the victory of common sense, then we must have doubts as to their ability to stand at the helm of a sovereign state.

2. The Czechoslovak Communist politicians contend that they received from the nation a mandate which they had honorably fulfilled. We must tell them openly that during the seven months of democratization they had never asked the people for a mandate authorizing these

politicians themselves to represent anybody anywhere. They never received a mandate from the people; they got it only from the neo-Stalinists in the Central Committee of the Communist Party.

3. The spontaneous support of the Czechoslovak people for the policy of the progressive wing meant resistance to foreign *diktat*, and gave nobody the authorization to sign a statement whose Stalinist-Beria-like jargon is just as incomprehensible as its substance is unacceptable. The neo-Stalinists who fear even the factory sirens—not to mention a general strike—accepted an antipeople compromise which conspicuously resembles Munich.

4. How the members of the Communist Party evaluate the Warsaw Letter and the Bratislava talks is their private business. The citizens of the state have to appraise the Warsaw Letter as a preparation for intervention, an appeal for civil war, an open interference in the internal affairs of a sovereign state. Only neo-Stalinists can sit down at the same table with the authors of such a statement, which attacks the basic rights of nations, states, and the people.

5. Deliberations of Communist parties are binding only for one-tenth of the population of Czechoslovakia. For nine-tenths of the inhabitants of Czechoslovakia they are not and will not be binding. If one polls the will of the Czech and Slovak nations in a referendum, he will know that the people reject the conclusions of the Bratislava meeting as the foundation for the life of the Czechoslovak Socialist Republic, and they will also reject any similar talks as undermining their own sovereignty.

6. The Bratislava talks represent a Waterloo of illusions about the character of the neo-Stalinists, and justify future reservations as to those "progressives" who want to exploit popular support only for their own goals. The neo-Stalinists have signed the proclamation of loyalty in exchange for a "sovereignty" which, however, is being undermined to its very foundations by that same proclamation. A guarantee is seen in the signatures of the representatives of foreign political parties, and not in the regular elections of a free people.

7. The withdrawal of Soviet armies from Czechoslovak territory was paid for with capitulation to the great-power policy of the USSR. The threat of intervention was not removed; on the contrary, it has

been deepened. The intervention was postponed into the indefinite future, that is all.

8. We shall soon discover the consequences of secret clauses or unofficial agreements. Disclaimers about secret clauses are only made when such secret clauses exist. The prohibition of KAN, of the K-231 club * and of the Social Democrats will be the first consequence of the "nonexistent" agreements; on the contrary, the recognition of these organizations will be a real proof that freedom of association actually exists, and that the aggressive antidemocratic demands of the Warsaw Letter have met with resistance.

9. The resolution of the present internal-political and foreign-political crisis lies only, and exclusively, in free elections, which can give a valid mandate to the politicians to act in the name of the people. If an old authoritarian like General de Gaulle can order regular elections within three weeks, in the agitated city of Paris, this should also be possible for young democrats within seven months after their assumption of power.

10. The source of power in the state of the Czechs and Slovaks lies not in diplomatic talks in Čierná and Bratislava, but only in the national assembly of a sovereign people. Such a national assembly, elected in secret elections, is an unpaid debt of the Czechoslovak neo-Stalinists to the people of Czechoslovakia. A parliament of submissive puppets is no obstacle to the neo-Stalinists, but it is a barrier to the sovereignty of the people and the interests of the state.

11. Maybe the neo-Stalinists have defended the sovereignty of the state for a few months, until a further conference of "friends" forces them to make further concessions. The representatives of the state want sovereignty for the state. The representatives of the people want sovereigny for the people. Herein lies the difference.

12. Dissolve the National Assembly, order free elections! Only in this way will you free yourselves, the nations, the state, the people, from the nightmare of Stalinism. The sovereignty of the people is

* As former political prisoners, the members of K-231 chose a name associated with the paragraph of the penal code under which they had been sentenced (Paragraph 231, for political crimes). Like KAN, K-231 was never legalized, although it was tolerated *de facto* as an illegal organization. Membership in KAN and K-231 was forbidden immediately after the occupation.—Ed.

more important than the agreements of neo-Stalinist apparatuses in Eastern Europe. Sovereignty of the people now! Let's be realistic! Let's want the impossible!

V. The Lesson of Bratislava

Beware of manipulators! Beware of the
bureaucrats!
—*Motto from Paris, May, 1968*

1. The first consequence of the Bratislava Declaration will be a substantial change in the political scene in future months. In the winter of 1967–1968 the main conflict was a matter of the internal problems arising among the factions of the Communist Party; in spring the conflict between civil rights and the power apparatus was sharpened. In summer, the focus of discrepancies was transferred to the central question—the position of the Czechoslovak Socialist Republic in the framework of the socialist camp. The armies of the friendly countries are ready to help solve this problem and to "enlighten" the people as to its rightlessness.

2. Should this conflict be resolved, then another more serious one will arise. At Čierná the Communists may have achieved self-determination for the Party and the right to conduct an independent policy within certain limits. In the eyes of the people they have gained considerably, because they allegedly succeeded in defending the sovereignty of the state. However, the unity of the nation which was created in the critical days has been radically shaken by the President's address to the nation after the Bratislava Declaration, so this unity has quickly disappeared in the wake of the declaration's disagreeable Munich phraseology.

3. A victory for the progressives at the upcoming September congress of the Party is almost certain, although the readiness to grant wide concessions to the centrists in the name of unity cannot be excluded. If the representatives of the reform wing are serious about the program of democratization, they will again be faced with the old conflict between the democratic requirements of the citizens, [and the requirements of] political groups and power apparatuses, which, to be sure, are now headed by new people. But the old tension will re-

(144)

main, unless democratic processes become the foundation for solving conflicts. This has not happened so far, and therefore a further sharpening of conflicts will follow, the more so as the government has to start carrying out economic measures.

4. Before the threat of intervention, both basic problems remained open—i.e., federalization and democratization. There is no decision as to the character of federalization, nor on the principal question of the recognition of the Social Democrats and other political parties. After freedom of speech, freedom of association becomes the main test of the seriousness of the democratization effort, incompatible with the National Front's decision not to agree to the creation of further political parties outside the National Front, and to consider political activity as activity *outside* the legal order.

5. The most important development for the future is the fact that the independent, spontaneous actions of the people have started to play a real role in creating state policy. The question is now no longer one of the internal differences within the power elite of a monopoly party, which decides in a sovereign way the limitations within which the people are allowed to express their will. The question is one of the first expression of the will of social groups that are not coordinated from the top. The continuation of this trend is bound to lead to the demand for free elections with independent candidates and separate lists of candidates, to civil equality, and to the demand that the parliament be dissolved and new regular parliamentary elections be held.

6. The Warsaw Letter and the Bratislava Declaration also bring about recognition, for the first time, of the conflict between the freedom of the citizen and the economic foundation of the socialist system. Or, in simple terms, the meaning of socialism is seen as a problem, as a theoretical dispute with far-reaching practical consequences. Only now the idea is coming to the fore that socialism is not identical with bureaucratic collectivism, that it is incompatible with the monopoly power of a neo-Stalinist elite; that state capitalism is just as dangerous as private-ownership capitalism; and that the replacement of socialism by statism was the greatest defeat of the working class and its independent organizations.

7. Thus modern Czech policy will be faced with the necessity of formulating a positive program much more essential than the one in

which the Czech National Council had presented itself to the people. A positive program of the new Czechoslovak policy will have to start with an effort to resolve central conflicts characteristic of European industrial societies, that is to say, how to cross the horizon of a consumer society, how to overcome the growing alienation of man in an industrial society, and how to defend human freedom before the technocracy of the managers.

8. Simultaneously, this solution cannot be separated from the problems of world and European policy. The idea of a free Czechoslovakia in the 1980's as a mature consumer society in an Eastern European socialist federation, and maybe even in a socialist Europe, seems unrealistic only to those who do not comprehend that the 1980's will bring further victories to independent socialism and to the idea of permanent revolution right in the cradle of socialism itself—in Europe. The general rehearsal took place this spring in Paris.

9. Together with the victory of the progressives, one must also expect remarkable personnel changes among leading politicians of the reform wing, who, true enough, were ready and willing to cast lots about succeeding Novotný but who may not want to acquiesce to the idea of a democracy aiming at limiting their own power. Democracy is based on the assumption that man is a creature of reason and that, by reasonable discussion, public opinion can be created which expresses the will of a sovereign people. Policy then is no longer mere power, but an autonomous sphere of human decision-making, a field of human rights and civil liberties.

10. To put it in a simplified form: we are to make a decisive step from democratization to socialist democracy. It seems that we have overcome the crisis of the third act. But, entering the peripeteia, or reversal, the fourth act of a tragedy, we must know that the differences have become wider and that in the classic tragedy the catastrophe comes just at the moment when total victory is within reach.

Prague, August 4, 1968

Appeal to the People* ᔕᔕᔕᔕᔕᔕᔕᔕ

1. We live in an occupied country, a country which was seized illegally; we live in a Soviet protectorate. This act of aggression is a criminal act. The reality of an occupation cannot be made to look pretty. A police regime of occupiers remains a police regime.

2. We live in an occupied country. We know that we have to fight. One does not negotiate with occupiers; one fights them.

3. The forms of this struggle with the aggressors are many and varied. But one thing is certain: a people cannot live on its knees.

4. Against whom are we fighting? We are fighting against the aggressors, the occupiers and the collaborationists who would like to legalize the aggression. Every occupation is illegal, every aggression is a criminal act, even under the charge of counterrevolution.

5. Is there a counterrevolution in Czechoslovakia and are there counterrevolutionaries? Yes, there are. They are those who direct the tanks of the Warsaw Pact armies. They are those who are today arresting the representatives of a sovereign state. Those are the only counterrevolutionaries in Czechoslovakia.

6. Who stands against them? The people and the idea of freedom, a very powerful idea, to which many armies have succumbed. The people are the greatest, the mightiest force. Who are the people? They are the workers in factories, the soldiers, and the intellectuals who are determined to defend their sovereignty, their freedom, and socialism. The people are everybody except the aggressors, the occupiers, and the collaborators.

7. What is the aim of this struggle? We are fighting for a socialist country, free and sovereign. We are fighting for human rights and for civil rights. We want nothing more than to live in accordance with

* Text of a speech by the author, who was in Vienna at the time of the Soviet invasion. The speech was broadcast by Viennese television, visible in southern Czechoslovak cities like Brno and Bratislava, and rebroadcast on August 23, 1968 by the Czechoslovak legal transmitters (denounced by the Soviets as "counterrevolutionary," "illegal" transmitters). It was published in a Frankfurt daily, the *Frankfurter Allgemeine Zeitung*, August 25, 1968.—Ed.

our ideas, and that is a right which is granted to every small African country. We protest against Soviet neocolonialism.

8. We have the courage to fight against terror because we are stronger than the aggressors and neocolonialists. The machinery of power and of aggression changes but the aspiration of man to be free remains.

9. One cannot sit on bayonets and one cannot rule from tanks. History has taught us that the Thousand-Year Reich lasted twelve years. Neocolonialism of the Stalinist type will surely last no longer. And everybody should be reminded of the Nuremberg trials.

10. Any organization created, in an occupied country, with the aim of supporting the aggressors is a criminal organization. To cooperate with such organizations is a criminal act against humanity, against the country, against the nations, and against socialism. All those who place themselves at the service of the occupiers and collaborationists are betraying the program of the Czechs and Slovaks; that is, Freedom, Sovereignty, Socialism. Truth shall prevail!

Manifesto Against Aggression * ~~~~~~

We, the Czech and Slovak artists, scientists, and journalists, enthusiastically accepted and supported the program of democratic reforms of Czechoslovak socialism. In the fateful hours of the occupation of the sovereign state of Czechoslovakia, we consider it necessary to proclaim certain basic convictions which we hold in common as intellectuals, as Czechs and Slovaks, as citizens of the Czechoslovak Socialist Republic.

1. We believe that as intellectuals we have one basic duty to our nation: *to speak the truth*. We refuse to compromise with truth and we shall not put expediency above the truth. The code of truth does not tolerate exceptions.

2. We trust the strength of ideas and we distrust power. We refuse to follow the dictates of power. We have no weapons but words and ideas, yet we are convinced that no force of oppression can withstand the thrust of thought. Today more than ever, we realize that an attack on ideas is an attack on man himself.

3. People may be deprived of all their civil rights but they cannot be deprived of their freedom to think. Totalitarian dictatorships may rob people of everything except their will to resist. Tanks can occupy territory but not the minds of men.

4. As Czechs and Slovaks, we know from historical experience that our country has several times led ambitious aggressors to a trapdoor of history. Czechoslovakia is in the heart of Europe and it cannot be transplanted without moral danger for the whole continent. This was demonstrated by Munich thirty years ago. Now, as at that time, the tanks of occupiers may be rolling toward another trapdoor of history.

5. Capitulation before violence cannot be justified. As citizens of Czechoslovakia, we denounce as an international crime the invasion and

* Statement adopted in Vienna by Czech and Slovak intellectuals, on the twenty-fourth anniversary of the Slovak National Uprising, August 25, 1968; published in *Die Presse*, Vienna, August 28, 1968, and in the Czech-language New York weekly, *Americké listy* [American papers], September 13, 1968. [This statement composed by the author was signed by various Czechoslovak intellectuals present in Vienna at the time of the occupation.—Ed.]

occupation of Czechoslovakia by the armed forces of the Warsaw Pact. It is not only the question of Czechoslovak sovereignty, but the question of whether invasion, aggression, and occupation will remain unpunished. This is not a fundamental question for Czechs and Slovaks only; it is a fundamental question for all peoples, nations, and states.

6. We commit ourselves to human freedom within democratic socialism. We deem this human freedom to be the highest value of mankind. We believe that individuals, movements, and states that wish to create a new culture, based on foundations other than those of human freedom, are in fact building nothing but modern forms of enslavement.

7. The violent acts of recent days have demonstrated again that totalitarian dictatorship represents the greatest danger to mankind. It is a matter of indifference under what ideology the dictators send their tanks into peaceful countries and for what ostensible motives soldiers shoot unarmed citizens.

8. At this moment, the occupiers have imposed extraordinary restrictions and the police already persecute the best minds of the nation. We ask ourselves now whether it is possible, in Central Europe, to have personal freedom and civil rights, generally respected even in the least developed countries. The criminal occupation of Czechoslovakia is comparable only to the most shameless examples of imperialistic aggression.

9. We are, therefore, addressing ourselves to the public of the world, in particular to artists, scientists, and other intellectuals, with the request that they come without delay to the assistance of free socialist Czechoslovakia.

10. We want to live in a free, socialist, sovereign Czechoslovakia, jointly upheld by workers and intellectuals, in a world without aggression, occupation, and war.

Fourth Act: Peripeteia

PROBLEMS OF NATIONS

Only those nations are free which do not
rob other nations of their freedom.

KARL MARX

Contents

Chronology

October 10

Meeting of "old Communists" (dogmatists) in Prague adopted favorable position on occupation and criticized top leadership for ideological softness, weakness, and incompetence.

October 18

Troop Stationing Treaty ratified by National Assembly, with ten abstentions and four votes against the treaty.

October 28

Students demonstrated in Prague, disregarding anti-demonstration appeal by leaders.

October 30

Federalization bill signed in Bratislava.

November 7

Anti-Soviet demonstrations held on fifty-first anniversary of October Revolution. Police intervene.

November 14–17

Central Committee of Czechoslovak Communist Party postponed the Fourteenth Congress; Lubomir Štrougal appointed to four Party positions.

November 18–20

Students in Czech institutions of higher learning held sit-in strike to manifest support for journalists' demands.

November 25

Regulations and restrictions imposed on travel abroad.

December 8–11

Czechoslovak-Soviet summit meeting held in Kiev.

December 16

New York *Times* correspondent Tad Szulc expelled from Czechoslovakia.

December 18

Protest strike threatened by metal workers if any leading political personalities removed from office.

December 20

Dubček warned of strict measures if "anarchistic elements" continued their activities.

December 21

Husák demanded that a Slovak become chairman of Federal Assembly.

December 27

High level Soviet delegation under Soviet Communist Party Central Committee Secretary Konstantin Katushev arrived in Prague.

January 16

Jan Palach, a twenty-one-year-old philosophy student at Charles University, immolated himself in protest against the Soviets.

Brezhnev as Saint Florian pouring water on a house representing
Czechoslovakia. (Baroque statues of Saint Florian are found in Czech
towns and villages. His protection is sought against fire.) ". . . But
there is no fire," Dubček objects.

The End of the Game *   ᖇᖇᖇᖇᖇᖇᖇᖇᖇ

SOVIET ARMY IN ACTION IMPRESSES WEST
Headline, New York Times, *September 10, 1968*

I. Results of the Aggression

1. Although the invasion of Czechoslovakia was carried out in a few hours, the full consequence of the Soviet adventure will emerge later—at the moment that the world realizes the shocking parallel with the Munich Treaty of 1938, an act of appeasement that merely postponed a world conflict by one year.

2. The most serious result of the Soviet occupation of Czechoslovakia is the alteration of the European scene. Regardless of statements by leading politicians who are seeking a continuity of the policy of bridge-building, it's clear that during the sticky Prague summer the era of the quiet postwar status quo ended. On the horizon of history, the specter of World War III has appeared, not because no great power would take risks for the sake of the Czechoslovak experiment, but because the Czechoslovak crisis dramatized the insoluble conflicts arising from the division of the world.

3. Another result of the Soviet occupation is the obvious fact that for the first time since the Hitler era, a great power has committed open aggression against its own ally. The destruction of sovereignty in a small European state raises the question of whether it is possible in today's world to defend the sovereignty of *any* small state.

4. The Czech invasion in fact inspired only a passive response among the nations of the world, including the United Nations. The United Nations not only did not stop the aggression, but it did not even make an attempt to stop it. Thus, in International Human Rights Year, the General Assembly accepted the most brutal violation of basic European

* Lecture at Columbia University, New York City; published in the daily *Newsday*, Long Island, September 21, 1968. German translation in the daily *Nationalzeitung*, Basel, December 8, 1968.

(156)

values and humanistic traditions, and the Secretary General made no effort whatsoever to visit Prague.

5. All this does not mean that the situation in Czechoslovakia is irrevocably lost. Indeed, there is every evidence that the people are unified in their determination to resist—at least passively—the occupation by Soviet troops, and the forces of humanism are in the forefront of this movement. The crucial question, of course, is how successful and long-lived such resistance can prove in the face of military rule and without any outside assistance.

6. The consequences of the occupation are equally important for the Soviet bloc. The occupation has already proved that the Stalinist concept has triumphed over revisionist alternatives and that the neo-Stalinists will mercilessly continue their imperialistic policy. Such a policy, of course, must inevitably lead to fascism within the Soviet state and to further acts of aggression. The Soviet Union is becoming a criminal state.

7. The Soviet occupation introduces colonialist methods into Central Europe and creates a new type of colonial empire, reflecting a total failure of Soviet policy toward its own allies. This failure testifies to the Soviet Union's inability to rule by means other than naked force, and the resulting tension will have far-reaching consequences. The most significant will be the erosion of the Soviet system, which is likely to be the major political development of the 1970's.

8. The Soviet intervention was aimed not only at a potential renegade but against a center of possible infection. The 500,000-soldier occupation army has also served to demonstrate Russia's readiness to fight the Soviet intelligentsia, which considered the Czechoslovak experiment as a possible alternative for its own society. The Soviet power elite is now more dangerous than ever, because it is frightened about its future.

9. The full consequences of the Soviet aggression will not be felt immediately, although they will have world-wide influence. One major point is that the Soviet action provided an argument that can be used in support of the United States' presence in Vietnam. However, the Soviet occupation might lead to a paradoxical result: the *end* of the war in Vietnam. Those advocating the war may finally realize that the real danger is not in Vietnam but in Europe. Important changes can now

be expected on the world scene, similar to those that occurred as a result of the Nazi-Soviet Pact in 1939. With whom will the Soviets then go—China or the United States?

10. Following the tragic night of August 21, it has become impossible to maintain the naive view of the European New Left, according to which the enemy of my enemy is my friend. The New Left in Europe no longer has the right to ignore the fact that Cuban Premier Castro approved the occupation of Czechoslovakia, just as East Germany's Walter Ulbricht did.

II. Consequences of the Occupation

Gegen Demokraten helfen nur Soldaten.*
KING FRIEDRICH WILHELM IV OF PRUSSIA, 1848

1. Although the consequences of the occupation are of a limited and local nature, they do touch upon the very roots of the Communist movement. The dialectics of history create, in the heart of Europe, a complicated situation that has defied the forecasts of the most enlightened of politicians. Thus, the Czechoslovak experience has both European and international importance, as the experience of a small state with the Soviets.

2. The Soviet occupation of Czechoslovakia means the establishment of a Soviet protectorate, regardless of the institutional form imposed. Czechoslovakia may follow the fate of Estonia, Lithuania, and Latvia, becoming a police state in which the fraternal Soviet police will assist in keeping order. Since August 21, in fact, the sovereignty of any Communist state has become incompatible with membership in the Warsaw Pact.

3. Czechoslovak policy can no longer be the policy of reform and no longer can it continue the program outlined in the spring by the leadership of the Communist Party. Any realistic policy must be based on the fact that Czechoslovakia's experiment is at an end as long as Soviet tanks remain on its territory. Everything else is an open or a disguised fraud.

4. The ideals which accompanied the creation of the Czechoslovak

* Untranslatable play on words: "Against democrats, only soldiers help."—Ed.

Republic have been exposed to a cruel test for the second time in thirty years. Munich in 1938 showed that there was no guarantee by Western democracies as far as the Czechoslovak state was concerned; by the same token, the summer of 1968 proved that Czechoslovak security cannot be guaranteed by the East, either. Any future alternatives for Czechoslovakia must take into consideration the possibility of creating a broader alliance of neutral Central European states that together would try to ensure their own security. A free Czechoslovakia is impossible with blocs dividing Europe.

5. For the Czech and Slovak peoples the occupation has even deeper meaning. Contrary to the traditional anti-Russian feeling in Poland, there have always been strong sympathies for Russia in Czechoslovakia. In the last twenty years, Czechoslovakians have entertained many ideological illusions about Soviet Communism. The occupation, however, means an end to such illusions and a change in social thinking; it also means the end of pro-Soviet sympathies and Pan-Slavic myths. The occupation will be educational in the sense that the masses will no longer differentiate between fascist and Soviet occupations.

6. Another result of the occupation has been the silencing of the intelligentsia. Censorship deprives intellectuals of all participation in the political game, and thus deprives the nation of their leadership. Despite these difficulties, the movement for human rights in Czechoslovakia has not yet capitulated. On the contrary, it is spreading—particularly among those who in the past were rather reserved toward the program of the intellectuals. Thanks to Russian tanks, the support for a morally sound and democratic Czechoslovakia has never been stronger.

7. An unresolved issue for the nation is the question of whether the capitulation of the Czech army in the confrontation with Soviet tanks was correct. While Czech army officers were crying, students and other young people stood up with bare hands against the tanks. The nation has found—after thirty years—further proof that submission without a fight does not pay. A state that does not defend itself cannot exist as a state, but only as a protectorate.

8. The Russian occupation means an end to the revisionist Communist movement in Czechoslovakia, a movement designed as an alternative to the totalitarian ideology and monopoly of power inherent in

neo-Stalinist Communism. The Czech Communist Party, as the leading political force, proved incapable of defending the country's sovereignty. Although the individual leaders of the Communist Party were admirably brave and honest under most difficult circumstances, the net result of the revisionist type of Communism is a total defeat.

9. In the light of the failure of the democratization movement, it must be said that attempts made by the European Left, in Paris and Prague, have ended in a common defeat, because the Communist parties as leading political forces are no longer capable of leading the leftist movement. To lead a radical democratic movement of intellectuals and workers does not mean to flirt with anti-American slogans and play with student provocations. To lead such a movement means to understand theoretically the perspectives of industrial society and those processes that are transforming the face of the world. A leftist movement can develop only outside the bureaucracies of Communist parties, only outside traditional revolutionary schemes. Only then can the movement gain the proper experience that may bring victory in the future.

10. However, the defeat of reformist communism and the concept of socialist democracy is not necessarily final. It is a defeat for the bureaucracy of the Communist Party, rather than for socialist and humanistic ideals. Any movement in industrial society that seeks to follow the path of socialism must absorb the experiences of 1968 in Prague and Paris. At the same time, it will have to take into consideration that the basic ideas of Marx's socialism and of European humanism are alien to Soviet Communism. The crisis of the European Left ends in an emancipating awareness that neither the revisionism of Prague nor the anarchy of Paris offers any solution. To admit this failure is a victory in itself.

III. *Possibilities for Resistance*

THE TEN COMMANDMENTS
1. don't know
2. don't care
3. don't tell
4. don't have
5. don't know how to
6. don't give
7. don't do
8. don't sell
9. don't show
10. do nothing

—*From* Večerní Praha, *August 26, 1968*

1. In occupied Czechoslovakia, there appear to be three possibilities for the future: a reign of terror by the occupying power, a collaboration government, or a mass passive resistance movement. Under occupation and a totalitarian dictatorship, an armed resistance is neither possible nor practical. Resistance must therefore adopt other forms.

2. Terror by the occupying power is made possible by the presence of tanks and the Soviet police, and the danger of the secret police is greater than that of police in uniform. The rule of fear through police repression is now being applied, since it is the only effective way to govern an occupied country. The Soviet terror is by no means an act of emotional revenge. It is a functional instrument applied in cold blood.

3. The Soviet occupiers know very well that a final act for the Czechoslovak tragedy has not yet been written and that their position in the country would be complicated by any useless terror. Any aggressor, after having carried out his aggression, is interested in one thing only: to give the aggression a legal status. At gunpoint he tries to extort the cooperation of the government and to achieve legality for the occupation regime. However, legal negotiation at gunpont is as invalid—from the very beginning—as the international behavior of the occupying power, although it represents, *via facti,* an undeniable fact of power policy.

4. Terror will increase in the near future as the population's resis-

tance against the occupation weakens. In the meantime, Soviet demagogy about so-called antisocialist forces in Czechoslovakia is preparing
the Soviet public for a great purge, a condition of which will be the
sealing off of Czech frontiers. Police terror in the Soviet protectorate
will undoubtedly follow, along with the emergence of new Háchas
and Heydrichs.*

5. Crime of this nature requires that legality be sought through a
quisling government. Any government in an occupied country has
only two alternatives: collaboration or resistance. Any government will
become a collaboration government if it adopts the "realistic approach"
of taking the lesser evil. The heroes of yesterday may become quislings
of tomorrow, regardless of their former personal prestige and merit.
History is as cruel as nature, and likes paradoxes.

6. The Prague government still has some space for maneuvering and
has not yet become a government of collaborators. It can still make
an appeal for passive resistance and refuse to legalize the aggression;
the parliament can cancel the Moscow Agreement. These steps are
expected by most of the people, including members of the Communist
Party. At the same time, the occupation army and police are also
ready. The Czechoslovak tragedy has not yet ended because the
Czechoslovak working class has not yet said its last word. It is entirely
possible that Czech workers will offer a parallel to the six-week general
strike of workers in Budapest that followed the suppression of the 1956
Hungarian uprising.

7. Only after the gradual liquidation of potential centers of resistance
in factories and in the Communist Party organization will a government of collaborators dependent on police terror be established in
Czechoslovakia. Such a government, of course, will again be in a difficult position because it will be considered only as a government supporting the aggression, and hence as a criminal operation. Czechs know
very well that membership in criminal organizations is punishable and
that people who commit themselves to occupiers are collaborators and
traitors.

8. The most topical alternative for the Czechoslovak people is passive

---

* Emil Hácha served as president for the protectorate established by Hitler in
Bohemia and Moravia; Reinhard Heydrich was the notorious *Reichsprotektor*
whose assassination resulted in the Lidice massacre.—Ed.

resistance, forms of which are being developed on the basis of the spontaneous opposition to Soviet occupation. This alternative is very promising. There is an atmosphere of national unity strengthened by the threats to national existence. This atmosphere creates a solid basis for actions to curb the terror of occupying forces and ease the conditions of collaboration imposed upon the government. The movement for human rights in Czechoslovakia is developing radical forms of resistance that can be expected to persist until the occupiers establish an open police state.

9. Under present conditions in Czechoslovakia, the unity between Communists and non-Communists—which made the reformist movement so strong and attractive—is still alive. Whatever one thinks of the role of Communist Party bureaucracies in the democratization process, it must be admitted that the unity of progressive Communists and non-Party members remains the major potential resistance force. No other way of fighting the occupation regime is yet apparent. Nevertheless, we should not ignore the fact that the first steps of the new government upon its return from Moscow were the abolition of non-Communist political groups and the encouragement of emigration for potential opponents. These steps are, of course, an indication that illegal resistance organizations may be formed.

10. The message of the Czechoslovak experiment may be found in its evidence that it is impossible to make Soviet Communism humanistic and that revisionism is a false doctrine that cannot stand up to the strategy of naked Stalinist aggression. Perhaps the value of the Czechoslovak events of 1968 is in their warning against the increasing danger of war. On the other hand, it might also be true that the crisis of Czechoslovak socialist society is opening new frontiers for freedom, democracy, and humanism.

All these possibilities of history reflect the fate of a small nation in the heart of Europe, marching toward tragedy with admirable resistance but with little hope, appealing in vain to the conscience of the world. The world, unfortunately, sees only the cold efficiency of the Soviet army in action.

Ten Commandments for an Occupied Intellectual* ൞൞൞൞൞൞൞൞൞൞൞൞൞

> Don't cry, don't ridicule, try to understand.
>
> BARUCH SPINOZA

1. Victory comes only when, after setbacks, we realize the logic of defeat. Revert to failure in order to understand it. In doing so, you are preparing your future victory. The game was lost through mistakes but, without risking mistakes, you can't play.

2. Failure is the most productive experience gained by people and by nations. A failure will either test your strength or break you down. In both cases, you will be closer to yourself. To realize one's failure is in itself a victory.

3. All cruelties have been committed in the name of noble ideals. Those who are most cruel are innocent since they don't know what they are doing. Oppose any violence, regardless of the motivation of these innocents and regardless of ideals.

4. Accept responsibility for your defeat, and face the new reality— in order to refute it. Have contempt for national sentimentality and for pretended martyrdom. Don't rely on the help of others; help yourself and don't feel self-pity.

5. Only by fighting will you manage to keep up a fighting spirit. When basic human rights are at stake, we have to fight without asking whether we can win. Don't be afraid of obstacles; they are put in your way in order for you to overcome them.

6. The national catastrophe has produced values which have been born "in the sun of hate." Your highest value is that of yourself as a man, of your awareness of man as a valuable entity. Personal values are irretrievable and can't be replaced by institutions.

* Private letters, sent to Czechoslovakia on October 28, 1968, the fiftieth anniversary of the Czechoslovak Republic; published in the Czech-language bimonthly, *Svedĕctví*, [Testimony], Paris, in 1968.

7. A free man seeks to be human. He doesn't want to rule or be ruled. Freedom is the very essence of man and finds its expression in human practice. The road to freedom cannot be found through power and force but through understanding the suppression of freedom.

8. Don't believe in what you want to believe, trust reality and your own strength to overcome it. Look upon the hysteria of ideologists with a feeling of calm superiority and contempt. Don't get your thinking institutionalized or nationalized.

9. To be radical means to keep faith in reason and to act and be committed for the sake of truth. Be aware that the criminals of the world are ruled by an even greater criminal—time. Do not get cornered into the safety of the crowd, into the security of illusion, and do not get under the protection of so-called realists.

10. Understanding of the proper context usually comes from the blue, suddenly. The occupation revealed the truth like a flash of lightning. Now you have to think and you will understand the logic of our time, the system of states and elites. Be open to the truth of reality and oppose it. "Don't cry, don't ridicule, try to understand"— and act.

Nation and History*

States are sustained by the ideas which
gave them birth.

T. G. MASARYK

The Present

In times of critical situations for nations, states, and even continents, history provides a clearer perspective for the future than the view of even the best politicians and statesmen. Whatever the tragedy or victory may be, sooner or later a force emerges, behind the deeds of statesmen and politicians, which is more powerful than these individuals. This force of history is the continuity of nations and states in time. Behind the triumphant victory of a dictator or the tragic catastrophe of a nation are linking determinants of social structures. These anonymous forces are capable of things no statesman could achieve, namely the transformation of victories into defeats, and tragedies into farces.

Human history reconstructs the phenomena of human time. The duration of a nation is recorded in the nation's history, and this history is a manifestation of the nation, an expression of its freedom to act, of its link with other nations and with determinants of landscape and economy. Thus, the destinies of nations are made by a unique combination of the three major movers observable in history—human freedom, social structure, and location. The more a nation is aware of its own past, the better it understands itself. Therefore, it should welcome those moments that enable it to free itself of illusions and make possible a genuine self-understanding. The total disillusion of the Czech and Slovak nations with the character of the Soviet Union is—in spite of whatever is happening just now—one of the greatest gains of both nations. After all, only dead illusions are good illusions. To become aware of a failure is in itself to overcome this failure.

*Lecture in New York City, to commemorate the fiftieth anniversary of the Czechoslovak Republic October 28, 1968; published in the Czech-language bimonthly, *Proměny* [Transformations], New York, in 1968.

(166)

History can test the worth of individuals, nations, and states much more exactly than any politician can, because it mercilessly reveals both the weaknesses and the strengths of men and of state structures or national character. One cannot lie before history because history itself is a sovereign judge. Only history verifies the vitality of nations. The thousand-year existence of Czechs and Slovaks as Western nations, the uninterrupted thousand-year existence of a Czech state, and the fifty years of existence of the modern state of Czechoslovakia are better proofs for the future than the occupying armies of the present moment. If the Czechs and Slovaks managed to absorb a thousand years of Western experience and, during the last fifty years, the experience of a modern democracy, of fascism and of Communism, then the destiny of these nations is of such relevance to the West and the whole world that only a very narrowminded politician can consider the Czechoslovak tragedy as a local and peripheral affair.

The elementary fact that Czechs and Slovaks are Western Slavs is both trivial and important. Czechs and Slovaks are not only Western ethnically but belong to the West culturally, while the majority of Slavs are Eastern both ethnically and culturally. Both identities are important. In fact, the whole past of Czechs and Slovaks has been full of tensions among disparate tendencies in national and state life.

Whatever tendency prevailed at various times, the Czech past has always been the past of a Western state and nation. To say it with a poet, "the French excitability and the Russian mist" have always been in conflict in the Czech national character. This tension has been present in the Czech past: now the tension between the West and East is the major problem of Europe. Is it a contradiction which has to be resolved by Soviet tanks, in an attempt to solve a puzzle of history? After all, Alexander the Great managed to undo the Gordian knot, not by untying it, but by cutting through it with his sword.

Czechoslovakia went through four crises during its fifty years of existence—in 1918, 1938, 1948, and 1968—and each time its sovereignty was at stake. This sovereignty was not a matter of individual social groups, classes, or the elite, but of the very existence of the state and the welfare of its two nations. At the same time, this state had been built on a philosophy that puts human rights, humanity, and social justice above nationalism. Following this philosophy, the Czech and

Slovak nations have always been eager to participate in Western civilization. This "orientation" was undercut during the last twenty years but it has never been lost or abandoned. Not even the new Communist power elite has been able to change this basic way of life of the two nations. Thus, any crisis of Czechoslovakia has become a crisis of European politics and Western values. The Soviet occupation of Czechoslovakia, therefore, does not merely confront Europe with the local tragedy of a minor state whose political structure has collapsed for the third time in fifty years; it poses a key question: Is Europe capable of guaranteeing the sovereignty of its own small states and its own values? To put it simply—has sovereignty in Europe become obsolete?

One thousand years of Czechs and Slovaks prove that the sacrifices made by these two nations were sacrifices for the West and in the name of freedom. The basic idea of the Czech state has been the idea of contacting and contesting * the West, based on the principle of cooperation among nations and political democracy. Czechs have paid a heavy price for embracing Western culture and its values. Their state has often been on the decline and they were dying—prematurely perhaps—for ideas derived from the West. Their victories and defeats have always been victories and defeats for the West. The present tragedy of Czechoslovakia can thus be considered as just another peripeteia of history, which is fond of paradoxes.

The descendants of revolutionary Hussites were forced to accept the Catholic religion. The victims of Germanization under Josef II (1780–1790) reacted by a great national awakening. Democratic Czechoslovakia was sacrificed at Munich in 1938 to the deadly enemies of democracy—the fascists. Reform Communists trying to restore human rights were sacrificed in Moscow in 1968 by a neo-Stalinist fascist-like bureaucracy. The totalitarian dictatorship will erode, not because of the errors committed by its policy makers, but because of irreparable flaws in the very structures of these dictatorships. Soon dictatorships will be clearly recognized as inefficient and unsuitable political structures for any industrial society, whether Western or Eastern. Mean-

---

* The leading Czech historian František Palacký used this term (*stýkání a potýkání*) to describe the ambivalent character of the relationship between Czechs and Germans.—Ed.

while, we must repeatedly ask the old question: Is it possible to enjoy human freedom at all under these totalitarian dictatorships?

Whether there is an answer to these paradoxes of Western civilization, whether it is possible to undo by democratic procedure the Gordian knot of world politics—all this has become, after the Soviet occupation, more controversial than ever before. The Czechs and Slovaks will survive their Soviet puppet state in the heart of Europe. However, the trend toward the use of force in settling disputes between the great powers makes the whole affair more controversial. Not only individual states but their communities as well, are sustained by the ideas which gave them birth. Western society may sometimes let a small state become a scapegoat to preserve world peace. But it cannot deny that it has done so.

The Past

A Celtic tribe, the Boii, once gave their name to the region—the home of the Boii, Bojohemum—which became Latinized into "Bohemia." The name remained fixed on the land in all early sources, though the Celtic settlers had long been replaced by Germanic Markomans, and later—probably in the sixth century—by waves of Slavs. Since earliest times the very essence of the small Slav formation in the heart of Europe has been reaching to its German neighbors, accepting them or rejecting them. The first great Czech historian František Palacký (1798–1876) saw the meaning of Czech history in this contact and contest. A permanent conflict took various forms in the past of the Czechs, and has never been limited to political conflict. "Contact and contest" must be applied to the relations between the Czechs and Slovaks, to Western values, and to the whole culture. In nationalistic history books of the nineteenth century the history of Western society is usually represented as the history of individual nations—French, Britons, Germans—and the common culture viewed as a set of natural cultures. For the two small nations of Czechs and Slovaks the past consisted of conflicts over specific Western issues, because the Czechs and the Slovaks were too small, as nations, to have any great political ambitions at any time during their existence.

The first state structure of Slav tribes who settled in and around

Bohemia in the sixth century is connected with the name of Samo, who was a Frank merchant elected leader by the Slavs, and whose rule lasted from about 623 to about 659. Greater Moravia, the first developed state, emerged later, in the ninth century. More important, however, than these temporary political structures was the far-reaching cultural change resulting from the adoption of Christianity, which began at that time and succeeded by the efforts of two Byzantine missionaries, brothers Cyrillus and Methodius, who arrived in Moravia in 863. Though Latin Christianity had been adopted by Czech princes in 845 in Regensburg, Saint Venceslav [Wenceslas], the Přemyslovic prince of Bohemia from 922 to 929, made a great effort to Christianize his people, and at the same time was forced to accept the subordination of Bohemia to the German king. His brother Boleslav, leading pagan national opposition, murdered him in 929. It was a great loss for Czech statehood, but the nation nevertheless benefited culturally from the seven-year rule of Venceslav.

The idea of Bohemian independence, which may have motivated the fratricide, gradually gained momentum during the rule of the Přemyslovic dynasty (till 1306) particularly when the title of hereditary king was granted to rulers of Bohemia by both the Roman pontiff in 1198 and the emperor in 1212. Bohemian kings became the most influential and powerful rulers within the Holy Roman Empire. In his attempt to obtain the Roman crown in 1273, Přemysl Ottokar II lost to Count Rudolf von Habsburg, and was killed on the battlefield in a final encounter in 1278. He was fighting for the idea of a Central European state, the very idea which the victorious Habsburgs adopted and developed. Like the assassinated Czech Saint Venceslav before him, the dead "iron and gold" king of the Bohemian battlefield of Marchfeld is another proof that Czech rulers fell fighting for the great ideas on which the future was built.

Human development loves paradoxes, and it might have been one of those "tricks of history" referred to by Hegel that exactly a hundred years after the death of Přemysl Ottokar II another king of Bohemia died in 1378 after having fulfilled the dream of the Přemyslovics—to base the power of the Holy Roman Empire on the strength of a rising Bohemia!

Roman Emperor Charles IV founded the oldest university in Central

Europe, the famous Carolina (or Charles) University: he continued the Přemyslovic policy of cooperation between Czechs and Germans, which had proved so fruitful in urban development and in the development of the arts. The reign of *"pater patriae"* Charles IV saw the culmination of the intensive activity of German settlers who had been invited to Bohemia by the Přemyslovics. His reign thus represents a stage of Czech history in which this wise and powerful ruler managed to achieve a harmonious relationship between the Czechs and Germans, to the benefit of the whole kingdom. Thus a key principle of the Bohemian state was reestablished—namely the cooperation of these two nations as a basis for state policy.

Another aspect of Czech national development, however, appeared later, during the Hussite Revolution, that glorious prologue to Protestantism. In the wars of resistance that followed the burning of Jan Hus in Konstanz in 1415, Czechs were fighting not only for their national ideals but also for their image of social justice and personal freedom, an image shared later by all those opposing the Catholic Church. When some established a communist order in the newly founded Hussite city of Tábor, the Czechs were proposing an ideal of social justice and personal freedom five hundred years before similar ideas penetrated Russia. It was a time in which Czechs were in the forefront of progressive thinking in Europe.

The two centuries of Czech protest, however, were crushed in 1620 after the Battle of Bílá Hora, or White Mountain, near Prague, in which the Bohemian rebels were defeated. The leaders of the Bohemian rebellion were executed in 1621, their properties were confiscated, their followers were given the choice of conversion or emigration, and a rule of terror was imposed. The second defenestration of Prague in 1618—when enraged Protestant noblemen threw three officials of the Royal Council out of the windows of Prague Castle—actually triggered the Thirty Years' War between the two religious blocs in the Europe of that time. This war accepted an earlier compromising principle of *"cuius regio eius religio."* [Whoever rules the country decides its religion.*] Czechs became victims of this compromise, victims of great-

---

* This was a medieval principle applied in international relations between Catholic and Protestant states after the Thirty Years' War. The head of each state decided the religion of his subjects.—Ed.

power politics, and victims of European peace efforts. Taking fully into consideration the differences between now and then, one cannot avoid asking whether the defeat of the present reform movement in Czechoslovakia is not repeating a general historical pattern and whether this repetition does not indicate that all the defeats of the Czechs have been defeats of the advanced Western concept of justice and freedom.

The baroque period which followed represents a "period of darkness," from which the Czech nation awoke only when alarmed by the reforms of Josef II (1780–1790). It was at that time that the national movement and its leaders awoke to a genuine national consciousness and later to a concept of political independence as well. It looks like another paradox that the repressive and absolutist Germanization of Josef produced the very opposite of what it intended—a vital Czech nation based on the recognition that the history of Central Europe has always been and will always be a history of Czechs, Germans, Slovaks, and Magyars, and that the Austrian monarchy with its slogan *"viribus unitis"* (strength in unity) was a reasonable arrangement, provided that it respected the autonomy of its individual peoples. This national philosophy of history was expressed by the "father of the nation," the Czech historian František Palacký, who stated that "if there were no Austria, we would have to create one." Palacký's true and reasonable concept was not destroyed by any unwillingness of the Czechs to cooperate with the Austrian Empire but by the incompetence of that monarchy to give a modern meaning to the idea of a Central European commonwealth of nations.

It was in the context of Western humanism and democracy that a new, independent Czechoslovakia was formed in 1918, following the fall of the dual monarchy. The spiritual father, founder, and first president of Czechoslovakia, Tomáš Garrigue Masaryk (1850–1938), was convinced that the future of the new state was bound up with the ideas of humanism, cooperation among nations, personal freedom, and human rights in general. Although Masaryk's republic suffered from all the critical problems of the postwar malaise—whether they resulted from national conflicts with a considerable minority group of over three million Germans or unemployment affecting a million people—the republic did manage to keep alive as an island of democracy amidst the cruel sea of fascism. Czechoslovakia, however, was sold out to fascist aggressors in Munich and one may assume that the lesson drawn from that sellout might have been one consolation to Europe, namely the recognition that deferring the resolution of a crisis is no solution, and that the appeasement of the aggressor does not pay.

In the following ten years, Czechoslovakia was continually changing political regimes. Its weakened power elite first tried some sort of cooperation with Hitler, then had to fight Hitler, and later to reform bourgeois democracy, but finally capitulated when confronted with Communist power in 1948. There is no other country in Europe which had experienced all possible political regimes in fifty years and whose middle-aged generation had tasted political democracy, fascism masked as nationalism, a clerical-fascist puppet order, Nazi occupation, a provisional regime of socialist democracy, Stalinist terror, de-Stalinized Communism, and reform Communism oriented toward democracy. Although suffering under fascism and Stalinism could not help but undermine the political will of Czechs and Slovaks, it has also brought about a hard-won, genuine experience on which to base the conclusion that all totalitarian dictatorships—be they of the far right or of the far left— are in essence identical. Furthermore, the same experience has shown that these extreme dictatorships, regardless of their differing ideologies, are simply not able to solve the problems of modern industrial society and that they represent a fatal danger to freedom—anywhere and anytime.

The Future

Nations never end by foreign occupation. As a matter of fact, occupation forces an occupied nation to seek new forms of existence and to look for new ideas to test. The Soviet occupation of Czechoslovakia has produced serious consequences for the whole Soviet zone of influence; by violating Czechoslovakian state sovereignty it has touched upon the very nerve of the Czechoslovakian state and Czech and Slovak being.

It seems to me that, fifty years after the disintegration of Austria in 1918, the Soviets will resume the Austrian effort to form a similar empire out of occupied states. They may very well proceed with such a plan for the simple reason that no one in Europe seems to be able or willing to challenge them. At the moment, it is evident that the principle of independence is no longer operative in their bloc and is being replaced by a gradual trend toward integration. This means that the *diktat* vis-à-vis Czechoslovakia will be followed by further *diktats*, even if perhaps applied in a more polite form. Some 120 million inhabitants of Soviet satellite states will thus pay the price for the fatal mistakes of American foreign policy which were made at the end of World War II.

Great Russian chauvinism is being expanded under the new Brezhnev Doctrine in a way Stalin himself would not have dared to carry out, and, in addition, the "legal" argument supporting that doctrine is something unknown to international law. The Czechs and Slovaks will have to live with it and they will be the victims of Soviet tyranny. Moreover, the Czechs and Slovaks will experience the Russian nagaika [whip] and Siberian camps and will be, at the same time, consistently taught how to rebel. Their teacher will be terror, as practiced by a people which has never experienced democracy, Western tradition, human rights. Czechs and Slovaks will only reinforce their awareness that they are part of the West and reject the East, where they do not belong. In their resistance they will find both new friends and new enemies. The most depressing consequence of the occupation will not be so much the permanent presence of Soviet troops but the influence of the internal fascistization of the Soviet Union, extending itself to the satellites, as a tendency toward a fascist-style technocracy. This is represented today, for example, by Gomulka's nationalistic and populistic Poland with its animosity against democracy, intellectuals, Jews. Imported from the Soviet Union, the process of fascistization will lead to internal conflicts and to a rapid degeneration of the Communist Party and its elite.

The consequences of the occupation for Czechoslovakia could hardly be more catastrophic if it had experienced a war. Černík's government has signed documents that the former boss of Czechoslovakia, Antonín Novotný, would never have dared to sign and submit to any elected state organ. By accepting the Moscow *diktat*, the Černík government legalized the occupation. This government has not protested to the United Nations and has taken a position which would have been taken by such conservatives as Indra, Kolder, or Bilák. Regardless of who they are, the harvest will be the same. In the past, new governments inherited the policies of their predecessors and were thus forced, willy nilly, to continue what they originally condemned. By the end of August, no one in Czechoslovakia would have believed that the same people who received such a tough lesson in Moscow would dare to submit to their parliament, on the fiftieth anniversary of Czechoslovakia on October 28, shameless documents attesting to acceptance of the Soviet occupation and the practical liquidation of state sovereignty. The Communist Party has accepted the Soviet *diktat*. The people have not, and never will.

The Communist Party alone is responsible for the capitulation and humiliation of both nations. Not even in the future will the Party be able to lead the people, the democratic movement, and the working class. The Communist Party, as a guarantor of the state and of socialism, failed completely because it did not have the courage—at crucial moments—to rely on the people and the people's democratic will. This failure occurred at a time of high revolutionary fervor, when Czechs and Slovaks were willing to support the Party and came as close as they ever had been to an authentic socialism. People can forgive politicians who weep, because people understand human tragedies. History, however, will never forgive. From the very beginning, radical students and intellectuals in Czechoslovakia did not trust the reforms aimed at keeping the public out of policy making, and at limiting reforms to a change of elite within the Communist Party. Their cool skepticism has been confirmed as a very realistic appraisal of all those who had been flirting temporarily with the concept of a socialist democracy.

The Soviet occupation will be more dire for the people than for the state. The only perspective left is a social system based on technocracy, bureaucracy, and dictatorship, a system as unbearable as it is inefficient. In addition, in the absence of any political reform, economic recovery will not be possible. Very soon, the degenerated political elite will be forced to rely more and more on terror without illusions while offering the apathetic masses at least a vision of a consumer society. While the intellectual elite of the country will be silenced, the degenerated power elite will suffer from uncertainty and a guilt complex and will be looked upon by the nation with silent contempt. Large-scale attempts to corrupt intellectuals will again be set into motion but, on the whole, intellectuals who had tried to play a role in politics will have no right to speak. The power elite will gradually lose its real power. It is only a question of time before it will be clear to the government and the governed that they have both been downgraded to the status of mere provincials who might be shipped to Siberia, to the Chinese borders— completely at the whim of the tsar, to satisfy the needs of his realm with the fraternal help of the armies, of the satellite provinces. The offer made to Dubček by Brezhnev, namely to place 250,000 Czecho-slovak soldiers on the Soviet-Chinese border, was by no means just a joke.

The disillusionment of Czechs and Slovaks with their leaders, the people's apathy and contempt, and the dissolution of the fictitious Czechoslovak nation into the Czech and Slovak nations, all this will have an emotional impact, as understandable as disillusion in love. Luckily, in this small country there are so many ingenious minds which will find ways to strengthen their nation's links with the West. Fully distrusting neo-Stalinist fascism, the intellectuals in socialist Czecho-slovakia will not fail to find theoretical and practical ways to decom-pose the totalitarian dictatorship, further to develop social democracy, and to get the Soviets out.

Western values are indivisible in both the Elbe and the Danube basins. Independence and democracy for people, social justice, freedom of expression, and the rights of individual man are threatened in all Europe, whenever they are threatened in any part of it. The idea of social democracy in Czechoslovakia, as expressed since January, 1968, belongs to the realm of Western ideals of freedom, independence, and socialism. The failure of these concepts under the pressure of Soviet tanks is not only a defeat for a country with an unfortunate location and strategic position, but a defeat for the West, for Western values and the Western spirit. It is true, Europeans do not want to take note of it, and only hindsight, one day, will tell them the whole story con-vincingly.

Czechs and Slovaks have learned the answer to the questions of whether freedom of man exists in totalitarian dictatorships and whether a people in Eastern Europe can enjoy sovereignty. The answer is no. This negative experience is one side. The other is the necessity to fight this experience with courage. Courage can change the behavior of the aggressor. We, Czechs and Slovaks, know our calamity. We ask the other peoples of the West: Can men be free and peoples independent in this time of totalitarian dictatorships? This question should be of some interest to you. After all, it's now your turn to answer—and not in theoretical terms alone.

The Gordian Knot* ~~~~~~~~~~~~

> Stalin was not a person. He *is* an obsolete
> institution which has been updated. This
> institution used to be operative in Russian
> internal life only, but now it is ravaging
> the new Russian colony of Czechoslovakia
> in a new and all-encompassing way.
>
> ERNST BLOCH, Neues Forum,
> *No. 167, Vienna, 1968*

1. Today, after the occupation of Czechoslovakia, we can see quite
clearly that the elitist-technocratic group of Communist reformers had
gone as far as its nature would allow. Its fear of the people, of the
workers and intellectuals, made it incapable of creating an alliance
for the common cause between those who work with their minds and
those who work with their hands. Such an alliance was diametrically
opposed to the elite's group interests, because it challenged its privileges
and called in question not only its policy but its very existence. Only
radical democrats and humanist socialists were able and willing to form
this decisive alliance as the basis for future political action. It was only
these people, whom simple-minded editors ridiculed as extremists, who
heard the rumbling of the tanks in the distance and tried to make the
sole move which, in spring, 1968, might have saved democratization—
*the mobilization of the working class for the defense of its own inter-
ests.* This attempt had such far-reaching implications that it fully de-
served the hatred it received from all the apparatuses; even among the
well-known progressives there was nobody who understood and supported this program.

2. After twenty years, it was very difficult for the intellectuals and
the workers to find a common language and to bridge the apparent
abyss between them, created and abetted by the Communist Party apparatus. The myth of the worker as the "new man" repelled the humanist intelligentsia by its falseness, while the worker who thought

---

* Lecture at Yale to commemorate International Students' Day, November 17,
1968; published in the monthly *New Politics*, New York, January, 1969.

realistically regarded the technical intelligentsia of his plant as the accomplices of the oppressive machine which was forcing him to produce more for less pay. Both ideological illusions, carefully fostered by the ruling organs, prevented the two basic social groups from coming to an understanding, until they realized that they were both manipulated and victimized by the ideology of the political apparatus—and now by occupation armies.

3. In the heat of the summer there came an important turning-point. The *Two Thousand Words* manifesto brought together the particular group interests of the intelligentsia and the general national and popular interests of a free, sovereign, and socialist Czechoslovakia. The clear threat to the state, the endless maneuvers and the criticism contained in the Warsaw Letter created a situation favorable to a temporary national unity, to an alliance of workers and intellectuals for a common cause and to mass support for the Communist Party. The Soviet tanks sealed this alliance of workers and intellectuals in reaction to the invasion and produced that remarkable and unparalleled conjunction of the interests of workers and intellectuals.

4. It was only at the end of June that with their *Two Thousand Words* manifesto the Communist intellectuals—perhaps too late—obtained majority support for democratization, by their proposal that it be based on the activity of the people themselves. They thus *went beyond the framework of the policy of the elite.* The elite unanimously rejected the *Two Thousand Words,* since the manifesto *represented the first formulation of the intellectuals' and workers' community of interests;* this alliance for the common cause grew steadily closer in the course of the next two months, as the slogans of socialism, sovereignty, and freedom became matters of vital concern to every citizen.

5. Looking back, we may wonder if the intellectuals' attempt to accelerate the internal democratization of the regime—especially as it was expressed in the *Two Thousand Words*—was right, or if a more moderate course of action might have prevented the Warsaw Pact's military action. But history does not care for the conditional in the pluperfect. History is a series of changing situations, each of which opens up many alternatives; but it is irreversible. At every step only one course can be chosen and this constantly, over and over again, eliminates all the other possible alternatives of the given situation. Per-

haps from this point of view we can say that the only possibility of resistance to the armed intervention lay in a much more intensive pursuit of internal democratization. Instead of reacting to the repeated army maneuvers and to the Warsaw Letter with a partial mobilization, and thereby taking the risk of conflict, the Communist leaders accepted a compromise in Bratislava and signed the death-warrant of their democratization. They were incapable, both for personal reasons and because of the class character of Czechoslovakia's political structure, of choosing the only alternative that could have saved them—a popular movement of workers and intelligentsia. This was the alternative advocated by some individuals in March and by the intellectuals as a group in June. It finally came into existence at the end of August, in the form of an absurd and heroic resistance; but then, in spite of its enormous potential strength, the movement was as tragically helpless as it was admirable.

6. A more cautious course of action might have deferred the intervention, but it was the very essence of the social changes in Czechoslovakia which was unacceptable to the Soviet leadership. The reaction to the reformist group's continual readiness to compromise led nowhere; the Soviet side regarded it as proof of weakness and not as a desire for a certain degree of democracy in the relations between nations and states. The moderate approach meant that the Soviet generals were repeatedly invited into a country whose government so readily proclaimed its fidelity to the military interests of the Warsaw Pact. So, finally, the generals were quite sure they were on safe ground and they decided to stay in the country, together with several divisions. A still more restrained course of action might have managed to postpone the crisis by a few months, but insofar as the Czechoslovak movement really was a democratizing and popular one, and insofar as it tended to break up the mechanism of the totalitarian dictatorship, there was absolutely no way of preventing the Soviet intervention except by accepting the risk of war, of open conflict.

7. Consequently, if today we seek the hypothetical alternative which could have prevented the intervention, we shall certainly not find it in greater moderation of the intellectuals' policy but, on the contrary, in more radicalism in the struggle for socialist democracy, in a more radical readiness to defend one's own country by force of arms. If the

Communists had prepared the country for the possibility of armed conflict, they might have prevented the intervention, because the Soviet leadership would have had to deal with a much more complicated politico-military problem than the occupation itself represented. The risks connected with war in the heart of Europe were so great, especially in view of the proximity of Germany, that the need to decide whether to risk outright war would have strengthened the more moderate group in the Soviet Politburo. The knowledge that we have to deal with a man of courage affects the way we behave; in the same way, awareness of the risk of conflict would have affected the strategy of the measures taken against Czechoslovakia. If Finland could defend itself, if Rumania and Yugoslavia are ready to fight for their national independence, there is no reason to doubt that the policy which ruled out armed struggle against the aggressor was fatally wrong. In dismissing General Prchlik, the Prague leadership made a grave mistake, because by the same token it ruled out the possibility that the country would defend itself and neutralized its only real force—the Czechoslovak army.

8. No shots were fired when the invasion came, because by then it was too late. As a glance at a map will show, any armed resistance could have lasted only a matter of hours or, at best, of days. At the same time, however, it must be said that the state could have and should have defended itself, because the final outcome of a war is never certain. For what is at issue is not only the actual occupation of the country, but also what can be done in the country once it has been occupied. The American experience in Vietnam shows clearly enough that, though the five Warsaw Pact powers might have conquered Czechoslovakia within a few hours, their military victory would have proved a radical defeat if during that crucial night the leading statesmen had had the courage to do their duty and defend the country's sovereignty by force of arms. What are armies for, if not to fight when their country is attacked by an enemy?

9. Finally, from the point of view of political strategy, we may wonder if the intellectuals' and politicians' big mistake was not to overestimate the danger of the conservatives at home and to underestimate the threat represented by the Soviet tanks. A moderate internal democratization coupled with a more intensive effort to get out of the sphere

of the USSR's power would perhaps have been successful. It must be recognized that the political leaders, the skeptical intellectuals, and the radical students were not ready to face the possibility of the USSR's repeating its performance in Hungary in 1956. This outcome seemed improbable until the Čierná Conference; even the professional advisors of NATO thought it was out of the question. Why? Because the brutality of Soviet foreign policy is beyond reason. The more absurd the picture the imagination paints, the nearer it will bring us to the truth about the nature of the Soviet state and its imperialist ambitions. History is a play of eventualities, but the politician must always bear in mind that, whatever action he happens to choose, it will be irreversible, and that a wrong move or political apathy will lose the game long before the tank columns arrive to impose their will on history and on nations.

10. More recent developments in Czechoslovakia have proved again that the community of interest between intelligentsia and workers is the most productive political idea for the socialist movements of the future. What in the spring of 1968 seemed a utopian projection by isolated intellectuals has become a reality in the months that followed. This experience indicates that, in modern industrial society, there exist conditions favoring a new type of political alliance; this alliance will come about only if the intellectuals are capable of formulating a Marxist-humanistic program in terms of the majority of the population, in terms of the unity of the blue-collar and white-collar workers. This is the solution to the problem of this Gordian knot.

Heads Against Tanks * ⌇⌇⌇⌇⌇⌇⌇⌇⌇⌇

> Whenever ideas were separated from in-
> terests, they were compromised.
>
> KARL MARX

Problem of Problems

1. The tragic fact of history—that interests always win over noble ideas—has been proven several times in the evolution of mass ideologies. Ancient world religions as well as modern socialism confirm that mass movements have always been transformed by history; in confrontation with reality, the human aim is distorted to such an extent that the new reality achieved in the name of the movement appears as a caricature of the original idea. By the end of 1968, the Czech and Slovak nations knew more than anybody else about the cruel dialectics of ideas and interests. In the history of Czechoslovakia the conflict between reality and ideas took the shape of a caricature of Marxism.

2. The original aims of the Marxist labor movement, as a program of transforming society, conflicted in 1968 with the interests of the power elites of Eastern Europe and with the great power orientation of one of the world's superpowers. The very meaning of socialism as a program of human freedom was exposed to its severest test of the last hundred years. This test is comparable only to that which occurred in the period following the defeat of the Paris Commune, and in the period of the Stalin-Hitler Pact. Out of Czechoslovakia emerged a problem not only for the great powers, but for the whole international socialist movement, and for world culture in general—the problem of the meaning of socialism.

3. In 1968, two small nations in Central Europe asked their neighbors,

---

* Lecture written December 24, 1968 for the striking students of the Philosophical Faculty, Charles University, Prague. The lecture appeared on the desk in the
corridor of the Faculty in Prague. It was published, in part, in *Svedĕctví*, Paris,
in 1968, and it was delivered at Northwestern University, Evanston, Ill., on January 18, 1969, to commemorate the immolation of Jan Palach.

Europe, and the whole world the following questions: Is it the purpose of socialism to achieve greater human freedom? Can a repressive totalitarian system be gradually transformed and democratized? Are basic human rights, national independence and sovereignty of people compatible with socialism? To put it theoretically: Is the original, authentic program of Marxian socialism compatible with the reality of present socialist states? Are its ideas compatible with the interests of power elites in socialist countries? Is it at all possible to build "socialism" without a Soviet occupation?

4. In the light of last year's experience, it can be said that these questions have received an unequivocally negative answer. This suggests that we should perhaps give up socialism, if it were not for the tremendous support of people, of nations, and of the socialist movement, which has given the opposite answer—despite the occupation. It seems to be a paradox that the key question of socialism becomes theoretically clear only when the Soviet system is well understood—as a system which has nothing in common with socialism but the name. Soviet society is monopoly socialism based on the violation of human rights.

5. The Soviet system has several features in common with old capitalism: a) hired labor; b) a power elite as a ruling class; and c) state organization. The basis of the Soviet system is the very mechanism of economic, political, and ideological oppression that Marx wanted to abolish. Marx, in fact, considered socialism impossible without the abolition of the state, of class rule, and of the hired labor system. The fifty years of the Soviet Union's existence offer a sufficient clue that the Soviet Union is nothing but a variation on modern industrial society, and that it has applied principles representing just the opposite of that socialism proclaimed by Karl Marx and characterized by the decline of the state, the abolition of the hired labor system, and of exploitation.

6. State monopoly socialism in the Soviet Union differs, however, from classic capitalism, not in the structure of production (the economic basis) but in the despotic character of the police state (the superstructure). The basic difference between the two major world industrial systems is to be found in the mechanism of political control applied by the ruling power elites. Whereas under the Western system the power elite has to recognize the basic human rights or at least to take into account the demands of citizens and organizations, the giant

Soviet state, which plays the role of the enterpreneur and has its bu-
reaucratic-police-military elite, is subject to no control whatsoever.

7. Marx considered the existence of the state under socialism incompatible with the freedom of man. Lenin tried to achieve a democratization of the state and a decline in the repressive mechanisms of state
power. Forty years of Stalinism created the very opposite of revolutionary freedom: a giant system of totalitarian dictatorship compared
to which tsardom resembles a liberal paradise. This distortion of the
original aims of Marxist socialism created at the same time a new class
stratification and enabled the emergence of a new privileged ruling
class of state and party bureaucrats. The Soviet system is based on the
economic exploitation of a right-less population, on the class rule of a
technocratic-state-party power elite, and on suppression of the human
rights of both individuals and nations.

8. Thus the Soviet system is not a historic fulfillment of Marx's idea
of socialism but is, in fact, a denial of Marx's vision of the future. The
Soviet state has become an obstacle to the promotion of socialist ideas
and to the liberating activities of political organizations, nations, and
the labor movement. The Soviet ideology is a mockery of humanism, a
theoretical liquidation of Marxism, and a caricature of genuine socialist
ideas.

9. The transformation of socialism into a system of bureaucratic
dictatorship, the transformation of the October Revolution into a new
form of class tyranny, and the replacement of revolutionary theory by
brutal force represent a revision of socialist humanism, and a total
revision of Marxism as a theoretical program for the liberation of all
mankind. Marxism—surpassed as a system but unsurpassed as a method
for the theoretical examination of social reality—has degenerated, in
the Soviet Union, into an institutionalized ideological lie, and become
a system of rigid rules which can be interpreted arbitrarily according
to the prevailing interests of the given power elite.

10. Authentic Marxism is in a position to explain this degeneration,
as well as the true nature of the controversial present reality and the
perversion of socialism in the Soviet Union. Authentic Marxists understand the nature of social developments and the interests behind the
transformation of the original idea. Soviet socialism, which has no faith
in man and in people as the moving force of history, is a perverse ideol-

ogy shared by the technocratic elites of totalitarian dictatorships, which will continue to prostitute the very meaning of socialism, namely the right of people to determine their economic destiny, their political system, and their personal freedoms. If it is true that the Soviet power elite has turned Marxism into nonsense, we then have to conclude that the nonsensical existence of power elites has to be abolished in order to restore the appealing idea of socialism—true human freedom. Without this unity of ideas and interests, history could be defeated by absurdity.

The Blind Alley of Czech Politics

What you have not lost, you have.
You have not lost your horns.
Therefore, you have horns.
—*An old Greek paradox*

1. Through the Soviet occupation we have not lost socialism, for the simple reason that we have never had it. We have only lost a chance to come closer to a society which would combine the state ownership of the means of production with a political system that makes possible a proper democratic control over the ruling power elite. Bearing in mind the ancient Greek paradox, we could also say that, by not losing socialism, we have obtained it now, thanks to the occupation, the newly introduced censorship, and the so-called "realistic" policy. In fact, we have socialism to the same extent that the man who believed in the ancient Greek paradox had horns. The "socialist character" of the state is confirmed by the reestablishment of censorship, by the extraordinary rights accorded to the police, and by the presence of Soviet tanks.

2. Unlike soccer players, Czech professional politicians have always thought that the nation could dribble through its history without scoring, without shooting. They have always maintained that the nation could survive best by adopting the attitude of "the good soldier Schweik," [in the World War I novel of that name by Jaroslav Hašek]. Thus Czechoslovakia, located in Central Europe, has been maneuvering between two giants—Germany and Russia—with admirable style, but

with no success. The popular "Czech lane" * of soccer, as adopted by politicians, has proved to be a useless trick.

3. The blind alley of Czech politics has its beginning in [the Communist coup d'état of] February, 1948, the greatest victory of the Czechoslovak labor movement and, at the same time, its greatest defeat. In a few months, victory had changed into the defeat of the aims followed for seventy years by both political parties of the Czechoslovak working class—the Social Democratic Party and the Communist Party. The consequences of the February, 1948 events resulted in the acceptance of the Soviet model of socialism, the imposition of a totalitarian dictatorship, liquidation of human rights and liberties, and the limitation of national sovereignty.

4. Once Czech policy became subordinated to the Soviet sphere of influence, the construction of socialism came to be subordinated to the falsification of Marx, as practiced by Big Brother in the Soviet Union. The creation of the power elite, the bureaucratization of production, and brainwashing in Czechoslovakia, although in essence similar to trends prevailing in the Soviet Union, had always been marked by one peculiarity, namely that Czechoslovakia was the only industrially advanced country ruled by Stalinists. This exportation of socialist tsardom to Central Europe proved to be catastrophic from all points of view—economic, political, and ideological.

5. Czech policy in 1968 tried to find the proper meaning of socialism in an attempt to combine socialism and democracy. This attempt has been impeded by the consequences of the post-1948 sovietization of the country, rather than by the February 1948 events themselves. The Czechoslovak power elite thought that it would find a solution of economic crises and political difficulties by respecting the national characteristics of Czechoslovakia. The political leaders, however, were unaware that by doing this they would provoke both nations to seek an answer to questions relating to the very essence of socialism. *They were unaware that they were questioning the very basis of Soviet power.* It was not the power elite but the Czechoslovak people and their intellectual spokesmen who presented a frightening alternative to the Kremlin:

---

* A soccer trick based on creating a favorable angle for an unexpected shot. The term *lane* in Czech (*ulička*), is also used to describe a "blind alley."—Ed.

either accept the dangerous idea of democratizing socialism and making Russia European, or intervene militarily in order to prevent not only the reforms but a disintegration of Russia's power. Once again, the Kremlin decided to play the traditional role of the tsars, that of being Europe's policemen.

6. The concept of Czechoslovak socialism as a democratic system which made political activity, and control over the power elite, possible for the masses, was in harmony with political democracy; it was a concept that became a phenomenon of European importance, and indeed of world importance. Socialist ownership, political democracy, and freedom of information seemed to be capable of overcoming the gap between the Soviet and the Western systems and of finding a simple definition for socialism: "Socialism is democracy and freedom." This concept, as a solution of the existing deadlock, was first adopted by a small group within the Czechoslovak power elite which took over the Communist Party. In its naiveté this group thought, however, that it would be enough to make some technocratic changes, to liberalize cultural life a little, and to make a few concessions similar to Khrushchev's de-Stalinization.

7. In its maneuvers against the overwhelming majority of Stalinists, this group of reformists managed to get strong popular support but at the same time antagonized the Soviet power elite which had been moving for quite some time in a direction the very opposite of Khrushchev's adventurous de-Stalinization policy. Moreover, the Czechoslovak power elite—in the eyes of the Soviet neo-Stalinists and technocrats—committed a mortal sin: it asked for support from outside the Communist Party and thus revised the Stalinist interpretation of the Party's role.

8. The conflict between different interpretations of Marxism developed into a conflict between power elites. The occupation resolved the conflict between elites and the various interpretations of Marxism in favor of the stronger elite. The Soviet invasion rendered a service in teaching the East European power elites collective gangsterism. At the same time, the invasion has shown again that at crucial moments the power elite is unable to escape its limitations, that it remains an elite composed of party bureaucrats and technocrats, and that it prefers its alliance within the Soviet bloc to political support from its own people. Both in theory and practice, the concept of a socialist democracy is in-

compatible with the neo-Stalinist version of socialism based on power elites and technocracy.

9. If a revolt in one single country is doomed to failure under the pressure of Soviet tanks, it necessarily follows that, in order to be successful, the next upheaval will have to be greater and will have to be extended to more countries. In any case, no nation—after the experience in Hungary and Czechoslovakia—will any longer believe in the illusions promoted by Czechoslovak reformists, according to which it is possible to transform a modern totalitarian dictatorship in a nonviolent way, by gradually applying reforms within the ruling power elite, without action by a broad democratic popular movement, and without armed resistance against an invading army. Marxists should not be afraid to swallow this bitter truth.

10. At the time of crisis, the Stalinist bureaucrats of the Party wake up from their "freedom dream" and turn back to "reality," to blind alleys and Shweikian maneuvers, again proving the falsity of whatever illusions are entertained by the freedom-seeking nation in regard to the Party machinery. While Party bureaucrats are again practicing their old ideology, though with some modifications, workers and intellectuals are also awakening from their "freedom dream." But their awakening is different. Modern nations, as alliances of workers and intellectuals, can no longer be stopped from working to exact structural changes from modern industrial society and thus realizing the very meaning of socialism.

11. A rebelling modern nation, an active popular movement with workers and intellectuals united, is losing—in present-day industrial society—its illusions and its dreams about freedom and starting to realize *its own genuine freedom,* the very opposite of freedom for power elites. It can no longer share the new ideological oscillation of the bureaucratic Party pendulum. It must insist—with stubborn intransigence—on the true meaning of socialism: the growth of freedom.

Fifth Act: Catastrophe

PROBLEMS OF MEN

> Profound thoughts arise only in debate,
> with a possibility of counterargument,
> only when there is a possibility of ex-
> pressing not only correct ideas, but also
> dubious ones.
>
> PROFESSOR ANDREI D. SAKHAROV, 1968

Contents

Chronology

January 19

Funeral of Jan Palach

January 20–23

Further protests by immolation: Josef Hlavatý, Plzeň; Miroslav Malinka, Brno; František Bogyi, West Slovak prison; Josef Jareš, Litobór.

February 25

Jan Zajíc, from Šumperk, Northern Moravia, set himself afire on the twenty-first anniversary of the "Victorious February, 1948."

March 28–29

Second Czechoslovak victory over the Soviet Union in World Ice Hockey Championship Competition, Stockholm; anti-Soviet demonstrations occurred throughout Czechoslovakia. Soviet airline Aeroflot office destroyed in Wenceslas Square, Prague.

March 31

Tass circulated *Pravda* article containing criticisms of Czechoslovak press, and attack on Josef Smrkovský as a participant in the Wenceslas Square demonstrations. *Komsomolskaya Pravda* published similar article April 1.

Czechoslovak Ministry of the Interior issued a report on the demonstrations. Serious disturbances occurred in Prague, Usti-on-Elbe, Bratislava and other large towns. Eighty-one windows broken in Soviet troops' barracks in Mladá Boleslav.

Soviet Defense Minister, Marshal Grechko, arrived in Czechoslovakia.

April 2

Czechoslovak Communist Party Presidium statement on the events of March 28 and 29 condemned the "acts of vandalism" and criticised the mass media, including the Party press, for generating "moods which grew into anti-Soviet hysteria." Party weekly *Politika* suspended. Presidium criticized Josef Smrkovský for "certain utterances at variance with the November Resolutions."

Minister-Chairman J. Havelka of the Federal Committee for Press and Information announced the reintroduction of press censorship and measures for reinforcement of Public Security Service.

April 3

Dubček condemned anti-Soviet demonstrations and appealed to population for calm, prudence, and discipline.

April 4

Czech Socialist Party weekly *Zítřek* suspended.

April 5

Executive Committee of the Party Presidium rejected "on principle" the statement of the Czech Journalists' Union.

April 6

Moscow Radio broadcast in Czech attacked the Czech Journalists' Union weekly, *Reportér*.

April 7

Moscow Radio broadcast in Czech attacked the Czech Socialist Party daily, *Svobodné slovo*.

April 8

Josef Vohnout, progressive chairman of the Czech Press and Information Office, replaced by a conservative Communist, Josef Havlín.

April 9

Military Council of the Ministry of National Defense decided to discipline soldiers who took part in the anti-Soviet demonstrations of March 28–29.

April 10

First Secretary Dubček praised the work of the Czechoslovak-Soviet Friendship Society.

April 11

Dr. Gustav Husák, in a speech at Nitra, in Slovakia, criticised the Communist Party leadership for its "lack of consistency, half-heartedness, and lack of unity."

April 12

Prague Radio announced that more Soviet troops would be transferred to Czechoslovakia. Later, Prague Radio announced that the earlier communique "in view of changed circumstances has no foundation."

Czech Trade Union daily *Práce* demanded the right of workers to express "opinions in their paper without fear that the editor will be persecuted."

April 14–16

Warsaw Pact antiaircraft defense exercises held in Poland, Czechoslovakia, and USSR.

April 16

Executive Committee of the Czechoslovak Communist Party Presidium declared that Bilák, Barbírek, Kolder, Piller, Rigo, Švestka, Lenárt, Kapek, Indra, and Jakeš had been "slandered" by allegations of "treason" and "collaboration," and blamed the mass information media.

April 17

At Czechoslovak Communist Party Central Committee plenum, Alexander Dubček resigned, the first secretaryship and was succeeded by Dr. Gustav Husák. New Presidium with eleven members elected. Dubček remained a member, but Smrkovský, Špaček, and other progressives elected to the Presidium in August 1968 were dropped.

Liberté, Egalité, Freundschaft!

(Liberty, Equality, Freundschaft!)
[East Germany's Ulbricht as "Marianne"]

Goliath's Arms * ～～～～～～～～～～～～～～

Ussuri! Ussuri!
New slogan from Prague, 1969

1. The occupation of Czechoslovakia is the expression of a new orientation in Soviet policy. The Soviet Union has achieved a military parity with the United States, has become a global power, and is advancing a new tactic. The global strategy is becoming evident first in the direct neighborhood of the USSR, in Eastern Europe, and on the Sino-Soviet border. But it is also becoming apparent in the Middle East, where the spheres of influence of both superpowers come into direct contact, making any crisis in this area extremely dangerous. The Soviet global strategy, based on the balance of atomic arsenals, is an aggressive, expansive policy which must lead to the same consequences as any other policy of this kind. Munich could not stop Hitler, and no diplomatic negotiation can stop aggressive force through any kind of agreement. If the Soviet Union treats its friend as she treated Czechoslovakia, what will be her dealings with her enemies?

2. The occupation looks like the end of a phase, but actually it is rather the beginning of a new process of change in Eastern Europe and the USSR, a beginning of structural change in Soviet state systems. The occupation stopped the political manifestations of this trend, but did not stop the development of dispositions favoring such change; it deepened the existing crisis of these systems and made reforms visibly imperative. The occupation proved that the structures of these societies are in motion, that a necessity for reform is becoming evident to both the masses and the elites, and that ideological camouflage and police repression are no longer workable as the normal methods of hiding shortcomings. In contrast to conditions in the nineteenth century, when a mere political revolution could cause profound changes, the present

* Lecture at the University of Michigan, Ann Arbor, published in the monthly, *Text*, Munich, in 1969.

economic structure of industrial societies cannot be destroyed at once, even by a successful political coup.

3. Trends toward structural changes in the Eastern Bloc are not caused merely by political crises and conflicts between the political elites of small countries and that of the Soviet superpower. The reason lies much deeper—within the economic and political system. The Soviet economy has become the economy of an advanced industrial state, the economy of a superpower, but essentially it is controlled by the same principles as at the time when no automation, atomic weapons, and computers existed. The necessity of reforming economic methods leads to theoretical disputes among economists as to whether it is enough to make changes in administrative management and in the method of control. The radical critics say the system is so bad that it cannot be repaired, and it is necessary to introduce an operational planning system to control the market as a whole, not the individual relationships within the market. All industrial states are facing similar problems in changing their economy, and the similarity of problems makes plausible those theories that posit the convergence of the economic systems of the West and East. From the viewpoint of economists it is important that both systems are, in an asymptotic way, approaching some kind of "ideal" model of an "optimal" economic system, in which even the problem of the difference between private and state ownership disappears, because ownership itself would be regarded as a set of social functions. From the viewpoint of politics it is important that the convergent trend does not necessarily mean a political rapprochement of the systems, that the convergence is irrelevant vis-à-vis politics, and that on the contrary it may heighten the conflicts or produce new and worse situations.

4. These economic and global political problems cannot be solved within the framework of the old social order because of the obstacle created by the dominant political institution of Soviet Russia—the Communist Party, as the chief force of conservatism and stagnation. Lenin created the Russian Communist Party as an instrument of revolutionary policy, as a party of professional revolutionaries leaning on mass movements, but he did not conceive it as a mechanism which should control a huge industrial economy of the modern state. Stalin's adjustment of the Communist Party to the new tasks (through the liquida-

tion of the old Leninist Party leadership, and through repression against the masses) could not create a system capable of mastering the problems of production and consumption in a modern industrial society, simply because the apparatus of the Party was originally conceived for entirely different social goals—for revolution and for the seizure of power within the state. The unnatural state of affairs was apparent to Khrushchev, but no changes were undertaken. As a result, the Party *de facto* stopped directing the society, and particular interests have become dominant. The Communist Party still claims for itself the leading role within the state, but actually the inflexibility of the regime and the system creates obstacles to its fulfillment of precisely this top decisive function. Czechoslovakia was a good example of how far this crisis went, and a nightmarish example of the risk connected with the reform of Soviet industrial society. Yet the necessity for this reform, which threatens nothing less than the decomposition of the Soviet state, is doubted by only a few.

5. The complexity of these problems caused by progress in technology promotes conflicting situations, based not only on the inability of individual persons, but also on functional changes within the society itself. Hence these problems cannot be solved by exchanging persons within the leadership of the Soviet Politburo. The rigidity and disfunctionality of the system leads by necessity to the birth of particular interests, to splits in the bureaucracy, to the formation of interest groups, and finally to the creation of alternative elites striving for political power. In that respect, Czechoslovakia was an alarming experience. Once the Communist Party reflects group interests, the new political elite is formed. Although its crises resemble rather the revolts of court cabals or the changing of Roman emperors, they create, in connection with generational conflicts, an opposition of intellectuals, and, in connection with nationality problems, an explosive situation of mass protest against the conservative forces of the Party apparatus and against the state bureaucracy. There is a prerevolutionary situation in the Eastern Bloc. *Mutatis mutandis,* its course will be a repetition of the Prague Spring of 1968.

6. The problems arising from structural change in Soviet society are new and without analogy. They generate new types of revolutionary and democratic transformation processes for which at least three char-

acteristics are decisive: a) a movement for a structural reform—regardless of whether it is called a democratization, a revolutionary movement or a reform movement—takes place in the form of a wave of changes combining "revolution," invasion, and "counterrevolution," reforms, occupation, and normalization, violent confrontation, resistance, and nonviolent activities; b) The movement itself shows a number of ambivalent features; their common program is the defense of human rights within modern society, an awareness of the necessity of reforming structures, and a new awareness that the power elites of Communist parties fail as the leading force of the society; c) The transformation is taking place within the framework of the given system of values, within the framework of the given ideology, as a revival of socialist democracy; the crisis in modern society creates objective opportunities for a new revolutionary process, for a mass opposition against totalitarian dictatorship in the USSR.

7. The future democratic movement for structural reforms, human rights, and humanistic socialism in the USSR has several specific features rooted in the history of Russia. The Soviet state totally disregards the fundamental human rights and freedoms. The Czechoslovak experiment therefore cannot be repeated as a program of socialist democracy, simply because the power elites of a totalitarian dictatorship must oppose democratization if they know where it leads. Any popular reform movement is unacceptable for the Soviet power elite, because the participation of people as a moving force in the formation of a historical process heralds the end of an elitist approach toward the masses. It means the end of this elite, the end of the given structure. The present Soviet leadership cannot allow any kind of democratization, because it knows that the crisis would be a big-power crisis and a world crisis.

8. Unfortunately, it seems that the generals will use these trends toward a protest and toward structural change for an old solution— that of Bonapartism. The elite of the Party bureaucracy, industrial technocracy, and the military establishment, leaders in industry, the state apparatus, and the army represent the same forces which have always been in the background of any totalitarian dictatorship. Differences between the interests of technocrats and those of the military within this dark coalition give us a certain hope that small things can cause an unexpected avalanche. Those who under these circumstances

do not understand the tremendous increase in the real danger of Soviet expansion and rely on reducing the tension through an agreement on spheres of influence will become victims of their own retreat.

9. The Soviet technocracy would like to replace militaristic expansion with a program for a consumer society of the Western type, overcoming its economic difficulties by means of an integration of the Eastern Bloc. This real alternative is unfortunately dangerous for Eastern Europe, because there are no forces in the world willing to oppose this program. The Soviet technocracy is well aware of the fact that the ideological goals of communism are only a mask for the growth of a tsarist empire. It knows that Soviet communism is dead and that a real power ascendancy for Russia depends directly on the retreat of the revolutionary ideology. The technocracy reasons in nonideological terms. It thinks about its domination realistically. A system of efficient exploitation and police repression, a state monopoly with a ruling class that carries on the tradition of tsarist ambition—this is the alternative appearing on the Soviet horizon of the seventies.

10. After the failed experiment of Communist intellectuals, we have to realize that people in Czechoslovakia are waiting for Godot, who is not coming. The game of socialist democracy is stalemated. No solution for the Czechoslovak stalemate can be found just now, and it would be futile to try to find one. Just as the program of democratization collapsed as a result of external causes, any improvement in the internal situation of Czechoslovakia can be brought about by external changes only. Who will play the actual role of stalemated king is more or less irrelevant, and the differences among all who may play the king will soon become negligible. A nuclear stalemate between the two great powers, a stalemate in the divided world and Europe, a stalemate in Berlin separated by a wall, and another "family stalemate" between the power elites in socialist states—these are too many negative factors, excluding any guarantee of stability for the 1970's. After the current wave of conservatism and technocratism now prevailing in the politics of both superpowers, Europe will be united under an independent European, humanistic, and socialist policy. Not even then will Godot arrive. However, the absurd game of power elites in totalitarian dictatorships will end.

David and Goliath

The eleventh commandment:
There are moments
There are hours between horror
And the last straw of truth
When you have to hate your neighbor
And you even have to kill him.
　　—JAN DAVID, "*Hands of Goliath*."
　　(Verses of an unknown writer in
　　Czechoslovakia, made public
　　after the Soviet invasion.)

1. In 1967, Czechoslovakia was a Stalinist totalitarian dictatorship; it will be the same in 1969, because no radical change is possible without basic changes in Stalinist institutions. A totalitarian dictatorship can be mild or tough, its politicians can be narrow-minded or bright, its economy can be good or bad—but under all circumstances it totally excludes the participation of the working class and the people in political decisions. The system of any ruling totalitarian party is a Stalinist system of executing political power, and this system cannot be "democratized," it can only be destroyed.

2. Neo-Stalinism is incompatible with the program of liberation of the working class, since only the working class itself can achieve its liberation. This can be accomplished by neither intellectuals nor revolutionaries, nor technocrats. The liberation of the working class can only be an act of this very class itself; it cannot be accomplished by the state or the Party. This was Marx's basic idea, and any retreat from his concept leads to a wrong path, that of despotic dictatorship. Although the role of the working class has changed in the course of modern history (any messianism is unjustified), the working class and its alliance with the intelligentsia nevertheless represent the major political force capable of carrying out a democratic program of structural changes.

3. The occupation of Czechoslovakia has revealed a new stage of development in the anti-Marxist policy of the Soviet power elite: an openly declared subordination of local power elites in East European colonies to the central power in Moscow, confirmed legally by an international treaty. The Soviet leaders have now instituted, as the basic principle of the "socialist commonwealth," the right of the

stronger power elite to intervene. This new Soviet attitude is a projection of the theory of the leading role of the Party, a projection of the theory of power elites into relations between nations. Both theoretically and practically this is a new phenomenon.

4. The Soviet Union has become a neocolonialist, imperialist world power; the situation has ripened for a new type of anticolonial revolt of nations. The occupation had not been ordered by primitive politicians as a miscalculated strategic operation based on false assumptions and lacking a political plan or any predetermined objectives. On the contrary, the occupation was a perfectly executed neocolonialist plan, another successful imperialist offensive, and a warning to potential opposition forces inside the Soviet Union.

5. The democratization movement in Czechoslovakia served as a proof that a spontaneous popular movement and a people's unity could force a regime to adopt more liberal attitudes and carry out reforms in the interest of the people. Communist Party leaders everywhere will be widely supported, if they decide—partly in response to the pressure of economic difficulties—to reform the Stalinist dictatorship on the basis of humanism and of socialist democracy. The Czechoslovak way has shown the Soviet people the only alternative to imperialism and oppression.

6. Industrial society has been developing at such a tremendous pace that none of the social systems can remain intact. If states want to respond to this dynamic modern economy, they have to conform to this trend regardless of the attempts made by power elites to retain the repressive system unchanged. The need for basic structural changes becomes more acute, and for a sociologist more urgent, the more the power elite tries to prevent any structural reforms, the more it relies on a routine response to deal with emergency situations, and the less capable it is of seeing individual events in a broader social context. The Soviet power elite does its best to create an explosive situation in its own country and to sharpen the potential conflicts between the industrial system and the repressive political mechanism.

7. The tension in the relationship between the economic structure and the political system is further sharpened by the national problem. More than half of the Soviet Union's population is non-Russian; it is ruled, however, with a tough centralist hand from Moscow. Although

a system of federal political power and a program of decentralization could easily solve the problem without any prejudice to the power, the prestige, and the territorial integrity of the state, such a program under the existing totalitarian system would be considered as something too risky to be attempted. The Soviet power elite is fully aware that such a program would not only mean the end of its rule but the disintegration of the Soviet state as well. The new Brezhnev Doctrine represents a deepening of the national problem in the Soviet Union; the camouflaged incorporation of Eastern Europe into the Soviet sphere of control will further magnify this principal problem of Russia.

8. Finally, within the Soviet power elite itself, there is a growing tension between the Party bureaucracy and the young technocrats, similar to the conflicts between the military and the intellectuals, writers and scientists. The conflicts within the bureaucratic dictatorship are growing and the new technical intelligentsia rightly considers the Party bureaucracy as an obstacle and as a parasitic group. Thus the main social trends sharpen the controversy within the Soviet power elite and make it more vulnerable. At the same time, these trends make democratic reforms inevitable. Achilles has his vulnerable heel, and the faster he runs, the better we can see it.

9. Both revolutionary theory and the philosophy of freedom will have to resolve a new and unique phenomenon, namely the changes in motivation of politically active social classes. Neither in Paris nor in Prague had the students and workers submitted materialistic demands only. They were more in favor of a "moral integrity," of finding their proper identity and overcoming defects in the structure of the industrial consumer society, defects which can not be drowned out by the noise of increasing production and consumption. The experience of Prague and Paris can be interpreted as a revolt against alienation, as a revolt in the name of human rights, as an attempt of alienated masses to build a new political alliance in order to transform the society as such, as a recognition that only by structural changes can modern society rid itself of its faults and difficulties.

10. David's wisdom in his fight with Goliath was his choice of arms that enabled him to use his superiority. All power elites, both in Czechoslovakia and in Russia, are vulnerable in any fight in which they cannot take advantage of their strength—i.e., of their organization of

the totalitarian system as the highest form of social repression. They are vulnerable in any fight in which they are exposed to the superior spontaneity, activity, and courage of the people. It is here that the elite fails, because it follows its own theory, according to which political activity is the privilege of a limited number of citizens. The populaton at large is condemned to the status of a second-rate, anonymous, silent mob.

11. Any political theory based on the dialectic contradiction of an elite and a mob, on an unchecked rule of leaders, is unsound. Power elites are slaves of their contempt for people to such an extent that they sincerely consider any manifestation of the people's will and any dissent as rebellion, indeed as counterrevolution. In their belief that revolution as well as counterrevolution is "produced," the power elites look for the nonexistent "producers" of coups d'état everywhere but in the creativity of people.

12. The more perfect the repressive system of a totalitarian dictatorship is, the more it is dependent on smooth coordination of all its parts, and the more vulnerable it becomes. The failure of a part may lead to a total failure. Therefore, the better we know the mechanism of a totalitarian dictatorship, the sooner we recognize its vulnerability, the easier it will be for the future democratic left to apply the superiority of democratic, popular revolution against the power of a modern state. And at the moment that the self-assured Goliath first sees the sling in a boy's hand, he will not realize that he is facing death.

13. History creates its personalities, including Goliath and David, who appear on the stage at crucial moments as if they were actors in a perfectly produced drama. The David of tomorrow may still study at Charles University, trapped by the occupation, confused by its absurdity, trying to understand the world, the people, and political systems. He may seem to be a little peculiar, but he is bright and he thinks. In ten years he will pull out his sling.

The Policy of Truth * ∽∽∽∽∽∽∽∽∽∽

> Comrades, in the system which has crys-
> tallized and stabilized itself in the course
> of the past 50 years and which to a cer-
> tain extent has gradually accepted changes
> and compromises, yet in substance re-
> mained firm, we are now experiencing
> *revolutionary changes, a revolutionary*
> *turn. Our party, our society, seeks another*
> *political system, the opposite of the polit-*
> *ical system that we have had so far.*
> GUSTÁV HUSÁK, *Spring, 1968*

1. The truth is the most dangerous enemy of any totalitarian dictatorship, and the lie, on the contrary, is its constant ally, because the absolute power of the bureaucratic elite is possible only thanks to misin-
formation about the conditions in which people live. *The policy of*
truth is therefore the most effective and most simple weapon against
the power elite, which must persecute the truth in a frenzy hardly
understandable to a Westerner but quite obvious to everybody who
knows that merely spreading truthful information destroys one of the
pillars of the power elite, because it destroys the lie about given conditions. The truth discloses that ideologies simply gamble with human
hope. For that, the truth is hated by all who regard it as a function of
power, who believe that truth is made. One cannot reach truth through
lying.

2. Stalinist Communists do not believe in the truth in politics. They
believe in historical laws which justify their lies. They believe in a
history which is to create a future which justifies everything, even the
occupation of their own country. Their functional lie is a "higher
truth" of history with which they identify themselves in the same
naive belief with which they blame the anonymity of a historical necessity, and *not themselves* for crimes, wars, occupation, and genocide.

*Lecture at the University of Miami, Florida; published in the bimonthly,
Svědectví, Paris, in 1969.

The faith in history as a sequence of predestined situations governed by laws is a faith in fate, in a modern kismet which makes them aggressive. Contrary to Marx, Brezhnevs and Husáks do not understand that freedom is the primary and fundamental need of man and that man creates history.

3. If, however, mankind is merely a function of historical necessities (laws), then man is just an instrument of a historical process manipulated by the apparatus of the Communist parties, an object without rights. On this point the Communist ideology contradicts the most revolutionary thoughts of modern times—the idea of natural, inalienable human rights. Man, as man, possesses certain rights. They are rooted in the human substance. They are *a priori* rights and are not derived from the state, God, or historical necessity. *Man can revolt against any kind of power in the interest of his natural human rights.* Human rights are an inalienable prerogative of man. They are valid always and unconditionally. They are also valid against the state, which cannot limit them by any legal act; it can limit them only through violence. In contrast to this unique and wonderful idea of human freedom, which molded the whole of European culture, any faith in historical destiny is a Byzantine conservative superstition of the heirs of tsarism. The best thoughts in the democratization process of the Prague Spring of 1968 were based on the tradition of truth, freedom, and human rights. What are their prospects today?

4. The Soviet occupation was the beginning of the disintegration of the reform wing of the Communist Party, *which adopted the self-destructive tactics of concessions to the occupants*, in the belief that by so doing they could save democratization. In the process of making ever more substantial concessions the reform wing disintegrated, lost the main functions within the Party and the state, and instead of bargaining hard it did the worst: it legalized the occupation, liquidated basic liberties, suppressed independent organizations, introduced censorship, eliminated the press, and atomized opposition groups. As a result of these catastrophic tactics the occupation power managed to achieve everything—in a bloodless way to be sure—that nations usually give up only unwillingly and after being defeated in war. In all truth, we have to state that the catastrophic decisions were made under the leadership of the soft-spoken and pleasant looking Alexander Dubček, not

by the "iron chancellor" and gloomy-looking "federalissimo" Gustav Adolf Husák.

5. The legalization of the occupation under Dubček's leadership and the introduction of a neo-Stalinist "Fascistoid" dictatorship are the more embarrassing considering the fact that, since the intervention, *the bureaucratic elite of the Communist apparatus had tried without cessation to break the neck of the popular movement* that had spontaneously helped the reform wing. Three big waves of popular resistance, in November, 1968 (after the fiftieth anniversary of the Czechoslovak Republic and during the student strike), in January, 1969 (the funeral of Jan Palach), and in March, 1969 (the hockey victory), were used by the power elite to keep aloof from the population and to stab in the back any action in support of the reform policy. The Communist bureaucracy managed to perpetrate a masterful fraud against human trust by making not the slightest attempt to resist the occupation power, in order to enhance the nation's wonderful unity. On the contrary, under very favorable international conditions the Communist elite rendered invaluable services to the comradely power elite of the USSR: it prevented the United Nations from taking up the occupation; it prevented the subject of the occupation from appearing on the agenda of the next conference of Communist parties; and it forced organs of the Czechoslovak state to legalize the occupation.

6. After the new general secretary was installed it was only logical that an *ex post* approval would then be given to the occupation, a new intervention prepared, and an open policy of armed and police repression introduced. To be fair, Husák inherited mistakes he was not guilty of. Regardless of the changing officials, the Party apparatus of the Communists was successful in surviving the crisis, consolidating the monopolistic dictatorship through purges, and preventing substantial political and economic reforms. This was achieved, of course, because *the crisis of the Communist apparatus turned into a crisis of both nations, into a general crisis of monopolistic socialism.* The apparatus achieved this only with the help of tanks and at an excessively high cost. The leadership of the Party has become a leadership composed of collaborators, traitors, occupants, and fascist opportunists. Anybody who ever expects anything else of the power elite of a monopolistic dictatorship must forget the old truth that power elites cannot trespass

(208)

the limits of their interests, and that a democratization managed by technocrats, bureaucrats, and *apparatchiks* has always been, and always will be, in the wrong hands.

7. The policy of a synthesis of freedom, socialism, and sovereignty, which regarded truth, freedom, and human rights as an inalienable heritage of European culture, a policy of the synthesis of democracy, socialism, and humanism, was destroyed in a single year by the same people who had brought it to life. It did not fail because it was wrong, but because bureaucrats and technocrats are incapable of leading a popular movement or of leaning on people in a time of crisis. *The monopolistic bureaucracy of the totalitarian dictatorship is unable to make a democratic revolution within socialism, is uncapable of continuing to develop the socialist revolution, and cannot transgress its class confines as a privileged caste ruling over a people with no rights.* It cannot do it even if it tries sincerely and hard. Only a popular, democratic movement based on a community of interest between workers and the intelligentsia can continue to develop a revolution through the democratization of the given social structure. Such a movement must be independent vis-à-vis the power elite of the totalitarian dictatorship and its technocratic mentality, and it must be free of the fateful illusion held by some Czech statesmen that they can reconcile the West with the East, the Soviet Union with Europe.

8. The policy of freedom, socialism, and sovereignty will emerge on the Czechoslovak horizon immediately, whenever new alternatives are created by the international situation. The seventies will be very propitious in this respect, because the USSR will enter into a period characterized by a general crisis of her Stalinist institutions, a crisis aggravated by the growing difficulties of her neocolonialism and her expansive militarism preparing for a preventive war against China. The distance between the Soviet regime and Marx's socialism is great. This distance is as great, in fact, as the distance between the Soviet regime and Marx's definition of an oriental despotism is short. This variety of despotism was based on the so-called Asiatic method of production, in which state ownership is not coupled with a classless society, but with the terror imposed by the elite and its despotic government, and in which social ownership is replaced by state ownership. The Soviet Union is in a prerevolutionary situation. Her response to growing social

requirements is an increased aggressiveness by her generals, new concentration camps, new trials, and neo-Stalinism.

9. The Kremlin harbors no inhibition concerning a preventive war against China because there is no power in the USSR which could prevent the generals from deciding to destroy Chinese atomic installations in Sinkiang. The Brezhnev Doctrine justified the future intervention *a priori*. The Soviet general staff did not hesitate to launch a *blitzkrieg* against Czechoslovakia, where no Soviet territory was in danger. It is a matter of common sense to see that an atomic *blitzkrieg* against China is near. Preventive wars have always been popular with bankrupt political cliques. *The bombs which soon will be dropped on Lop Nor will surprise only those politicians who suffer from incorrigible illusions as to the death of Stalinism.*

10. There is a future for the policy of freedom, sovereignty, and socialism in Czechoslovakia and Eastern Europe whenever, in the seventies, Western Europe begins to represent an independent economic and military power capable of coping with the neocolonial aggression of the USSR. The Soviet Union, preoccupied with the problem of China, will be unable to control Eastern Europe forever. The modern industrial society itself generates the need for a democratization of the state economic structure and of political decision-making. One may expect with justification that *the present Czechoslovak crisis is just a symptom of a general crisis of monopolistic socialism, including that in the Soviet Union.* History does not repeat itself and time is irreversible. There will not be another Prague Spring in 1978, but what will happen by 1978 will be much more revolutionary than we can imagine today. Surrealism has moved from art into politics, and the fantasies of Salvatore Dali fade, when they are confronted with the reality of Soviet neo-Stalinism.

11. A respect for hard fact is one of the good qualities of scientists. One of the least appreciated but most important facts of present-day Eastern Europe is the fact that the Chinese People's Republic is also a power factor of prime importance in that area. If anybody saves Rumanian independence it will not be the American President, but the huge Chinese army poised on the Soviet frontier. If anybody can soften the trend by which Czechoslovakia is being transformed into a Russian province, it will be the warning of Radio Peking against the Soviet fas-

cist oppression of Czechoslovakia, rather than the United States' eager-
ness for negotiation with the USSR. Ten years ago, Albanian policy
seemed to be ridiculous and five years ago Rumanian policy seemed insignificant. Will East European politicians be forced by an unholy
Soviet-American alliance to regard China as a possible ally in securing
the independence of small nations?

12. The Czechoslovak democratization died of the illusion that the
USSR would keep her solemn declarations about national independence,
state sovereignty, and equality among Communist parties. What an
irony of history to see a repetition in Prague of a similar situation to
that of February, 1948, when the non-Communist politicians expected
that Communists would act according to democratic rules. They were
astounded when Communists acted like Communists. Czechoslovak politicians in 1968 were astounded in a similar way when they were kid-
napped and taken to Moscow, and when they discovered that gangsters act like gangsters. Illusions in politics are deadly dangerous. Only
dead illusions are good. The death of an illusion about Soviet Communism is the positive result of the Czechoslovak experiment.

The Extremism of Truth

What is truth?
PONTIUS PILATE

1. Truth is the criterion of science. But what is truth in politics? Was
the Russian Revolution of 1905 a defeat for the Bolsheviks, a prologue
to their victory, or a compromise between the tsar and the liberals?
Was the Prague Spring of 1968 a defeat for the reform movement, a
victory for an ideology of revolt, a compromise by power elites, or all
of them mixed together? We still do not know who has won and
whether the boomerang of events will not destroy the one who threw
it. Only if we exclude particular viewpoints in favor of indisputable
facts are we able to come nearer to the truth. Indisputable remain the
goals of the Action Program of the Communist Party of Czechoslovakia, the actual results of this program, and the historical lessons
which can be derived from a confrontation of the promises contained
in the program with the actual results of the Prague Spring.

2. The result of the program of socialism with a human face is a

total bankruptcy, a total collapse of the goals of structural reforms, of socialistic democracy, of Marxist humanism, and of the movement for civil and human rights. If we accept its practice as a criterion of the truth of the political movement we have to admit that the "revisionist" interpretation of Marxism failed completely because it neglected the power factors of the military blocs and the division of the world, and because it wanted to achieve political change merely by ideological postulates. The attempt to change the oppressive character of the dictatorship, the attempt to return to the European concept of Marxism and to Europeanize socialism ended in a great European crisis in which numbers of mechanized divisions were the triumphant political argument. This argument could again be used in a move to destroy Europe.

3. The bankruptcy of the program of the Communist Party turned into a national bankruptcy because the Communist Party, which held, and still holds, the monopoly of power, transformed itself into an oppressive mechanism without any popular base, into an antinational power apparatus in the service of the occupation forces. The Communist Party has the total responsibility, not only for establishing totalitarian dictatorship in a democratic Czechoslovakia, for the Sovietization of its European culture, and the subsequent debacle of its economy, but also for Czechoslovakia's occupation and transformation into a Soviet protectorate, its waning sovereignty, and its integration into the neo-colonial Soviet Bloc. Any politician who might try, in the future, to collaborate with Communist power elites must take into account the possible long-range effect of such action—the Soviet occupation of his own country.

4. The bankruptcy of the Czechoslovak experiment cannot be explained merely by the ineffectiveness of the Communist Party and the local degeneration of a power elite. It also means the collapse of the theoretical-ideological concept on which the experiment was based. It means the collapse of "revisionism," and a victory for the elitist version of "Panzer-Marxism," operating as the power apparatus of a military-administrative superpower complex. The "Panzer-Marxism" of the technocratic Eastern European elites has degenerated into an open ideology of aggression and exploitation, which does not even have to pretend that it pursues social justice and advocates broader freedoms as

its revolutionary ideal. Authentic Marxism has become incompatible with the theory and practice of Communist parties. Whoever wishes to be a Marxist cannot be a member of the Communist Party.

5. What kind of lesson should we draw from the confrontation of the noble goals of socialist democracy with the cruel reality of the result—with the Soviet occupation? The program of structural reform within industrial society, the program of transforming a totalitarian dictatorship into a direct democracy of producers is *the most significant political idea of our time*. However, if structural change keeps the power elite intact, no managerial technocracy, not even the most successful one, can lead human society out of its crisis. A Jenghiz Khan coupled with a computer is still a Jenghiz Khan. Structural changes in an industrial state-capitalistic society are incompatible with managerial technocracy, just as a socialistic democracy is incompatible with elitism of any kind, simply because there is no socialism or democracy without fundamental civil rights. Is then a socialist democracy possible?

6. A socialist democracy is possible only as it arises from a community of interest between the workers and the intelligentsia, as a system of permanent and effective control over the power elite, as a direct democracy in which creativeness is the guarantee of permanent change, as a permanent transformation of industrial society which fosters its development into a society with broader freedoms. Socialist democracy is impossible as a power monopoly by the apparatus of any political party, simply because a power monopoly requires an elitist approach to the masses of citizens. Because the masses are regarded as objects of manipulation, the basic prerequisites for socialism as well as for democracy are ruled out. The Communist power elite will never accept socialist democracy and its pluralistic political system—unless a built-in system were to prevent the free play of political forces. This boils down to the unwillingness of this elite ever to give up its power.

7. The mutating Stalinists of the state monopolistic system were, are, and will be unable—intellectually or practically—to fulfill their promises and take their own programs seriously. They do not know any other way of ruling than by power, censorship, police, and tanks because they are afraid of independent acts by their own people and their own intelligentsia. As soon as the intelligentsia steps beyond the horizon

of any elitism, as soon as it passes the threshold of power-elite interests, it gains the support of the masses, but tanks and police start to operate. In the future, the intelligentsia must create its own variant form of socialist democracy; it must know that revolutionary processes, like wars, begin where the previous one comes to an end. The revolutionary process of tomorrow will begin as a movement for the unity of workers and the intelligentsia, for human rights and socialist democracy—against the apparatus of the totalitarian dictatorship. The leaders of this revolutionary process must be aware of the fact that any concession to the apparatus of the elite is a fateful error.

8. Some questions remain to be answered. Was it possible to carry out a structural reform of the totalitarian system in a democratic way? Was the effort of combining socialism and democracy an attempt to square the circle? Is it possible to democratize the Soviet system, the Communist Party, and Soviet power? Was the Czechoslovak experiment a dead-end street for European, democratic, and humanistic thinking in an era characterized by a new apportionment of the world? Was it an archaic illusion in an era of three superimperialisms? The truth will be revealed by history only. And while the skeptical Pilate shrugs his shoulders to permit the crucifixion of salutary ideas, two small nations will also be dying, crucified on the Soviet-American agreement regarding the globe as a property of the elites. The truth of socialism with a human face is dying in pain.

9. The Czechoslovak experiment foundered on its own paradoxes—on the bizarre role assumed by the Communist Party, which tried to act in the guise of a democratic organization, on the naive belief of the power elite that its adversaries could be drowned peacefully in a wave of popular enthusiasm for democracy, and on the clash between the illusion of Marxist humanism and the reality of mechanized divisions. Division commanders are the final interpreters of the meaning of Soviet Communism, regardless of the changing emotions of the leading politicians of a small country, regardless of their uniformly gay or somber faces, and regardless of whether they regard the Soviet Politburo as benefactors or as a bunch of gangsters.

10. The Czechoslovak experiment foundered on its effort to accomplish the impossible: the Europeanization of Russia and the humaniza-

tion of Soviet Communism. With the full knowledge of our defeat, we have to continue our work because the challenge of Marxism as a philosophy of truth lies here. Whoever may try to accomplish this task will encounter the same fools who said of Confucius: "This is the one who knows it cannot be done but still does it."

The Truth about the Occupation[*] ✌✌✌✌

> *We have the preconditions for raising society to a higher level of socialism.* And we are sure that what we are doing will set an example for the comrades in other socialist countries who term what we are doing a great experiment. *We think it is a project, a deliberate project, which hitherto has not been carried out by any socialist society.*
>
> JOSEF SMRKOVSKÝ, *Spring, 1968*

1. A year ago, the first secretary of the Communist Party of Czechoslovakia was a beloved national hero. Today, the first secretary of the same institution is the most hated of collaborators, collaborator number one. *Time, the most demoniac of categories in politics,* has transformed the Czechoslovak social scene to such an extent, in the course of a single year, that the most skeptical of pessimists have been surpassed in their estimates of how low the Communist Party apparatus could fall, and how base the power elite of a totalitarian dictatorship could be. The unimaginable has become reality: the Soviet intervention was legalized, and approved *ex post*, and its first anniversary is to be celebrated by organizing its even more successful repetition—by the same party which was the hope of the majority of the nation a year ago.

2. Soviet occupation brought a number of significant changes in political life, in social structure, and in the consciousness of people. All the changes resulted from the organic weakness of the occupation regime and its representatives, and they are a proof *that the occupation did not arrest the growth of the resistance against the totalitarian dictatorship and that, on the contrary, it turned the resistance into a mass movement.* The occupation did not stop the trend toward structural reform in the East-European regimes. It only built an obstacle on the road to reforms and made social conditions far more explosive than in

[*] Lecture at the University of Virginia, Richmond; published in *Die Presse*, Vienna, August 21, 1969.

1967. It is clear today to both the power elite and the occupied people that the system must rot right down to its foundations and that it cannot be saved through reforms. The power elite of the totalitarian dictatorship are organizing their own extinction. We congratulate them.

3. When the Communist Party lost its mass base, its core—the power elite of the apparatus—transformed itself into an instrument of occupation, collaboration, and normalization, into a gangster club which can seek its power only in the police. The strongest European Communist Party, with almost two million members, ends up in a total isolation of its leadership which cannot rely either on the nation or on its members, but only on the occupation tanks. *In any new crisis of the regime the power elite of the Communist Party will seek support in a militaristic intervention by foreign troops.* In doing so it will change the character of its rule and the character of the Communist Party: the political leadership of the state takes on the role of an apparatus collaborating with the occupation power. The Communist Party changes into a party of the neofascist, neo-Stalinist type. The highest stage of Stalinist Communism is fascism.

4. The Communist Party sank into its deepest crisis, from which there is no exit, because the efforts of the leadership to normalize the situation are precisely the efforts that deprive it of the trust of even its own Party members. The collaborationist, antinational, and occupation nature of the system, which is based on a totalitarian dictatorship by the monopolistic bureaucracy, becomes so evident that no lies and no ideological camouflage can hide the repressive militaristic-fascist police character of the regime. *The total crisis of the Communist elite becomes a total crisis of the neo-Stalinist dictatorship*, the existence of which now depends exclusively on the armed intervention of the occupiers, an intervention which the power elite itself must organize. The militaristically oriented police dictatorship is the immediate executor of Soviet power in the province entrusted to it, and the system's policy is now (and in the future will be even more) based on the primitive mentality of the power realists; from now on, only the armored divisions of the occupiers guarantee their monopolistic power.

5. By a kind of diabolical and malicious dialectic, this bankruptcy of the Communist Party elite creates favorable conditions for a democratic change in the area of socialism, and for the defeat of this power

elite in the future crisis of the seventies. Precisely the dead-end situation to which the Communist power elite has condemned itself brings to life new political trends. *In the future, a revolt against the violence of the technocrats' and bureaucrats' managerial socialism is not only possible, but even realistic and necessary. The dead-end situation provides the exit.* A year ago, only a handful of intellectuals understood *that the only chance of saving democratization was to promote its development from below, in opposition to the monopoly held by the technocratic Party bureaucracy, not in cooperation with it.* It is clear today that the future belongs to a democratic revolution based on socialism. The incompetence of the conservative power elites, who are corrupted by power, deception, and personal rivalries, has, by radicalizing the masses, prepared the way for a revolutionary solution. A year ago, the intelligentsia was radical. Today, the radicalization of the working class creates a much more explosive situation.

6. The degeneration of the Communist apparatus and the repressive nature of the totalitarian dictatorship is not merely a result of political errors and tactical clumsiness. A hardening of the dictatorship is indispensable for economic reasons. A drastically deteriorated standard of living is only a secondary phenomenon, in view of the chronic and unremovable defect in the production relations of the monopolistic bureaucratic system of managerial socialism. Everywhere in Eastern Europe stagnant consumption faces an insoluble contradiction in regard to the development of production. The social contradictions brought about by the system of monopolistic bureaucracy cannot be solved within the system of monopolistic bureaucracy. A prerevolutionary situation is created vis-à-vis social conditions themselves—not only in the consciousness of people; this situation cannot be resolved by the neo-Stalinist dialectics of the *nagaika* and *tschabaika.**

7. The occupation of Czechoslovakia initiated *a period of general crisis for monopolistic socialism* in Eastern Europe. There is no exit from this situation, because the road to reforms was rejected by Mos-

---

* *Nagaika:* Russian whip. *Tschabaika:* popular salami sausage. "The dialectic of the *nagaika* and *tschabaika*" is an allusion to the policy of Napoleon III, "Vive les saucissons!" and to Bismarck's policy of "the sugar and the whip." Both were aimed at destroying the morale of the workers through simultaneous bribery and repression.—Ed.

cow. Willy-nilly, the power elite of the Czechoslovak state will become trapped in the fundamental contradiction of the system, the growing demand for consumer goods and the stagnation in production. The militaristic and imperialistic direction of production will increasingly limit the existing consumption level. The devastating contradictions of monopolistic socialism must lead to a repressive policy against the working class and the majority of the population, simply because, within the system of monopolistic socialism, the power elite must manipulate manpower just as it manipulates any other production resource. Through police repression it must ensure the docility of the labor force.

8. The political bankruptcy of the Communist Party and the general crisis of the monopolistic bureaucracy's totalitarian dictatorship offer an excellent prospect to democratic socialism in the seventies. In the first place, the great majority of Czechs and Slovaks knows today that twenty years of violence produced no advantage at all, that Communism threw both nations backward and caused a general and total bankruptcy. Still, before the occupation some might have believed that the limitation of personal freedom was compensated by an economic development. Today, we know that *the loss of freedom has been and will be an absolute step backward.* Whenever basic human rights are endangered the society as a whole is the loser regardless of whether the graphs of national income rise or fall. Any power will degenerate if citizens lack their basic civil and human rights.

9. Another basic experience of both nations—an experience which cannot be erased from the mind of two generations—is the knowledge of the surprising weakness of the totalitarian dictatorships' repressive apparatus in a crisis situation, when the most perfect systems crumble almost overnight. *In the critical year of 1968, the Czech and Slovak people solved one of the most difficult riddles of modern history: how to disintegrate a totalitarian dictatorship through internal forces generated by a community of interest between workers and the intelligentsia, and through the unity of a nation opposed to the power elite.* The Czech and Slovak people have learned where the Achilles' heel of a bureaucratic police dictatorship is located, but they have also experienced six thousand tanks riding against two thousand words. Will

Brezhnev send three tanks for every word of protest when Brother Mao commences to aid him against revisionism, as Brezhnev aided Dubček, with an armed intervention?

10. Victorious revolutions begin where defeated revolts end. In this way the historical cycle is closed by the constantly renewed struggle for broader freedoms. *During the days of occupation, the democratization process ended with the proclamation of a slogan calling for a neutral, socialist Czechoslovakia. This is a correct slogan, the only alternative protecting Czechoslovakia against becoming a Russian province of the Soviet neocolonial empire.* A neutral Czechoslovak socialist republic with a democratic political order, a neutral, sovereign state with a foreign policy independent of any bloc seems to the realistic power holders today as chimerical as democratization seemed to them under Stalinism. The policy of the status quo is always the worst policy.

11. Two European nations [the Czechs and the Slovaks] have proved that they have had enough of the dialectics of the Russian whip and that they were ripe for neutrality, democracy, and socialism. But they also know well that their problems are part of the larger power game of European and world politics. *To retreat is not shameful, but it is shameful to give up.* The small mongoose defeats the much stronger snake by retreating repeatedly and attacking at the moment that is fatal for the snake. When the mongoose faces two snakes, the snake of a totalitarian dictatorship and the snake of an occupation army, it must retreat until it can accomplish a deadly attack on one enemy at a time. This it will do unless both snakes destroy themselves in a fratricidal struggle for the purity of Communism.

The Trip to the Moon * ∾∾∾∾∾∾∾∾

The Soviet revisionist clique is like a
notorious prostitute who insists on having
a monument erected to her chastity.
—Radio Peking, 1969

A unique historical event took place in the heart of Europe in 1968:
the Czechoslovak Democratic Revolution based on a socialist society,
a revolution following the best traditions of the Paris Commune, the
Russian Socialist Revolution, and the Hungarian uprising. More precisely, only the first stage of this revolution against the bureaucratic
police dictatorship took place. This was the phase which began as only
an intellectual revolution and as an overture to the transformation of
the system, but which, just before the occupation, grew into a revolutionary movement calling for a radical structural change in Stalinist
institutions. The democratic revolution of the Czechs and Slovaks
strove for a structural reform of the modern Eastern type of industrial
society ("socialist" society) and achieved an almost incredible thing
in proving that after a twenty-year-long, intensive repression there still
existed in the bureaucratic police state revolutionary forces capable
of an offensive action.

To the Czechs and Slovaks the problem of whether a revolution is
possible in a modern industrial society equals the question of whether
it is possible to land on the moon, at the time that the astronauts are
already on their way back to Earth. The landing on the moon has
become a historical reality. We need no speculative analyses as to
whether the moon trip is possible. Likewise, after the Czechoslovak
Democratic Revolution based on a modern industrial society there is
no need for analyzing the historical facts of the dizzy flight of two
small European nations to a broader freedom. If then somebody asks
whether a revolution is possible in a modern society we may answer

* Contribution, International Dialogue Committee, first meeting, on "The Possibility and Impossibility of Revolution in Modern Industrial Society," Vienna,
July 21-26, 1969; published in the monthly *Forum-Dialog*, Vienna, in 1970.

without reservation: yes, such a revolution is possible and realistic, and it can be successful. Its course revealed several basic facts which probably do not apply to the Eastern type of society only. However, here we are concerned only with the positive and negative experiences of democratic revolution in the Eastern type of industrial society ("socialist" society).

Experience 1 The character of the revolution differs basically from that of previous known revolutions, especially in three points:

a) The revolution is not just a political change. It is understood as being a radical structural change of the system, as a transformation of the social order, combining revolution and reform, its course being a sequence of revolutionary reforms, not merely a change of persons or of parties in power.

b) The revolution is seen as more than a short-lived process. It is a permanent revolution, a sequence of changes requiring a long period of time and a long, or possibly permanent, effort by a democratic, revolutionary movement which is not an opposition within the system, but an opposition against the system.

c) The revolution does not take place as a change in the political orientation of the state or a change in the program of the government (although it includes both these points), but as a mass performance by spontaneous groups, quickly realizing that their problems can not be solved within the framework of the existing system of economic and political power. The modern concept of a democratic revolution is incompatible with the elitist practices of professional revolutionaries, the experts on coups.

Experience 2 From the economic point of view, the revolution is made possible by a sudden crisis. This crisis is the expression of the latent contradiction between the explosively growing production forces and the archaic production relations in every modern industrial society. This latent contradition exists even where there is a constant growth in the standard of living, because new contradictions created within the ruling power elite lead to repressive measures and a limitation of fundamental civil rights. This latent crisis—which does not exclude a moderate growth in prosperity and the standard of living of the masses—unifies all basic segments of the population, creating a unified and unifying front against the elite. Under these circumstances secon-

dary events generate an avalanche-like sequence of spontaneous movement in the direction of radical reforms, and cause sudden and surprising crises of the whole political system, a democratic revolution.

Experience 3 The affluence of the consumer society is unable to suppress a movement for broader freedoms, civil rights, and a new quality
of life, even though it is possible to use armed force to defeat the representatives of the resistance and occupy the country. Modern democratic
revolutions do not originate in economic depressions of the prewar
type. They are brought about by a latent crisis of the whole system,
a crisis that frustrates growing hopes and creates a revolutionary consciousness despite possible economic prosperity. The argument that, in
the modern industrial society, the revolution lacks its social base and
its driving force is wrong and without substance. Its base is created in
the form of an alliance between the old and new left, as a community
of interest among whole strata and classes of the population, precisely
within the process of developing a movement for structural change.
In a latent way, the social base of the revolution is given by the structure of modern industrial society itself and is developed in the process
of implementing revolutionary reforms, in the process of democratizing
and transforming the system.

Experience 4 The movement for structural reform takes place as a
democratization of existing institutions, as a sudden discontinuity in the
functioning of the system. The system is paralyzed, but not uprooted,
because the advocates of democratization understand they cannot
simply take over; on the contrary, by expanding the movement they
must create pressure situations for enforcing reforms. Democratization
itself creates entirely new and very effective forms of political pressure, generated through spontaneous activity in the form of new action
centers, political clubs, self-governing bodies of workers, mass protests,
and revolutionary movements calling for a structural transformation.
The critical moment comes when an attempt is made to implement the
basic points in the program. This attempt produces a repressive wave
which, however, is too weak to stop spontaneous masses.

Experience 5 When the democratic revolution arrives at the threshold of its second phase, during which it is necessary to introduce the
first practical measures touching on the structure of the given system
itself, the democratization process enters its decisive crisis. If it is a

local, isolated movement limited by national boundaries the popular revolutionary movement draws counterrevolutionary (Stalinist) forces against itself. It cannot resist these forces without international support, without allies, without a world movement for structural reforms, and without the support of democratic forces within its own bloc. Parallel democratization movements in the present superpowers—especially a democratization movement in the USSR—are necessary to enforce radical structural changes, even when the change within the system expresses the will of almost the entire population and is close to success. On a national scale, democratic revolutions must fail under the tanks of the superpowers. The movement for structural reform in modern industrial societies must become international and transcend the boundaries of the various regional power blocs in order to be successful.

Experience 6 An armed intervention stops the revolutionary process and prevents the implementation of structural reforms, but it deepens the latent crisis of the regime because, when it occurs, the repressive bureaucratic and police nature of the system becomes perfectly clear. The occupation power must establish its power base, composed of the police, the army, and the party apparatus, must introduce the monopolistic system of a single party, must reimpose censorship of information, and make contacts between the individual revolutionary groups impossible. For some time, the spontaneous activity of radical groups maintains a nonviolent resistance, but, because the alternative to armed resistance is unreal and cannot be effective under censorship, it is forced to withdraw after a few acts of desperate individual heroism. The society as a whole is thrown back into the conditions of the pre-reform phase, but with such a sharpening of revolutionary consciousness that even an avalanche of consumer prosperity cannot extinguish the will to resistance at the first possible occasion. The intervention provides the democratic transformation with a latent mass base, a political treasury for the future revolution.

Experience 7 During the crisis the members of the Communist Party oppose the Party apparatus, but they are still decisively under the influence of the bureaucratic elite of the Party and trade-union apparatus. As a unit the Communist Party does not act as a revolutionary force, but as the party of order, as a disciplined organism of the bureaucratic elite, betraying its own program and the revolutionary consciousness of the masses, and organizing a colossal fraud to justify intervention. The bureaucratic elite becomes the direct instrument for collaboration with the occupation power and the former national heroes actively assist the occupiers, legalizing the loss of sovereignty. The dialectics of history reveal the ambivalent Janus face of the Communist Party, for which the masses had provided mellowed human features. But the familiar warlike grimace of the apparatus soon emerges, proving that it is impossible to give Communism a human face, for the same reason that it is impossible to square the circle.

Experience 8 The occupation crushed a mass illusion as to the democratic nature of the Communist Party and as to the possibility of establishing socialism with a human face under the aegis of this Party. The Communist Party has been and will be a bureaucratic-elitist organization, the substance of which is incompatible with a democratization or democratic movement, with spontaneous, creative political activity by citizens. The present Communist parties are bureaucratic police apparatuses for manipulating masses. They are not political parties and even less are they spokesmen for social reform movements. Any future effort to democratize the system must always clash with the insurmountable limits of the Communist Party as a Stalinist institution, with its deeply antidemocratic and antipopular substance, with its elitist nature as an institution. Democratization is possible with the Communists participating in a pluralistic political movement, but is impossible under the leadership of the Party apparatus, which always has defended and always will defend the interest of the Soviet bureaucratic elite and that of its own bureaucratic elite. The Communist Party is consistent when it uses police to suppress mass demonstrations. It is inconsistent when it plays with slogans about a human face. If Communism has a human face it ceases to be Communism.

Experience 9 On the eve of its second phase the democratic revolution clashed with the chief enemy of structural changes in Europe—with the tanks of the Soviet power elite, with the counterrevolutionary forces of the Russian state which does not observe Lenin's principles, but follows Hitler's conviction that *Grausamkeit imponiert . . . Terror ist der wirksamste politische Mittel* (Cruelty makes an impression . . . terror is the most effective means). Again, the democratic revolution was wrecked on the Soviet "Fascistoid" dictatorship, which for the last fifty years has made the establishment of socialism in Europe impossible. The reason why capitalism is still alive in Europe is the horror spread by the inhumanity of the regime that wants to replace capitalism. The Russian state has become an organ of the bureaucratic counterrevolution, an organ for wars of intervention against Czechoslovakia, China, and Europe, and it will proceed on this road despite liberal illusions that Stalinism is dead.

Experience 10 The most important lesson of the Czechoslovak democratization is the fact that if it becomes impossible for the democratization movement to carry out radical structural reforms, "Fascistoid" dictatorships will enforce their own solution. Revolutions that fail lead to fascism, neo-Stalinism, and the strengthening of repressive totalitarian dictatorships, the highest form of organized repression in the world. The Czechoslovak democratization was wrecked by an internationally organized gang of Warsaw Pact military elites, which regard states as their property. It was wrecked by the solidarity of the Stalinist monopolistic bureaucracy of the Eastern Bloc and by illusions about the Communist Party as a leading force of democratization. Alternatives, then, become threateningly simple: either a democratization of modern industrial society or fascist barbarism.

Historical experiences are paid for with blood, occupations, and wars. But the only lesson drawn from history is that people refuse to learn from it. With this bitter Hegelian dialectic reinforced by the tragic ignorance of the Czechoslovak experiment that is prevalent in the ranks of the Western Left, we have to return to the speculative question of whether a revolution is possible in modern industrial society. Yes, it is possible, it is even real and necessary as an alternative to the fascist barbarism of occupation, preventive wars, and totalitarian dictatorships. Of course, the revolutionary process has new forms, and of essential importance is the question of whether the advocates of structural reforms will correctly perceive prerevolutionary situations and the preparatory phases of structural changes, and whether the Czechoslovak experiment in history will be the dress rehearsal for a democratic revolution in Russia and Europe. The Czechoslovak people were the first in the world to experience the initial stage in the transformation process of modern industrial society; the preparatory phase of structural change, a democratic revolution as an absolutely new type of the revolutionary process, a new attempt to transform the structure of the socialist state.

In a time in which people are reaching for the moon a revolutionary answer to the problems of modern industrial society may seem archaic. Indeed, revolution is archaic compared with a technology that is turning fantasy into reality. However, it is not archaic, considering the fantastic reality of the hunger of half mankind, and the reality of aggressive wars, of totalitarian dictatorships, and of the dimensions of human alienation. As long as man continues to seek freedom and social justice, as long as he continues to seek ways to overcome misery, hunger, fear, war, and violence, revolution will not be archaic, even though it will be declared as such time and time again.

At this moment two Americans stand on the moon, thousands of kilometers from the Earth of man. People are jubilant the world over. At the same time, fifty kilometers from Vienna, Soviet tank divisions are poised in an occupied country whose people are silent. Americans on the moon, Russians in the heart of Europe. And the rest is silence.

Ten Commandments for a Rock-bottom Intellectual * ∾∾∾∾∾∾∾∾∾∾∾∾∾∾∾∾

To the students of Charles University, Prague

> Everything we experience is good.
> OSCAR WILDE, *in a letter from jail*

1. To be at rock bottom means to be more oneself; man is permanently touching the bottom of himself. Naked before death, before others and before yourself, you know what you are: you are the bottom of the universe. The deeper you are anchored in the universe, the more you are alone: *at rock bottom you are always alone.*

2. The more you live, the more you are pained by the world, as you are wounded by society and by yourself. But the sharper the pain is, the more profound existence is. We are rich only in the wounds of life. The value of existence is its depth, its bottom: *the intensity of life is given by pain.*

3. The heavier a stone is, the faster it drops toward the bottom. Love for the depths leads to the bottom. But to touch bottom is the privilege of the profound. The bottom is silence. And through silence you come closer to the truth. With reason at an end and the void of the universe before you, *you go anywhere for the truth, even to rock bottom.*

4. Man's meaning is formed out of the meaninglessness of existence, and to be at rock bottom is to be man. To be at rock bottom confers the freedom to rebel against not being at rock bottom; in the essence of yourself you have rebellion. Rebellion is the destiny of man; *rebellion is the logic of the paradox of human existence.*

5. In the name of life we are constantly in rebellion against a given reality, in rebellion against death. Rebellion is your link to the world, it is your first human act, your fundamental self-determination. So

* Article written in Vienna, August 21, 1969; published in *Text*, in 1969.

long as you live, your rebellion is your integrity: *your integrity lies in rebellion.*

6. The more you are at rock bottom, the more human you are and the closer you are to yourself as a rebel. Awareness that you are at rock bottom is your sole strength, is the Archimedean point of your rebellion. Rebellion is the nonexistence of salvation because rebellion alone is salvation. *Your salvation is in rebellion.*

7. Life is the test of your possibilities in history, of your imagination, of your courage, of your intellect. In history there is neither decisive defeat nor decisive victory, there is only the dialectics of upheaval. History is the prize of time and of the continuity of change, just as *man is the prize of time and of change.*

8. In the trap of history you realize how bitter it is to be in the trap of history, at the bottom of existence. Man is the prisoner of history, but his rebellion against history makes history. With the failure of all hope, powerless and beaten, you are the prop of history: *history rests on the beaten.*

9. In rebellion against history and striving after the impossible, you the beaten are at this very moment making history. At the bottom of yourself, at the bottom of the universe, you are rebellion against history because you are man, the potentiality for everything. History has only the meaning that man gives it: *history is the art of the impossible.*

10. The universe is infinite. Man is a finite being, the antithesis of infinity, a scar on the universe. The more you are at rock bottom, the more you scar the universe by your concreteness, by your life, by yourself. Man is rebellion against the bottom, against the universe, against history. *Man is rebellion, the scar on the universe.*

Vienna, August 21, 1969

Catharsis

CONCERNING JAN PALACH

And here gallop Picasso's bulls.
And here march Dalí's elephants on spiders' legs
And here rides the knight of La Mancha.
And here the Karamazovs carry Hamlet.
And here is the core of an atom.
And here is a cosmonaut's base on the moon.
And here stands a statue without its torch.
And here runs a torch without a statue.
And it's very simple: Where the man ends,
The flame begins.
And then in the silence can be heard the mumbling
of worms in the ashes. For
In essence billions of people
Are keeping silent.
 MIROSLAV HOLUB, *Jan Palach's Prague*

Jan Palach

Jan Palach's Last Letter ～～～～～～～～

Because our nations are on the brink of despair
we have decided to express our protest
and to wake up the people of this land.
Our group is composed of volunteers
who are willing to burn themselves
for our cause.
It was my honor to draw the lot number one
and thus I acquired the privilege of writing the first letter
and starting as the first torch.
Our demands are:
1/ immediate elimination of censorship
2/ prohibition of the distribution of *Zprávy*.*
If our demands are not fulfilled within five days
by January 21, 1969
and if the people do not support us sufficiently
through a strike of an indefinite duration
more torches will burn.
Remember August.
In international politics a place was made for Czechoslovakia.
Let us use it.

TORCH NUMBER ONE

* Soviet occupation journal.

To Jan Palach, living torch number one ∿∿

by Jan Zajíc, living torch number two

A playful afternoon,
They carry nearby a Prometheus.
Eyes are a broken dike.
I cry in the rain on a sidewalk,
For everything . . .
. . . That silence roars on my behalf
. . . Silence tears my ears,
all know it and are silent.
Their mouths are stifled by fear
Of life and death.
This is January 69 . . .

I hear your cowardice,
It cries in the fields,
It roars in towns,
It whimpers on crossroads,
It trembles from fear of death
And it does not feel that death warns and lures.
Bells toll from the spires of churches.
For the nation, for the country.
In the name
Of your life
I burn
Jan

February 26, 1969, Prague, Europe

Selected Bibliography

Selected Bibliography[*]

Aptheker, Herbert. *Czechoslovakia and Counter-Revolution: Why the Socialist Countries Intervened.* New York, 1969.

Beckmann, Petr. *Whispered Anecdotes: Humor from Behind the Iron Curtain.* Boulder, Colorado, 1969.

Beer, Fritz. *Die Zukunft funktioniert nicht: Ein porträt der Tschecho-slowakei: 1948–1968* Frankfurt, 1969.

Bernieres, Luc. *Blindés sur Prague . . . et pour les Tchèques commença la nuit la plus longue . . .* Paris, 1968.

Bertleff, Erich. *Mit blossen Händen: Der einsame Kampf der Tschechen und Slowaken 1968.* Vienna, 1968.

Biagi, E. *I giorni di Praga.* Rome, 1968.

Blumenfeld, Yorrick. *Seesaw: Cultural Life in Eastern Europe.* New York, 1968.

Bongiorno, Arrigo. *L'Utopia bruciata–Praga 1968.* Milan, 1968.

Bonnoure, Pierre. *Histoire de la Tchécoslovaquie.* Paris, 1968.

Buchanan, Alastair, et al. *The Soviet Threat to Europe: An Analysis of Soviet Potentials and Intentions by Experts of Six Countries* (Introduction by Lord S. Oswald). London, 1969.

Chapman, Colin. *August 21st—The Rape of Czechoslovakia.* Philadelphia, 1968.

Conspirators!: A Documentation. East Germany, 1968.

Csizmas, Michael. *Prag 1968: I. Dokumente; II. Analyse.* Bern, 1968.

ČSR: The Road to Democratic Socialism, Facts on Events from January to May 1968. Prague, 1968.

The Czech Aggression Against Nazi Germany: A Legend That Almost Happened (With Some Authentic Text). New York, 1969.

Czechoslovakia and the Brezhnev Doctrine. Prepared by the Subcommittee on National Security and International Operations of the Committee on Government Operations, U.S. Senate. Washington, 1969.

Daix, Pierre. *Journal de Prague, Decembre 1967—Septembre 1968.* Paris, 1968.

Domes, Alfred. *Prag—21. August 1968: Eine Sammlung von Dokumenten zur Besetzung der Tschechoslowakei und ihre Folgen.* Bonn, Brussels, New York, 1969.

Drama nel cuore dell'Europa. Milan, 1968.

Dubček, Alexander. *Il nuovo corso in Cecoslovacchia.* Rome, 1968.

———. *K otázkám obrozovacieho procesu v KSČ* [On Questions Con-

[*] Co-author, William Brzorád.

cerning the Regeneration Process in the Communist Party of Czechoslovakia]. Bratislava, 1968.

———. *O narodnostní otázce* [On the Problem of Nationalities]. Prague, 1968.

Ello, Paul, ed. *Czechoslovakia's Blueprint for Freedom: Dubček's Statements—The Official and Original Documents Leading to the Conflict of August, 1968.* Washington, 1968.

Fabiánova, Božena. *Rok 1968. Necht' mluví fakta* [The Year 1968. The Facts Should Speak]. Prague, 1970.

Farrell, R. Barry, ed. *Political Leadership in Eastern Europe and the Soviet Union.* Chicago, 1970.

Feiwell, George, R. *New Economic Patterns in Czechoslovakia.* New York, 1968.

Fiš, Teodor. *Mein Kommandeur General Svoboda: Vom Ural zum Hradschin.* Vienna, Frankfurt, Zurich, 1969.

Frei, Bohumil. *Tschechoslowakei: Geschichte und Staat.* Munich, Vienna, 1968.

Fritz, Ermarth. *Interventionism, Security, and Legitimacy: The Challenge to Soviet Interests in Eastern Europe, 1964–1968.* Santa Monica, Cal., 1969.

Garaudy, Roger. *Le Grand Tournant du socialisme.* Paris, 1969.

Garaudy, Roger. *La Liberté en sursis.* Prague 1968. Paris, 1968.

George, Richard T. de. *The New Marxism: Soviet and East European Marxism Since 1956.* New York, 1968.

Goess Franz-Beer, Manfred R. *Prager Anschläge, Bilddokumente des gewaltlosen Widerstandes.* Frankfurt, 1968.

Goldštůcker, Eduard. *Liberta e socialismo.* Rome, 1968.

Grass, Günther and Kohout, Pavel. *Briefe über die Grenze: Versuch eines Ost-West Dialogs.* Hamburg, 1968.

Griffith, William E. *Eastern Europe After the Soviet Invasion of Czechoslovakia.* Santa Monica, Cal., 1968.

Grünwald, Leopold. *ČSSR im Umbruch. Beiträge, Kommentare, Dokumentation.* Vienna, Frankfurt, Zurich, 1968.

Guyot, Rémi. *La Mutation tchécoslovaque.* Paris, 1969.

Haefs, Hanswilhelm. *Die Ereignisse in der Tschechoslowakei vom 27. 6. 1968 bis 18. 10. 1968: Ein dokumentarisches Bericht.* Bonn, Vienna, Zurich, 1969.

Hagelstange, Rudolf. *Der Krak in Prag: Ein Frühlingsmärchen.* Hamburg, 1969.

Hall, Gus. *Czechoslovakia at the Crossroads.* New York, 1968.

Hamšík, Dušan. *Spisovatelé a moc* [Writers and Power]. Prague, 1969.

Hartmann, Bernd. *The Events in the CSSR in the Light of Marxism.* Cologne, 1968.

Hensel, K. Paul, et al., eds. *Die Marktwirtschaft in der Tschechoslowakei: Mit Dokumenten.* Stuttgart, 1968.

Horlacher, Wolfgang. *Zwischen Prag und Moskau: Augenzeugenbericht —Analyse*, Dokumente. Stuttgart, 1968.

Hrbek, Jaromír. *Manifest pravdy* [Manifesto of Truth]. Prague, 1969.

James. R. *The Czechoslovak Crisis 1968*. London, 1968.

Josten, J. *21.8.1968. Anno humanitatis*. London, Cologne, 1968.

Kamberger, Klaus, ed. *Der Fall ČSSR: Strafaktion gegen einen Bruder-staat, Eine Dokumentation*. Frankfurt, 1968.

Klokočka, Vladimír. *Demokratischer Sozialismus: Ein authentisches Modell*. Hamburg, 1968.

Kohout, Pavel. *Aus dem Tagebuch eines Konter-Revolutionäre*. Lucerne, Frankfurt, 1969.

Kuby, Erich, et al. *Prag und die Linke*. Hamburg, 1968.

Lemberg, Eugen and Rhode, Gotthold, eds. *Das deutsch-tschechische Verhältnis seit 1918*. Stuttgart, 1969.

Leonhard, Wolfgang. *Die Dreispaltung des Marxismus: Urspung und Entwicklung des Sowjetmarxismus, Maoismus und Reformkommunismus*. Düsseldorf, Vienna, 1970.

Levine, Isaac Don. *Intervention: The Causes and Consequences of the Invasion of Czechoslovakia*. New York, 1969.

Liehm, Antonin. *Gespräche an der Moldau: Das Ringen um die Freiheit der Tschechoslowakei*. Vienna, Munich, Zurich, 1968.

———. *Trois générations: Entretiens sur le phénomène culturel tchéco-slovaque* (Introduction by Jean-Paul Sartre). Paris, 1970.

Littell, Robert, ed. *The Czech Black Book*. Prepared by the Institute of History of the Czechoslovak Academy of Sciences. New York, 1969 (also in Czech, French, and German).

Loebl, Eugen. *Geistige Arbeit—die wahre Quelle des Reichstums: Entwurf eines neuen sozialistischen Ordnungsbildes*. Düsseldorf, 1968.

———. *Sentenced and Tried: The Stalinist Purges in Czechoslovakia*. New York, London, 1969 (also in French and German).

Loebl, Eugen and Grünwald, Leopold. *Die intellektuelle Revolution: Hintergrüne und Auswirkungen des "Prager Frühlings."* Düsseldorf, 1969.

London, Artur. *L'Aveu: Dans l'engrenage du procès de Prague*. Paris, 1968 (in German: *Ich gestehe*. Hamburg, 1970).

Longo, Luigi. *Sui fatti di Cecoslovacchia*. Rome, 1969.

Lotar, Peter, ed. *Prager Frühling und Herbst im Zeugnis der Dichter*. Bern, 1969.

Lukaszewski, Jerzy, ed. *The People's Democracies After Prague: Soviet Hegemony, Nationalism, Regional Integration?* Bruges, 1970.

Journalist "M". *A Year Is Eight Months* (Introduction by Tad Szulc). New York, 1969.

Mandrou, Robert. *Les Sept Jours de Prague, 21–27 août 1968*. Paris, 1969.

Marcelle, Jacques. *Le Deuxième Coup de Prague: Le renouveau socialiste tchécoslovaque à l'épreuve de la liberté*. Paris, 1968.

Maxa, Josef. *Die kontrollierte Revolution: Anatomie des prager Frühlings.* Vienna, Hamburg. 1969.

Mayer, Milton. *The Art of the Impossible: A Study of the Czech Resistance.* Santa Barbara, Calif., 1969.

Mezernik, A. G. *Invasion and Occupation of Czechoslovakia and the U.N.* Washington, 1968.

Mňačko, Ladislav. *Die Aggressoren: Von der Schuld und Unschuld der Schwachen.* Vienna, Frankfurt, Zurich, 1968.

————. *La Septième Nuit.* Paris, 1968 (in German: *Die siebente Nacht.* Vienna, Munich, Zurich, 1968).

Norden, Peter, ed. *Prag, 21. August . . . Revolution, Intervention, Invasion.* Munich, 1968.

On Events in Czechoslovakia. Facts, Documents, Press Reports, and Eye-Witness Accounts (the "White Book"). Prepared by the Press Group of Soviet Journalists. Moscow, 1968 (also in Czech, French, German, Russian, and Spanish).

On the Situation in the Czechoslovak Socialist Republic. Berlin, 1968.

Pelikán, Jiří, ed. *Le Congrès clandestin: Protocole secret et documents du 14e congrès extraordinaire du P.C. tchécoslovaque, 22 août 1968.* Paris, 1969 (in German: *Panzer überrollen den Parteitag.* Vienna, Frankfurt, Zurich, 1969; also in Czech).

————. *Das unterdruckte Dossier: Bericht der Kommission des ZK der KPTsch uber politische Prozesse und "Rehabilitierungen" in der Tschechoslowakei 1949–1968.* Vienna, Frankfurt, Zurich, 1970.

Pell, Clairborne. *Czechoslovakia 1968: Report to the Committee on Foreign Relations, U.S. Senate, July 1968.* Washington, 1968.

Pitter, Přemysl. *Geistige Revolution im Herzen Europas.* Zurich, Stuttgart, 1968.

Portfolio for Peace. Excerpts from the Writings and Speeches of U Thant, Secretary-General of the United Nations, on Major World Issues, 1961–1968. New York, 1968.

Pustejovsky, Olfrid. *In Prag kein Fenstersturz: Dogmatismus (1948–1962); Entdogmatisierung (1962–1967); Demokratisierung (1967–1968); Intervention (1968).* Munich, 1968.

Radimský, Ladislav. *Než bude pozdě* [Before It Is Too Late]. Toronto, 1969.

Randle, Michael. *Support Czechoslovakia.* London, 1968.

Reden zum IV. Kongress des tschechoslowakischen Schriftstellerverbandes, Prague, Juni, 1967. Frankfurt, 1968.

Reitzner, Almar. *Alexander Dubček, Männer und Mächte in der Tschechoslowakei.* Munich, 1968.

Remington, Robin Alison. *Winter in Prague: Documents on Czechoslovak Communism in Crisis.* Cambridge, Mass., 1969.

Rok šedesátý osmý v usneseních a dokumentech UV KSČ [The Year 1968 in Resolutions and Documents of the Central Committee of the Communist Party of Czechoslovakia]. Prague, 1969.

Rőll, F. and Rosenberger, G. *ČSSR 1962-1968: Dokumentation und Kritik*. Munich, 1968.

Sager, Peter. *Prag 1968: Analyse, Tatsachen, Meinungen*. Bern, 1968.

Sakharov, Andrei. *Progress, Coexistence, and Intellectual Freedom*. New York, 1968.

Salomon, Michel. *Prague: La révolution étranglée; Janvier–août 1968*. Paris, 1968.

Schmidt-Háner, Christian and Műller, Adolf. *Viva Dubček: Reform und Okkupation in der ČSSR* (introduction by Heinrich Bőll). Cologne, Berlin, 1968.

Schwartz, Harry. *Prague's 200 Days: The Struggle for Democracy in Czechoslovakia*. New York, 1969.

Selucký, Radoslav. *Reform-Modell ČSSR: Entwurf einer sozialistischen Marktwirtschaft oder Gefahr für die Volksdemokratie?* Reinbek bei Hamburg, 1969.

Šik, Ota. *Fakten der tschechoslowakischen Wirtschaft*. Vienna, Munich, Zurich, 1969 (also in French).

———. *Plan and Market*. Prague, 1967.

Skibowski, Klaus Otto. *Schicksalstage einer Nation: Die ČSSR auf dem Weg zum progressiven Sozialismus*. Dűsseldorf, Vienna, 1968.

Škvorecký, Josef. *Nachrichten aus der ČSSR. Dokumentation der Wochenzeitung "Literární Listy" des tschechoslowakischen Schriftstellerverbandes, Prag, Februar–August 1968*. Frankfurt, 1968.

Slánská, Josefa. *Bericht űber meinen Mann: Die Affäre Slánský*. Vienna, Frankfurt, Zurich, 1969 (in French: *Rapport sur mon mari*, Paris, 1969).

Šlingová, Marian. *Truth Will Prevail*. London, 1968.

Soldi, Fiorini. *Viaggio a Praga*. Milan, 1968.

Spender, Stephen. *The Year of the Young Rebels*. London, 1969.

Studer, Hans, K., ed. *Tschechoslowakei, August 68: Die Tragődie eines tapferen Volkes*. Kilchberg/Zurich, 1968.

Sviták, Ivan. *Man and His World: A Marxian View*. New York, 1970.

———. *Verbotene Horizonte*. Freiburg, 1969.

Svoboda, Václav. *Genosse Aggressor: Prag im August 1968*. Vienna, Frankfurt, Zurich, 1968.

Swerling, Anthony. *The Rape of Czechoslovakia: Being Two Weeks of Cohabitation With the Soviet Allies, August–September 1968*. Cambridge, 1968.

Tatu, Michel. *L'Hérésie impossible: Chronique du drame tchécoslovaque*. Paris, 1968.

Tchécoslovaquie: Les Ouvriers face à la dictature, 1938–1948–1968. Paris, 1969.

Tigrid, Pavel. *La Chute irrésistible d'Alexander Dubček*. Paris, 1969.

———. *Le Printemps de Prague*. Paris, 1968.

———. *Praga 1948—Agosto '68*. Milan, 1968.

Tschechoslowakei: Einmarsch von Truppen aus 5 Staaten des Warschauer Paktes, vergablich auf ein Hilfe-Ersuchen tschechoslowakischer Funktionäre. Bonn, 1968.

Tschechoslowakei 1968. Zurich, 1968.

Die Tschechoslowakei 1945-1968. Berlin, 1968.

Una chiesa che ha deciso: Cecoslovacchia, 1948-1968. Milan, 1968.

La via cecoslovaccha al socialismo (Il programa d'azione del partito communista cecoslovacco). Rome, 1968.

Vichniac, Isabelle. *L'Ordre règne à Prague*. Paris, 1968.

Weissenborn, N., ed. *Prag und die Linke*. Hamburg, 1968.

Weisskopf, Kurt. *Les Coups de Prague, 1938-1968*. Paris, 1968.

Whelan, Joseph G. *Aspects of Intellectual Ferment and Dissent in Czechoslovakia*. Prepared at the request of Sen. Thomas J. Dodd for the Committee on the Judiciary, U.S. Senate. Washington, 1969.

Windsor, Philip and Roberts, Adam. *Czechoslovakia 1968: Reform, Repression, and Resistance*. New York, 1969.

Zeman, Z. A. B. *Prague Spring*. New York, 1969.

For titles dealing with the period prior to 1968 we refer the reader to *East Central Europe: A Guide to Basic Publications*, edited by Paul L. Horecky, Chicago, 1969; and *Czechoslovakia: A Bibliographic Guide*, by Rudolf Sturm, Washington, 1967.

New York, May 1970

Publications Sponsored by the
Research Institute on Communist Affairs

Diversity in International Communism, Alexander Dallin, ed., in collaboration with the Russian Institute, Columbia University Press, 1963.

Political Succession in the USSR, Myron Rush, published jointly with the RAND Corporation, Columbia University Press, 1965.

Marxism in Modern France, George Lichtheim, Columbia University Press, 1966.

Power in the Kremlin, Michel Tatu, Viking Press, 1969, was first published in 1967 by Bernard Grasset under the title *Le Pouvoir en URSS* and also in England by William Collins Sons and Co., Ltd., in 1968.

The Soviet Bloc: Unity and Conflict, Zbigniew Brzezinski, revised and enlarged edition, Harvard University Press, 1967.

Vietnam Triangle, Donald Zagoria, Pegasus Press, 1968.

Communism in Malaysia and Singapore, Justus van der Kroef, Nijhoff Publications (The Hague), 1967.

Radicalismo Cattolico Brasiliano, Ulisse A. Floridi, Istituto Editoriale Del Mediterraneo, 1968.

Stalin and His Generals, Seweryn Bialer, ed., Pegasus Press, 1969.

Marxism and Ethics, Eugene Kamenka, Macmillan and St. Martin's Press, 1969.

Dilemmas of Change in Soviet Politics, Zbigniew Brzezinski, ed. and contributor, Columbia University Press, 1969.

The USSR Arms the Third World: Case Studies in Soviet Foreign Policy, Uri Ra'anan, The M.I.T. Press, 1969.

Communists and Their Law, John N. Hazard, The University of Chicago Press, 1969.

Fulcrum of Asia, Bhabani Sen Gupta, published jointly with the East Asian Institute, Pegasus Press, 1970.

Le Conflit Sino-Soviétique et l'Europe de l'Est, Jacques Lévesque, Montreal University Press, 1970.

Communist China and Latin America, Cecil Johnson, Columbia University Press, 1970.

Between Two Ages: America's Role in the Technetronic Era, Zbigniew Brzezinski, Viking Press, 1970.

Communism and Nationalism in India: M. N. Roy and the Comintern, John P. Haithcox, Princeton University Press, 1971.

The Czechoslovak Experiment: 1968–1969, Ivan Sviták, Columbia University Press, 1971.